Rudyard Kipling
to Rider Haggard

Also by Morton Cohen

RIDER HAGGARD
His life and works

Rudyard Kipling

Rider Haggard

Rudyard Kipling
to Rider Haggard

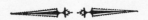

THE RECORD OF A FRIENDSHIP

Edited by

MORTON COHEN

Rutherford · Madison · Teaneck
Fairleigh Dickinson University Press

Associated University Presses, Inc.
Cranbury, New Jersey 08512

6881
Printed in the United States of America

To the memory of
my mother, father, and sister Annette

Contents

THE RECORD

Illustrations

A note on the text

This volume contains all the material touching upon Rudyard Kipling's friendship with H. Rider Haggard that I have been able to find. It comprises forty-nine letters from Kipling to Haggard; two letters from Haggard to Kipling; twenty-seven entries in Haggard's diaries; one letter from Kipling to Andrew Lang; one from Haggard to his wife; one from Kipling to Ida Hector, Haggard's secretary; and descriptions of other holographs that have survived, particularly the plot outlines and character sketches for three of Haggard's novels on which Kipling and Haggard worked together. Many letters have not survived because Kipling scrupulously burned incoming mail when he had finished with it. Other papers that would have thrown more light upon the friendship have undoubtedly gone the way of the missing letters. Of the two letters from Haggard that survive, one he dictated to his secretary about eight weeks before he died. In it he takes a long retrospective look over much of his life, and for that reason Kipling probably cherished it and kept it from the flames. The second survives as a copy that Haggard made and kept. Most of the letters printed here consequently reflect the flow of Kipling's thought. But Haggard's diaries afford frequent glimpses into his own mind, and because Kipling's letters are often replies to Haggard's, they too reflect Haggard's thinking.

Unless a note indicates otherwise, Kipling's letters to Haggard are in the Norwich Public Library, with Haggard's diaries and the letter from Kipling to Lang. The holograph material concerned with plotting Haggard's books is in the James McGregor Stewart Kipling Collection, Dalhousie University Library, Halifax, Nova Scotia. Haggard's letter to Kipling dated November 10, 1912, is in the Huntington Library, San Marino, California, and the one dated March 2, 1925, remains among the Kipling Papers owned by Mrs. George Bambridge. One Kipling letter (undated, p. 28 below) is owned by a private collector, Mr. H. Dunscombe Colt of New York. Unless my notes say otherwise, I possess photographic copies of the letters and documents in the text.

Haggard reproduced one of Kipling's letters in his autobiography, Professor C. E. Carrington quoted from a few of them in his biography of Kipling, and Miss Haggard and I also quoted from them in our biographies of her father. But these are the first of Kipling's letters to be edited for publication. Miss Haggard and I have quoted from her father's diaries, but the entries here are more numerous and extensive than those published before.

In transcribing the letters and diary passages and preparing them for publication, I have sought to make as few editorial changes as possible and still produce a readable text. I have spelled out ampersands, expanded the abbreviations in Haggard's personal shorthand, and silently corrected a few obvious misspellings and *lapsus calami*; but where an error has some intrinsic interest, I have retained it. The Kipling letters are printed in full; what seem to be ellipses are his own stylistic devices and do not represent omissions in the text.

The missing letters leave gaps in the record of the friendship, and I have tried to supply explanatory links where I felt they would be helpful. I have also tried to sketch briefly what the men did when too busy to write or when meeting too frequently to bother writing.

When I began work on this manuscript, I tried to keep footnote superscripts out of the text entirely, but I soon realized that, at best, the reader would find the search for a footnote (even the search to determine whether or not I had supplied a note at a given point) difficult and confusing, and I have settled for the small annoyance of the superscripts. I have, however, kept superscripts, footnotes, and citations to a minimum. To this end, I have not given references to information I have taken from the following standard sources: *Encyclopaedia Britannica*, *The Columbia Encyclopedia*, *Dictionary of National Biography* and its supplements, *Who's Who*, *Who Was Who*, *The Oxford Companion to English Literature*, and *An Encyclopedia of World History*. Finally, I have glossed only those words not included in either the *Oxford English Dictionary* and its supplement or *Webster's New International Dictionary* (2nd ed.).

May, 1965

Morton Cohen
The City College
The City University
New York

Acknowledgements

I take considerable pleasure in recording the debts of gratitude that I have incurred in the past four years while preparing this book for publication. Without the help of Kipling's daughter, Mrs. George Bambridge, and Miss Lilias Rider Haggard, I should not have been able to undertake the work at all. Since 1954, when I began my study of Sir Rider's life, Mrs. Bambridge and Miss Haggard have been continually patient with me and have responded more than kindly to all my requests. For permission to publish for the first time the complete texts of Rudyard Kipling's letters to Sir Rider, I am immensely grateful to Mrs. Bambridge, as I am to Miss Haggard for her permission to print her father's letters and diary entries. Sir Godfrey Haggard has also been a source of encouragement and frequent help.

For access to unpublished papers I am indebted to the owners, among them Mr. H. Dunscombe Colt, New York City; the Huntington Library, San Marino, California; the University of California Library, Los Angeles; and the James McGregor Stewart Kipling Collection, Dalhousie University, Halifax, Nova Scotia. Particular thanks go to Mr. P. Hepworth, Norwich City Librarian, and his staff for repeated and cordial help with the Haggard papers lodged in the Central Library, and to Miss Jean M. Kennedy, Senior Archivist of the Norfolk and Norwich Record Office.

I wish the following persons to know that I am grateful to them for their help: Mr. Michael Bowe, Mr. Andrew Haggard, Earl Baldwin of Bewdley, Mrs. Audrey Alley Gorton, Col. R. E. Harbord, Rev. H. W. Howe, Sir Harold Nicolson, Mr. R. F. Rattray, Dr. E. G. Stanley, the Earl of Swinton, and Professor A. W. Yeats. For sharing with me their knowledge of Kipling and their critical insights into his life and works, I wish to thank Professors C. E. Carrington and Bonamy Dobrée and Dr. J. M. S. Tompkins. I should also like to acknowledge the editorial assistance of Messrs. Alan Bennett, Robert Fromer, A. J. Martin, Daniel Olivarez, and Professor Robert Sonkin.

I am grateful to Professor David A. Robertson, Jr., for suggesting the idea for this book; and to Professor Jerome Hamilton Buckley, whose advice and approval I repeatedly seek and ever value. My editor and friend, Miss Dorothy Tomlinson, has been enthusiastic about this book from its beginnings, and she has given me much-needed support. Mr. Peter Watt has solved many knotty problems for me, and Mr. James Petrie, librarian at The City College, has often helped to make my search for information fruitful.

Three friends have shown a continuing interest in my work and have offered counsel whenever I needed it: Roger Lancelyn Green, to whom I am indebted for the services of an authority on the life and works of both Kipling and Haggard; Cecil Y. Lang, for the constant help of a master stylist and brilliant nineteenth-century scholar; and Richard N. Swift, for his professional editing skills and eminent good sense.

Short Titles

Carrington	C. E. Carrington, *The Life of Rudyard Kipling* (New York: Doubleday, 1955)
Chandler	Lloyd H. Chandler, *A Summary of the Work of Rudyard Kipling* (1930)
Cloak	Lilias Rider Haggard, *The Cloak That I Left* (1951)
Days	H. Rider Haggard, *The Days of My Life*, C. J. Longman, ed., 2 vols. (1926)
Rider Haggard	Morton Cohen, *Rider Haggard* (1960)
Scott	J. E. Scott, *A Bibliography of the Works of Sir Henry Rider Haggard* (1947)
Stewart	James McG. Stewart, *Rudyard Kipling: A Bibliographical Catalogue*, A. W. Yeats, ed. (1959)
Something	Rudyard Kipling, *Something of Myself* (1937)
Works	The Outward Bound Edition of Kipling's Works, (36 vols., New York: Charles Scribner's Sons, 1897–1937)

Introduction

"From all outward appearances, they should have been enemies, not friends," a critic remarked recently when we were talking about Rudyard Kipling and Rider Haggard. And he was probably right. In 1889, when Kipling and Haggard met, Haggard was at the height of his popularity with English readers. In the previous four years, *King Solomon's Mines*, *She*, *Allan Quatermain*, and five other titles had appeared. Kipling was still unknown, trying to appeal to essentially the same public that Haggard held firmly in his grip. Haggard might easily have seen Kipling as an upstart and refused to have anything to do with him. In the early 'nineties he could understandably have resented Kipling's transplendent rise to fame, which outstripped even his own. For his part, Kipling might have recognized his superior craftsmanship and considered Haggard unworthy of success. Once established, Kipling might easily have broken away from Haggard, as he did from almost all other literary associates. Instead, he and Haggard found each other congenial from the start, and their relationship grew and deepened through the years. Neither man ever saw the other as a challenger or a competitor, and the winning and losing of readers and fame had nothing to do with their friendship. It travelled its own course, away from the world of letters, indeed surprisingly divorced from it.

"They were such different people, or so it seemed," my friend went on. And he was again right. Haggard, a tall, handsome man with sparkling blue eyes and a booming voice, came from a large family, liked company, and thrived in the limelight. He dressed well, fought openly for causes, and had about him the dash of the romantic heroes he created in his adventure stories. Kipling, an only son, was short, slender, bespectacled, and shy. He did not make friends easily, nor did he want many. Although he spoke his mind frankly and openly in his work, he did not enjoy appearing in public, and in later years he grew more and more a recluse. He was soft-spoken, studious and high-strung.

But their differences presented no problem; however apparent, they were merely surface qualities. The friendship took root in their similar experiences and reached into the deeper ground of similar intellectual

1

and emotional points of view, similar political and social attitudes, and strongly sympathetic religious feelings.

Though still young men when they met in London (Haggard was thirty-three, Kipling twenty-three), they had already travelled far and experienced much. They found that they shared, in many ways, similar backgrounds. Both had come from good families, and although each had a sound education, neither had been to the university. Instead, they had spent what would have been their university years in distant British dependencies, Haggard in South Africa, Kipling in India, each discovering himself and a life's work, receiving and recording impressions of distant peoples and exotic adventures. In time, both met with unrequited love, but ultimately each made a suitable match. Both Haggard and Kipling raised small families on country estates, close to the land. Each lost his first-born child and, after Kipling's son was killed in World War I, they shared another grief, the death of an only son. They both took to writing early, both about the far-off corners of the Empire.

Kipling's letters to Haggard and Haggard's diary entries bring us closer to both men's minds and hearts than I could hope to do with descriptive statements. But a glance at the two lives up to the time they met in 1889 helps put this meeting in context and supplies a basis for understanding and appreciating the friendship that ensued.[1] Henry Rider Haggard, born on June 22, 1856, was the eighth of ten children of William Meybohm Rider Haggard, the eccentric squire of Bradenham Hall, Norfolk, and his wife Ella. When Rider Haggard was only ten years old, his domineering father thunderingly dismissed him as dull and "only fit to be a greengrocer."[2] In the elder Haggard's view it would have been folly to spend much money in educating this "whimsical" boy, and instead he went to Ipswich Grammar School, and from there, when he was sixteen, to London to prepare for the Foreign Office.

During the summer of 1875, Haggard's father, learning from *The Times* that an old friend and Norfolk neighbour, Sir Henry Bulwer, had been appointed Lieutenant-Governor of Natal, offered Sir Henry the services of this ineducable sixth son. Bulwer agreed to take him, unseen, to South Africa as a member of his official party, and soon, the nineteen-year-old found himself Sir Henry's general household manager in Natal.

[1] Sources for Kipling's biography are his own *Something of Myself* (1937); and C. E. Carrington, *The Life of Rudyard Kipling* (1955). For Haggard's: his own *The Days of My Life* (1926); Lilias Rider Haggard, *The Cloak That I Left* (1951); Morton Cohen, *Rider Haggard* (1960).

[2] *Days*, I, 5.

He worked hard and gave a creditable account of himself. He came to know the strange natives and the stranger Boers. He hunted wild game and travelled through jungle and over veld. He matured, and both he and his superiors grew confident of his abilities. In 1877, when the British annexed the Transvaal, he was selected to run up the British flag at the official ceremony in Church Square, Pretoria. In the same year, he was appointed English Clerk to the Colonial Secretary's Office and could write home that he was finally earning an income. Soon afterwards, at twenty-one, he was appointed Master of the High Court of the Transvaal, and although he had no legal training whatever, he did a laudable job of wiping out corruption in the courts and revitalizing a degenerate legal system. Political tension was rife in South Africa: the British, the Boers, and the Zulus were fixed in a death struggle for possession of the land. Haggard kept a close eye on political developments and thought seriously about his own future. During his only holiday at home, he met, courted, and wed Louisa Margitson, the heiress of Ditchingham House and a small Norfolk estate surrounding it, which remains to this day the property of the Haggard family. In 1880, returning to South Africa with his wife and a retinue of servants, he settled down to ostrich farming, but that proved a venture for which neither temperament nor experience had equipped him. Moreover, the British were now at war with the Boers, and a future in South Africa was less than promising. In August, 1881, they returned to England.

Family responsibilities weighing heavy upon him, Haggard entered Lincoln's Inn to read for the Bar. While studying in London, he also wrote his first book, *Cetywayo and His White Neighbours, or Remarks on Recent Events in Zululand, Natal and the Transvaal*, a denunciation of the Government's shilly-shallying with England's interests in South Africa. But in order to get it published he had to pay his publisher £50, and a year after the publication date only 150 copies had been sold. Haggard nevertheless kept writing during his leisure time: reading for the Bar did not provide an adequate outlet for his energy. Then he stumbled upon fiction as a means of expressing himself. While he and Mrs. Haggard were in church one Sunday morning, they noticed sitting near them, as Haggard himself put it, "a singularly beautiful and pure faced young lady."[1] Later, they decided that this young lady deserved to be a heroine in a novel, and they each began to write a story about her. Mrs. Haggard gave up after she had written two or three sheets; Haggard wrote on

[1] *Days*, I, 209.

until he completed his first three-decker, which he called *Dawn*. Finding a publisher was not easy, but Hurst & Blackett finally brought it out in 1884.

Dawn is a weird mixture of the novel of manners and what George Saintsbury called the "elements of occult arts and astral spirits."[1] The *Athenaeum* reviewer saw in it a combination of "fatal facility . . . imagination . . . [and] courage."[2] Although once again his work did not sell, the few favourable notices were enough to encourage him to return to his writing desk. His next effort was *The Witch's Head*, another hodgepodge of autobiographical detail and aimless excursions into the grotesque. But at one point, when the hero has to escape from England, Haggard sends him to Africa, and once Haggard is back in Africa, he writes from the heart. Immediately the reader is enthralled by a new kind of adventure story in a strange, distant world. It is an exhilarating experience that places *The Witch's Head* far above Haggard's earlier novel.

Haggard was finally called to the Bar but, once there, he found the ennui of the law unbearable. While his need to earn a living kept him rooted to his profession by day, his demand for adventure and escape kept him at his writing desk in the evening. In 1885 he read *Treasure Island*, a new, popular book, and when his brother chanced to ask him his opinion, Haggard replied recklessly that, though it was certainly a good story, he himself could write a boy's book just as good. His brother challenged him, and for the next six weeks Haggard spent his evenings at his pedestal desk, in his house in Kensington, winning the wager with a tale of African adventure. The result was *King Solomon's Mines*, the first adventure story in English to exploit the African setting, and the harbinger of a genre. It took the fog-bound London reader far from the British Isles to a land where the sun was as bright as the jungle was dark; it introduced him to primitive cultures, dangerous missions, and narrow escapes. The reader hunts big game, finds treasure, and defeats or outwits wild animals, primitive natives, and the natural elements. It is an astonishing adventure story with excitement, suspense, and massacre on almost every page. The English public gobbled it up.

King Solomon's Mines appeared in September, 1885, and changed all for Rider Haggard, and although he did not give up his legal practice immediately, the barrister was subordinated to the author. Now that his pen had struck the right vein, he devoted as much time as he could to

[1] *Academy*, XXV (March 22, 1884), 200.
[2] LXXXIII (March 22, 1884), 372.

his writing and completed three more works of fiction in the next six months. The last of these, even stranger and more popular than its predecessors, was the famous *She*. It contains all the elements of the early African stories, but with a difference. For here we get something new, the mysterious white queen of a savage race of black Africans. She is a magical ruler, too, and has been alive for two thousand years when the English adventurers discover her. The book was a *succès fou*, and Haggard's name, and that of his heroine, Ayesha, were heard everywhere.

By 1887 Haggard no longer doubted what his life should be. He gave up his law practice and set himself to writing full time, producing at least a book a year until his death. It was a brief two years after the publication of *She* that he met Kipling.

Joseph Rudyard Kipling was born December 30, 1865, in Bombay, where his father, John Lockwood Kipling, a kind, cultivated, gifted man, was professor of Architectural Sculpture in a new art school. When Rudyard was five, his parents brought him and his three-year-old sister to England to begin their formal education. The children were lodged "as paying guests" in Southsea at the house of a retired merchant naval officer "whose name had been obtained from an advertisement in the newspaper."[1] For over five years the boy suffered half-blindness, emotional hunger, and repeated thrashings in what he himself later called the "House of Desolation," until "some sort of nervous break-down" brought his mother from India.[2] Supplied with proper spectacles, he entered, at the age of twelve, the United Services College at Westward Ho!, where an old family friend was headmaster. Here he found order, friendship and understanding, and although he still yearned for family affection, he had much to content him. He could now indulge his passion for literature, for his masters did not interfere with his voracious reading habits. "Gigger," as Kipling was known (from "Gig-lamps," his spectacles), shared a study with George Beresford (M'Turk) and "Stalky" Dunsterville, and before long he was sharpening his wit in daily repartee with William Crofts ("Mr. King"), the master who taught him Latin and English literature. But these "verbal duels marked a deep-seated bond of sympathy between this enthusiastic teacher and his talented pupil," and it was Crofts who early recognized Kipling's literary talent and gave his reputation as school poet an official stamp in

[1] Carrington, p. 10.
[2] *Something*, p. 17.

dubbing him "Gigadibs, the literary man."[1] Soon Kipling enjoyed the freedom of the headmaster's "brown-bound, tobacco-scented library." The Head prohibited nothing, recommended nothing, and Kipling found there "a fat arm-chair, a silver ink-stand and unlimited pens and paper." On the shelves were scores of books, particularly "hundreds of volumes of verse. Then the Head, drifting in under the pretence of playing censor . . . would read here a verse and here another of these poets, opening up avenues. And, slow-breathing, with half-shut eyes above his cigar, would speak of great men living, and journals, long dead."[2]

In September, 1882, Kipling left Westward Ho! to join his parents in India. Just before his seventeenth birthday, he took a job as assistant editor of the *Civil and Military Gazette*, an influential newspaper in Lahore. Like Haggard in Africa, Kipling in India awoke to his own possibilities and to the remarkable, strange world to which fate had brought him. Although he "never worked less than ten hours and seldom more than fifteen per diem," he thrived.[3] "The re-discovery of India was a complete and absorbing occupation" for him. And his manner of life was different from anything he had known earlier: "He had his personal servant, . . . his own quarters in his parents' bungalow, his horse, . . . and a trap in which he drove down to the office."[4] In this vast subcontinent his imagination burgeoned, and poems and stories seemed to flow from his pen, even as he perfected his journalistic craft.

Although Kipling found his identity as a serious writer for the first time in India, he had been producing verses and tales since childhood. When he was fifteen, and at Westward Ho!, his parents had brought together some of his earlier work and printed it in India for private circulation as *Schoolboy Lyrics*. He wrote a good deal at the United Services College, much of which appeared in the *College Chronicle*, and in fact, while still there, he sold his first literary piece to "a London newspaper for no less than a guinea."[5]

Kipling's first important book was *Departmental Ditties*, published anonymously in Lahore in 1886, a collection of light verse that had appeared in the *Civil and Military*. It was "immensely popular in India"

[1] Carrington, pp. 20–25.
[2] *Stalky & Co., Works*, XVIII, 265–66.
[3] *Something*, p. 41.
[4] Carrington, p. 38.
[5] *Ibid.*, p. 29.

and soon a second edition was called for.[1] Some copies of the first edition found their way to London, and Andrew Lang noticed the book in his monthly column in *Longman's Magazine*, calling the pieces "quaint and amusing." He likes the brevity of the individual poems, and he suggests that "the Radical should read 'Departmental Ditties' and learn how gaily *Jobus et Cie.* govern India." One poem he finds worthy of Bret Harte and another ("In Spring-time") he likes "so much that (supreme compliment!)," he quotes it entirely.[2] Next came *Plain Tales from the Hills* (1888), containing thirty-two stories that had already appeared in the *Civil and Military Gazette* and eight new ones. The book found a ready public in the East. Kipling now had a reputation, and both the high quality of the stories and their local and topical interest won for him a wide audience. In the following months, new stories appeared as part of a series of six volumes inaugurating the Indian Railway Library. Kipling's biographer records that "these little books in grey paper covers created the first Kipling boom; they were carried by travellers and tourists, all over Asia and all over the world, getting the notice in London and New York that *Departmental Ditties* and *Plain Tales* at first failed to get."[3] Little wonder, for the first contained stories about the Soldiers Three, and the others offered "The Story of the Gadsbys," "The Man Who Would Be King," "Baa, Baa, Black Sheep," "A Wayside Comedy," and other equally distinguished tales.

Kipling's years of apprenticeship came to an end early in 1889, and although these had been "years of hard work and a reasonable amount of sickness,"[4] they served him well. For he had done more than learn a profession: through his work he had grown familiar with a new way of life, one that was more remote and more engrossing than anything he could have dreamed of at Southsea or Westward Ho!. India had mesmerized him, and he had spent his six years there trying to come to terms with its mysterious attractions. By the time he was ready to set sail, he had acquired a wide range of experience and a keen insight into the East. He

---

[1] Carrington, p. 62.

[2] "At the Sign of the Ship," VIII (October, 1886), 672–78. Lang would be the first to write a book article of Kipling's work after Kipling arrived in London. "An Indian Story-Teller," dealing with Kipling's stories up to 1889, appeared anonymously in the *Daily News* [November 2, 1889, p. 4.], and was followed by "Anglo-India," a review of the new edition of *Departmental Ditties* [*Ibid.*, March 15, 1890, pp. 4–5].

[3] Carrington, p. 75.

[4] *Something*, p. 75.

knew India's strange mixture of peoples, her incongruous combination of beauty and ugliness, her social chaos, and her deep elusive personality. And, whether he was aware of it or not, she had branded him. For not only was he to take the Indian swastika, the symbol of good luck, as his personal seal—he was to bring to bear upon his conduct the rules he had evolved in India and upon his work the knowledge and inspiration whose source lay in the East.

At the end of his "Seven Years' Hard," Kipling, "ripe for a change,"[1] decided on a journey to England, taking the long route by way of Rangoon, Hong Kong, Japan, and the United States. On Saturday, October 5, 1889, he arrived at Liverpool, "stepped into a waking dream,"[2] and began to rediscover the England he had left as a schoolboy seven years earlier.

If he bought a copy of The Times for his journey up to London, and it is unthinkable that he did not, he read among international news about the Shakir Pasha's coup in Crete, of wholesale expelling of Jews from Russia, of two train accidents in Germany, and of a cyclone in the Gulf of Mexico. The home news was that the Queen had donated £50 to King's College Hospital; the police had raided the East Finsbury Institute, leading sixty to seventy people away on the charge of illegal horse betting; two people had been killed in a tragic railway accident on the previous evening near Manchester; a pit disaster had occurred at Penicuik; and the Church Congress was meeting at Cardiff. The letters columns contained a number of complaints on the unpunctuality of English trains, the weather for Friday was reported as having been unsettled with rain everywhere, and the forecast for Saturday was showery. Kipling might also have read that at the Haymarket in London, Beerbohm Tree was appearing in A Man's Shadow, a play translated from the French by Robert Buchanan; at the Lyceum, Henry Irving and Ellen Terry were playing in The Dead Heart, a story of the French Revolution; and at the Savoy, the D'Oyly Carte Company were doing The Yeoman of the Guard. If he chanced to pick up Macmillan's Magazine, he found there an instalment of Mrs. Oliphant's Kirsteen. The English Illustrated Magazine for October contained Swinburne's "On the South Coast," Mrs. Molesworth's "English Girlhood," and G. B. Shaw's "Wagner in Bayreuth." The current issue of Nineteenth Century contained "Marie Bashkirtseff" by W. E. Gladstone.

[1] Something, p. 74.
[2] Ibid., p. 77.

When Kipling arrived in London, a twenty-three-year-old unknown, he had few friends and almost no money. What he possessed, however, was the experience of his apprentice years, an extensive knowledge of the world, untapped energy, a proven talent for putting words together—and a great desire and need to find work. He took lodgings in Villiers Street at Embankment Chambers, whence he could look out over the Thames or walk down Fleet Street to meet one of the few newspaper men he knew in London. But the set with which he would soon become associated, and whose members would do much to establish him and advance his reputation, was in fact largely contained within the walls of the Savile Club, then at 107, Piccadilly, in a "beautiful little house"[1] looking across Green Park to Buckingham Palace.

Rider Haggard had been elected to the Club in 1887, the year that *She* appeared, and although the Savile's records do not go back far enough to tell us who his sponsors were, we do know that Andrew Lang, one of London's most influential critics, had a hand in his election, for on February 1, 1887, he wrote Haggard, "You were elected to the Savile, in a triumphant manner."[2]

Lang was also instrumental in bringing Kipling into the Savile and consequently in touch with Haggard. After Kipling "had not been more than a few days in London,"[3] he somehow met Lang. Having read and admired Kipling's Indian tales and poetry, Lang was eager to help the novice establish himself. Just as six years earlier he had guided Haggard to Cassell's, who published *King Solomon's Mines*, so he now steered the young Kipling to Sampson Low, whom he persuaded to publish some of Kipling's work that had already appeared in India. And, at almost the same time, he shepherded the shy, moustached stranger into the Savile circle.

Kipling must have known of Haggard before Haggard knew anything about him, because in his short story, "Her Little Responsibility," which appeared in August, 1889, he took the liberty of paraphrasing a passage from Haggard's *Cleopatra*, published only two months earlier.[4]

---

[1] Henry Newbolt, *The Later Life and Letters of Sir Henry Newbolt*, Margaret Newbolt, ed. (1942), p. 10.

[2] Andrew Lang to Rider Haggard in an unpublished letter dated February 1, [1887], in the Lockwood Memorial Library, University of Buffalo.

[3] Carrington, p. 103.

[4] Kipling was in America when *Cleopatra* was published (it appeared simultaneously in England and the United States in June, 1889). In *Cleopatra* Hermachis, the Egyptian priest-hero, philosophizes: "For though that thing

Though neither could remember exactly when they first met, the meeting must have occurred within a few days of Kipling's arrival in London. Lang and Haggard, in the four years since *King Solomon's Mines* appeared, had become close friends and, when Kipling arrived on the scene, they were collaborating on a Greco–Egyptian romance to be called *The World's Desire*. Lang could easily have brought the two story-tellers together at the Club. Later Kipling was to remember that "at 'the little Savile' ... [there was] Rider Haggard ... [who] could tell tales, mainly against himself, that broke up the tables."[1] And during his earliest days in London, when he was still recording his first impressions in letters to his close friends in India, he wrote, "London is a vile place, and Anstey and Haggard and Lang and Co. are pressing on me the wisdom of identifying myself with some set."[2]

The set was of course the Savile, or one of the groups within it. And a splendid set it was, including at one time or another: Grant Allen, Max Beerbohm, J. A. Blaikie, Robert Bridges, Edward Clodd, Sidney Colvin, Austin Dobson, Thomas Anstey Guthrie, Thomas Hardy, Anthony Hope Hawkins, Maurice Hewlett, Henry James, William J. Loftie, Justin McCarthy, William Cosmo Monkhouse, Walter Raleigh, George Saintsbury, J. K. Stephen and H. G. Wells. Visitors included John Addington Symonds, Charles Eliot Norton, and Oscar Wilde. Wilde actually sought membership in the club, but did not get the unanimous voice necessary for acceptance.[3]

Desirable companions for writers are editors and publishers, and the Savile boasted a good many of them. Virtually every important journal was represented at one time or another, and everyone who held an

---

we worship doth bring us ruin, and Love being more pitiless than Death, we in turn do pay all our sorrow back; yet we must worship on, yet stretch out our arms towards our lost Desire, and pour our heart's blood upon the shrine of our discrowned God.

"For love is the Spirit and knows not Death." Kipling in turn, in "Her Little Responsibility," has a disreputable San Francisco drunk paraphrase the "priest-chap" in Cleopatra: "That priest-chap says a very true thing about [love] .... You can't stop when it's once started, and when it's all over you can't give it up at the word of command. I forget the precise language." [*Cleopatra* (1889), p. 324; "Her Little Responsibility," *Abaft the Funnel* (New York: Dodge, 1909), p. 16.]

[1] *Something*, p. 85.

[2] Carrington, p. 108.

[3] Rupert Hart-Davis, ed., *The Letters of Oscar Wilde* (1962), p. 224.

important post on the *Saturday Review* was reputed to be a member. A number of weeklies were, in fact, born at the Savile and were staffed almost exclusively by Savilians, among them Henley's *Scots* (later *National*) *Observer*, which one Savile member called "an overflow *Saturday Review*,"[1] and J. K. Stephen's *Reflector*. Representing English publishing at the Savile were C. E. Appleton (*Academy*), Frederick Greenwood (*Pall Mall Gazette*), W. E. Henley (*Scots Observer*), R. H. Hutton (*Spectator*), Sidney James Low (*St. James Gazette*), Norman MacColl (*Athenaeum*), William Minto (*Examiner*), John Morley (*Fortnightly Review*), John Murray, Kegan Paul, W. H. Pollock (*Saturday Review*), Owen Seaman (*Punch*), J. K. Stephen (*Reflector*), Leslie Stephen (*Cornhill*), and H. E. Watts (*Melbourne Argus*).

It was a club full of vitality, whose members were sharp, vigorous, creative, and productive. The Club's conversation was free and easy; it brought men closer together than they would be at other London clubs and paved the way for relaxed, intimate relationships. Certainly it was a lively fellowship. "I doubt whether any club, except, perhaps, the Garrick, ... has ever been regarded with such personal affection," wrote Saintsbury.[2]

The benefits that accrued to the members as a result of the casual life at the Savile were numerous, and Rudyard Kipling and Rider Haggard could not have been indifferent to them. The Savile had in fact become one of the literary counting houses of London, where great works were inspired and sometimes executed, where hopeful writers sought out editors and publishers, where authors' rights and copyright reform became burning issues, where literary reputations were made as well as broken, and where, over pipes of tobacco and glasses of sherry, a handful of men casually, even haphazardly, helped steer the ship of English letters for a quarter of a century. Literary talk and gossip were plentiful. A number of collaborations were conceived and some were even brought to term at the Savile.[3] A chance conversation sometimes gave birth to a major literary enterprise.[4]

[1] George Saintsbury, *A Scrap Book* (1922), p. 153.

[2] George Saintsbury, *A Second Scrap Book* (1923), p. 329.

[3] Lang and R. L. Stevenson collaborated. Walter Besant and W. H. Pollock wrote plays together. Lang and Henley collaborated, as did Henley and Stevenson. Brander Matthews collaborated with F. Anstey and with W. H. Pollock. Lang and Pollock wrote together. Charles Villers Stanford and Brander Matthews collaborated on a ballet that was never produced. Stanford and George H. Jessop wrote a comic opera based on Sheridan Le Fanu's ballet

The Club's connection with men of letters had been established early in its history, when it occupied a "set of very pleasant rooms" on the first floor at 9, Spring Gardens, with a view of Trafalgar Square. There, in 1868, the Savile had its beginnings when a number of Eclectic Club members decided to form a new group, "a mixture of men of different professions and opinions" devoted to "a thorough simplicity in all arrangements," a phrase which some members later interpreted to mean "plain living and high thinking."[1] The Club apparently took the rooms near Trafalgar Square because its founder wished to be within walking distance of Whitehall. It remained nameless for about a year and led "a precarious kind of chrysalis existence,"[2] writes one of its early members. Soon, however, they decided to call themselves the New Club, but surrendered that name for Savile when they moved to "a very delightful old house"[3] at 15, Savile Row in the autumn of 1871.

The Club thrived in its new quarters, and its membership rolls grew steadily. It took a motto, *Sodalitas convivium* (not, as rumour had it, in deference to Sidney Colvin's initials, but rather to those of the club itself).

From the beginning, members agreed that they should talk to one another without being formally introduced,[4] sometimes with amusing consequences. Brander Matthews, an American with a standing invitation to the Club, recalls an incident that occurred at dinner one evening when H. O. Arnold-Foster, the military expert, sat at one of the two long "ordinary" tables. During the meal another member noticed that Arnold-Foster had engaged a stranger sitting next to him in animated

---

Shamus O'Brien, and this was produced with great success. [John Connell, *W. E. Henley* (1949), pp. 15, 87–89, 93, 101–104, 120, 124, 325–28; Roger Lancelyn Green, *Andrew Lang* (1946), pp. 64–65, 113–14, 243; Brander Matthews, *These Many Years* (1917), pp. 421–22; Brander Matthews, *With My Friends: Tales Told in Partnership* (1891).]

[4] According to Brander Matthews, the idea for the first collection of Thackeray's letters was hatched at the Savile Club. See Matthews, *These Many Years*, pp. 301-305; Gordon N. Ray, *Thackeray: The Uses of Adversity* (1955), I, 4-5; *A Collection of Letters of W. M. Thackeray, 1847-1855* (1887).

[1] [Herbert Stephen,] *The Savile Club, 1868 to 1923* (1923), pp. 1–4.

[2] Sidney Colvin, *Memories & Notes of Persons & Place, 1852–1912* (1921), p. 119.

[3] Saintsbury, *Second*, p. 327.

[4] Colvin, p. 119.

conversation. Later, the observer approached Arnold-Foster and said something to indicate that he had noticed the lively exchange over dinner.

"Yes," Arnold-Foster said, "that was a very intelligent man next to me; and he seemed to be very much interested."

"What were you talking about?" the observer asked.

"Oh, I was just explaining some of the latest discoveries in astrophysics."

The observer smiled and said, "I should think that he might be interested in that. Don't you know who he is?—Sir Robert Ball, the astronomer royal for Ireland."[1]

The Club's founder, Auberon Herbert, younger brother of Lord Carnarvon, though still in his twenties, was secretary to Sir Stafford Northcote. He in turn persuaded his brothers, Lord Carnarvon and Robert Herbert, Assistant Secretary of the Board of Trade; John Murray; Henry Sidgwick; and others to become charter members. And soon they added to the rolls the names of Leslie Stephen, Alfred and Walter Morrison, James Bryce, Thomas Woolner, R. H. Hutton, Sidney Colvin, Henry Irving, Herbert Spencer (who joined, reportedly, because he could play billiards at the Savile on Sunday, a privilege denied him at the Athenaeum[2]). By 1873 Walter Besant could observe that the Club "was full of young writers, young dons, and young scientific men."[3]

Robert Louis Stevenson helped considerably to give the Club a distinct literary personality. He joined in 1874, during the Club's sixth year, and made it his London headquarters for the next five years. Around him clustered the early generation of Savile literary lights, Colvin, Lang, Appleton, Pollock, Saintsbury, Bob Stevenson, Edmund Gosse, Morley, Minto, and many other colourful figures. Stevenson was the "radiating centre of good talk," Colvin tells us, "a kind of ideal incarnation of the spirit of the society."[4] And Gosse recalls that "Louis pervaded the Club; he was its most affable and chatty member; and he lifted it, by the ingenuity of his incessant dialectic, to the level of a sort of humorous Academe or Mouseion."[5]

[1] Matthews, *Many Years*, p. 420.

[2] Edward Clodd, *Memories* (1926), p. 51.

[3] Walter Besant, *Autobiography of Sir Walter Besant* (1902), p. 175.

[4] Colvin, pp. 120–21.

[5] Edmund Gosse, *Critical Kit-Kats* (1897), p. 281.

The eleven years the Club spent in Savile Row were years of development, and when, in 1882, it moved to larger quarters, it was not only fully grown, but also showed signs of additional distinction and genius. With confidence, the Club bought from Lord Rosebery a house in Piccadilly "with Byronic and other memories."[1] It contained a double drawing room on the first floor that ran the length of the building and a guests' dining room for special occasions.[2] A visitor entering the Club for the first time might get this impression: "It was green. It was tastefully decorated with playbills and umbrellas; and the coats and hats of many rising authors depended at regular intervals upon the walls. On one hand, in a glass case, a manner of porter waited."[3]

During the Club's years in Piccadilly, Saturday luncheons were red-letter events for a group of the members, many of them writers, some either on the staff of the *Saturday Review* or regular contributors to it. These luncheons were always held at the same table in a bow window at the front of the house, and the conversations that began over the mid-day meal often lasted into the late afternoon or evening.

The list of those who attended these luncheons over the years is fairly long, though it covers more than one generation of members. The luncheons themselves were intimate, with seldom more than ten or twelve present. At one time or another there were Grant Allen, Eustace Balfour, Besant, Charles Brookfield, Clodd, Colvin, Martin Conway, A. J. Duffield, Gosse, Egmont Hake, Henley, Lang, Charles Leland (Hans Breitman), William Loftie, E. H. Palmer, Pollock, Saintsbury, James and Herbert Stephen, R. A. M. Stevenson, R. L. Stevenson, H. E. Watts, Gordon Wigan, and, of course, Haggard and Kipling.

As a centre of creativity, the Club was inevitably the eye of many a literary hurricane, and in the early 'nineties neither Kipling nor Haggard was ever far from the Savile storms. Walter Besant, one of the very first to "discover" Kipling, knew the dangers that waited for a newcomer within the Savile's walls, and he warned Kipling about the risks of controversy. "He advised me to 'keep out of the dog-fight,'" Kipling later recalled. "He said that if I were 'in with one lot' I would have to be out with another; and that, at last, 'things would get like a girls' school where they stick out their tongues at each other when they pass.' That was true too," Kipling adds. "One heard men vastly one's seniors

---

[1] Saintsbury, *Second*, p. 327.

[2] Edmund Gosse, *Silhouettes* (1925), pp. 379–80.

[3] Robert Louis Stevenson. *Diogenes at the Savile Club* (1921), p. [2].

wasting energy and good oaths in recounting 'intrigues' against them, and of men who had 'their knife into' their work, or whom they themselves wished to 'knife.' ... It seemed best to stand clear of it all."[1]

Many of the disagreements that arose among the members of the Savile shook the very rafters of the house. Literary schools arose within the Club itself, and the battle between "the crocodile of Realism and the catawampus of Romance" was waged within the Savile's walls. Editors competed both secretly and openly for the services of the latest literary stars. Novelists boomed their own names and, in fits of jealousy, struck out at their rivals. When one of the Club's book reviewers wrote an unfavourable notice of another member's latest novel, men put down their pipes and billiard cues, took up their pens, and waged internecine war. Accusations of logrolling, plagiarism, and mediocrity mingled with accusations of playing to the gallery. And the blows struck at the Savile frequently echoed through the columns of London's dailies and weeklies. Men stormed into the Club waving a copy of the latest paper in search of the "libellous" author. Others stormed out and sent in their resignations.

The members naturally took note of all literary happenings, especially when fellow Clubmen were involved. "A great sensation was created among us one day," writes one of the Saturday lunchers, "when an elaborate article appeared in a quarterly of repute violently and virulently attacking Gosse. He did not appear at lunch-time the next Saturday, but came dancing in afterwards. 'Behold the crushed worm,' said he. There was an uncomfortable silence till Walter Pollock replied, 'It's a long worm that has no turning.' The tension was relieved and all was well."[2]

When one Savilian fell out with another, he would sometimes write and even publish a parody on his opposite number. When William Black attacked an American woman writer for failing to see "in his beloved Scotland the marvellous sunsets he delighted in depicting," Brander Matthews, in turn, regretted in print that "a British novelist had been discourteous to an American lady." Black, though not mentioned by name, caught the reference, and in his next novel, he created a character by the name of Professor Maunder Bathos.[3]

At first Kipling succeeded in standing clear of most of the wrangles.

---

[1] *Something*, p. 84.

[2] William Martin Conway, *Episodes in a Varied Life* (1923), p. 253.

[3] Matthews, *Many Years*, p. 289.

But even in his earliest London days, he could observe in a letter to India that "the long-haired literati at the Savile Club are swearing that I 'invented' my soldier talk in *Soldiers Three*. Seeing that not one of these critters has been within earshot of a barrack, I am naturally wroth."[1]

And within a year of his arrival in London, he was at the very centre of an international tempest in which all literary London, including many Savile members, had a vested interest. Because no adequate Anglo–American copyright law had yet come into being, many American publishers pirated the works of popular British authors. In 1890 Kipling's *Barrack-room Ballads* made him the literary man of the hour both in England and the United States, and now that his reputation was made, American publishers were raking through all of his printed works, even his Indian newspaper pieces, and pirating them. This infuriated Kipling and many of his friends, and when, in September, 1890, the large and dignified house of Harper and Brothers printed "Krishna Mulvaney" without so much as a by your leave, the battle for adequate copyright laws began in earnest, Kipling in the front line of assault.

Kipling's part of the war was fought out in the columns of the *Athenaeum*. Norman MacColl, its editor, fired a barrage at Harper and Brothers, and then the American publishers wrote a reply for the following issue. Kipling in turn wrote an answer to the Harper statement, in which he called the publishers outright pirates, "like Paul Jones." And then, the blow that would seem to come directly from the Savile Club itself was a letter that appeared, also in the *Athenaeum*, over the signatures of Walter Besant, Thomas Hardy, and William Black, three of the most eminent men of letters of the day, defending Harper and Brothers, in spite of the unfortunate Kipling incident, as publishers who generally carried on their affairs in a manner beyond reproach.[2] Despite Kipling's policy of avoiding the literary battles at the Savile, this was more than he could abide, and he wrote a bitter ballad called "The Rhyme of the Three Captains," a masterpiece of satirical allegory on the preceding events and the current state of sea-going publishing. It too appeared in the *Athenaeum*, on December 6, 1890.

Kipling must have found some of his relationships at the Savile strained as a result of the copyright war. But, heated as the attacks were, they seemed not to impair any friendships permanently. For even while the remonstrances were appearing in the *Athenaeum*, Kipling's name was

[1] Carrington, p. 109.

[2] *Ibid.*, pp. 126–27.

formally proposed for membership to the Savile by Andrew Lang, and among his sponsors, at the very time that the Harper controversy raged, were two of the "Three Captains," Thomas Hardy and Walter Besant. On the night that Kipling was elected to the Club, he celebrated the event by dining with the same two members, a fact he himself remembered and recorded some forty-five years later.[1]

It seems, then, that in spite of the "dog-fight" and the Harper controversy, Kipling's relationship with the Savile and its members was amicable; when he came up for membership in late 1890, he certainly lacked no supporters,[2] and by his own confession, he took "great pride" in being a member.[3] He was frequently present at the Saturday luncheons, he often dropped in when he was in London, and he remained a member for fourteen years, until 1905, three years after he had moved to Sussex. It is perhaps surprising that in this highly competitive atmosphere, friendship could flourish at all. But so it did between Kipling and Haggard, though their fellow Clubmen seemed to set every obstacle in their way. Primarily, they saw Kipling as a challenger to Haggard's fame, which, in 1889, was at its height. "We'll tell you all about Rudyard Kipling—your nascent rival," Henry James wrote to Stevenson in Samoa. "He has killed one immortal—Rider Haggard."[4] And John Addington Symonds wrote in a letter to Horatio F. Brown: "Did I tell you of my making the acquaintance of Rudyard Kipling. . . . The Savile was all on the *qui vive* about him, when I lunched there . . . with Gosse. Rider Haggard appeared really aggrieved at a man with a double-barrelled name, odder than his own, coming up. Literally."[5]

[1] *Something*, p. 83.

[2] The Savile's Candidates Book contains a page that records Kipling's election to the Club. His name, qualifications ("Author of Plain Tales from the Hills, Departmental Ditties, etc."), and address are entered in Andrew Lang's handwriting. Two dates appear, presumably the date of proposal (October 25, 1890) and the date of election (January 30, 1891). Following Lang's signature as proposer, appear dozens of signatures scrawled by Kipling's supporters. They include Walter Besant, J. A. Blaikie, Sidney Colvin, W. M. Conway, Edward Clodd, Austin Dobson, Thos. Hardy, W. E. Henley, Henry James, A. Egmont Hake, J. W. Mackail, Justin McCarthy, E. B. Iwan Müller, Walter H. Pollock, George Saintsbury—and H. Rider Haggard.

[3] *Something*, p. 83.

[4] Janet Adam Smith, ed., *Henry James and Robert Louis Stevenson: A Record of Friendship and Criticism* (1948), p. 184.

[5] Horatio F. Brown, ed., *Letters and Papers of John Addington Symonds* (1923), p. 228.

The Press too pitted one against the other—or damned them both in the same breath: "It is a pathetic fact," wrote an anonymous columnist in *Harper's,* "that with such artistic and important books in our reach, the great mass of us prefer to read the Rider Haggards and the Rudyard Kiplings of the day."[1]

And then there is the jingle that J. K. Stephen composed, when, one afternoon at the Savile, he bolted from a talking circle and on the spur of the moment scribbled off these immortal lines:

> Will there never come a season
> Which shall rid us from the curse
> Of a prose which knows no reason
> And an unmelodious verse:
> When the world shall cease to wonder
> At the genius of an Ass,
> And a boy's eccentric blunder
> Shall not bring success to pass:
>
> When mankind shall be delivered
> From the clash of magazines,
> And the inkstand shall be shivered
> Into countless smithereens:
> When there stands a muzzled stripling,
> Mute, beside a muzzled bore:
> When the Rudyards cease from kipling
> And the Haggards Ride no more.[2]

But this sounds with as much humour as wit, with as much sense as nonsense, all deftly exposing the undercurrent of the professional jealousies running through the Club. Kipling and Haggard, however, were not hurt by wagging tongues. They both wished that they themselves had written the Stephen verses, and the gentle abuse became a standing joke between them. From the first they found in each other an attraction and mutual sympathy that raised their relationship above the traffic of the literary marketplace. "From [the time we first met] . . . we have always liked each other," wrote Haggard.[3] "I took [to Haggard] at once,"

---

[1] "Editor's Study, "*Harper's New Monthly Magazine,* LXXXI (October, 1890), 801.

[2] "To R. K.," *Lapsus Calami* (1891), p. 3.

[3] *Days,* II, 27.

wrote Kipling, "he being of the stamp adored by children and trusted by men at sight."[1]

Kipling and Haggard enjoyed the Club, warts and all. Its foibles, its limitations, and above all its homey air provoked a mixture of old-shoe affection and jocular self-criticism. Stevenson wrote of it with an appropriate mixture of levity and tenderness (rather than, perhaps, the strictest accuracy):

> This is the place known by fame to many; to few by sight. Now and again, Gladstone or Hugo, the Primate of England and the Prince de Galles, may tread, not without awe, its hallowed flooring. But these, great though they are, are not its true inhabitants. Here gather daily those young eaglets of glory, the swordsmen of the pen, who are the pride and wonder of the world, and the terror and envy of the effete pensionaires of the Athenaeum. They are all young; and youth is a great gift. They are all clever authors; and some of them, with that last refinement of talent, old as Job but rare as modesty, have hitherto refrained from writing. They are old friends, though they may slate each other in anonymous prints. And they are all Rising.[2]

Certainly the Club's reputation grew apace in London circles. One member records overhearing a stranger in the Inns of Court say, "Oh, I know the Savile; I've dined there. It's an awful swell club. They won't elect you unless you're an atheist or have written a book."[3] And they must have chuckled at the skit on the Savile in an evening paper: A tourist wandering down Pall Mall expresses to a constable curiosity about "the venerable appearance" of the gentlemen going in and out of the Athenaeum. When the policeman tells him that they are usually old by the time they are allowed to enter the sacred precincts, he asks, "But what did they do till then?" "Oh," says the policeman, "they've a little place to wait in, up in Piccadilly somewhere."[4]

But although the Savile was little and many did wait there until the Athenaeum beckoned, most of its members, including Kipling and Haggard, had a warm regard for it and benefited from its numerous advantages. Haggard appeared at the Savile regularly in the 'eighties and

---

[1] *Something*, p. 85.

[2] Stevenson, pp. [4–5]. I have silently corrected two printing errors in the Stevenson fragment.

[3] [Stephen], p. 35.

[4] Saintsbury, *Scrap Book*, pp. 326–37.

'nineties. Here he asked Brander Matthews if he might publish *She* over their combined names: "he hoped to be able to secure an American copyright if a citizen of the United States could claim to be its joint author."[1] Here Haggard would, from time to time, meet with Henley, who, he tells us, "was extremely fond of war and fighting . . . [and] would insist upon my telling him stories by the yard about Zulus and their blood-thirsty battles and customs."[2] Here he was host at luncheons and dinners, and he could later recall a particular dinner in the early 'nineties at which he entertained Lord Goschen, Mr. Balfour, Lord Lytton, and a number of literary men. "I remember," he wrote, "that it was a most pleasant feast, at which seventeen or eighteen people were present, and one that, to my great relief, went off without a hitch."[3] He could recall also an incident in the later 'nineties that marked a significant decision for the literary world: "One day . . . I was in the little writing-room of the Savile Club, that on the first floor with ferncases in the window where one may smoke. . . . Presently Thomas Hardy entered and took up one of the leading weekly papers in which was a long review of his last novel. He read it, then came to me—there was no other in the room—and pointed out a certain passage.

"'There's a nice thing to say about a man!' he exclaimed. 'Well, I'll never write another novel.'

"And he never did."[4]

Another member could later recall the day when Haggard told him where he had got the idea for the famous Place of Death in *King Solomon's Mines*:

> One day when . . . [Haggard] and I were lunching together [at the Savile] he produced a gold ring and told me that it was the ring that first opened the world of romance to him, and then he related the story which he incorporated in "King Solomon's Mines." The actual story was as follows. When Haggard was a boy there lived in the neighbourhood of his home a certain old retired sea-captain, who used to electrify him with all manner of wonderful tales of his own doings and experiences. The best of them, which he was never tired of hearing again, was the story of the Ring. The old skipper's ship had

[1] Matthews, *Many Years*, p. 278. Actually Harper's published *She* in the U.S. under Haggard's name in 1886.

[2] *Days*, I, 276.

[3] *Ibid.*, II, 24.

[4] *Ibid.*, I, 272–73.

been laid up for some months at Callao. He relieved the tediousness of inaction by accepting the hospitality freely offered him by residents in and about Lima. He was taken into the country one day to the sugar estate of a friend. Operations were going on there for the removal in whole or in part of a great mound. As they were watching the diggers a hole was breached into what proved to be a great cave or chamber within the mound, whose existence had not been suspected. What was their astonishment on peering in to behold a dozen or so of mummies seated as in life around a table, with the host or some superior person at their head. As the invaders watched in astonishment and some horror, the whole company fell to dust on the floor. Only one object survived. It was the golden ring which was on the finger of the chief. The ring was given the skipper and he wore it to his dying day. When Haggard was grown up and his friend was long dead, he bethought him of this ring. After elaborate inquiries he discovered it in the possession of a lady, a descendant or relative of the skipper. Haggard bought it of her and used himself to carry it about. I have worn it on my own hand and examined it in every detail. The ring is now in the gold room of the British Museum, to which Haggard presented it.[1]

Some of Kipling's appearances at the Club have also been recalled by his fellow members. One remembers being in the card room correcting the proof of a story destined for a provincial newspaper when

Rudyard Kipling came in and asked to look at it. He spoke most kindly of the tale, but had many suggestions to make with regard to the telling. "Don't you see how much stronger that would be?" he asked after suggesting an excision and a transposition. "D'you mind if I alter it?" And, so saying, he whipped out a pencil and set to work; and having once put his hand to the plough, so to speak, he persevered, and in a few minutes the whole virgin expanse of proof was furrowed and hoed and harrowed and manured and top-dressed by the master. I packed up and despatched the corrected sheet there and then.

The result was unexpected. I received a most abusive letter from the editor, saying that if I imagined his compositors had nothing better to do than to try and decipher Chinese puzzles I was gravely mistaken; that they had been put to great inconvenience to fill in at the last

[1] Conway, pp. 255–56. A somewhat different version of this story appears in Haggard's diary on December 4, 1920.

moment the space my story should have occupied; that they certainly shouldn't use it now, and were extremely sorry they had paid for it; and that they were writing to [my agent] ... to complain. I had not the Christianity to write and tell the editor that what he was discarding as worthless rubble was, in reality, sparkling with Kipling nuggets.[1]

Both Haggard and Kipling left testimonials to their years of convivial membership at the Club. "The Savile was a very pleasant club," Haggard wrote. "... Often as I walk down Piccadilly I look at the table through the window and think of many things."[2] And Kipling was to write that "one heard very good talk at the Savile. Much of it was the careless give-and-take of the atelier when the models are off their stands, and one throws bread-pellets at one's betters, and makes hay of all schools save one's own. ... [But] at 'the little Savile' I remember much kindness and toleration."[3]

[1] Charles H. E. Brookfield, *Random Reminiscences* (1902), pp. 28–29.
[2] *Days*, I, 273.
[3] *Something*, pp. 84–86.

THE RECORD

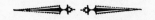

The earliest letter that bears upon the Kipling–Haggard relationship is one to Andrew Lang that Kipling wrote exactly three weeks after he arrived in England. The letter, a verse parody in the manner of Bret Harte's "Plain Language from Truthful James," is written in the context of the Savile Club gossip about Lang and Haggard's year-old collaboration on a romance about Odysseus' latter-day wanderings, and Kipling may very well have intended Lang to read it aloud for the amusement of the inner circle at the following Saturday luncheon. The letter suggests that when Kipling had last spoken with Lang, perhaps earlier in the day at the Savile, they had jokingly speculated about a journey or lecture tour in the United States that Lang and Haggard might make together in 1890 to help publicize their forthcoming book. In the parody, Kipling has Truthful James, Harte's crusty commentator on the American scene, tell of the confusion that results when the American public mistakes Lang for Haggard and Haggard for Lang.

The Grange, West Kensington, W.[1]
October 26, 1889

Dear Mr. Lang,
    No. There were no adventures. What happened after your tour was told in March 1890 by Bret Harte in the Argonaut[2] in this manner:—

---

[1] The Grange, North End Road, Fulham, was the home of Edward and Georgiana Burne-Jones, Kipling's aunt and uncle (Kipling's mother and Georgiana were sisters). Samuel Richardson had once lived there; the Burne-Joneses bought it when they married in 1860, and it became "the gathering-place of the Macdonalds [Kipling's mother's family] and all their set for more than thirty years." [Carrington, p. 4] Uncle Ned and Aunt Georgie were two of Kipling's dearest relatives, and the Grange one of his favourite places to visit. Writing later of his unhappy childhood in Southsea, Kipling added: "But, for a month each year I possessed a paradise which I verily believe saved me. Each December I stayed with my Aunt Georgie . . . at the Grange . . . [where] I had love and affection as much as the greediest . . . could desire." [Something, pp. 11–15; Angela Thirkell, Three Houses (1931), pp. 15–27]
    [2] The San Francisco Argonaut, a popular weekly, would be a likely place for a set of Truthful James verses to appear, and Kipling is easily able to recall the name of the paper from his visit to the United States. Harte's "Plain Language from Truthful James," known also as "The Heathen Chinee," was first published in 1870 and soon became his best-known poem. Andrew Lang had already written a parody ["From Truthful James to Mr. Bret Harte," first published in the St. James's Gazette, March 7, 1888; collected in Old Friends: Essays in Epistolary Parody (1890), pp. 120–22], and Robert Louis Stevenson also parodied it in a letter he wrote in 1884 [RLS: Stevenson's Letters to Charles

I reside at Table Mountain and my name is Truthful James
I am not versed in lecturin' or other sinful games.
You will please refrain from shooting while my simple lyre I twang
To the tale of Mister Haggard and his partner Mister Lang.

They were high toned litterateurs and two most unhappy men
For they started to enlighten our enlightened citizen;
And thanks to the reporter who the interviewing fixed
Mister Lang with Mister Haggard got inextricably mixed.

Now our sunward-gazing nation gets its information slick
From the daily mornin' journal—an' it reads darnation quick
So if that information be inaccurately wild
Some eighty million citizens are apt to be beguiled.

In the ears of Mister Haggard whom they hailed as Mister Lang
The societies of Boston ethnologically sang
And they spoke of creature-legends, and of totem, myth and sign
And the stricter law of Metre—Mister Haggard answered "*Nein*."

Then emboldened by his silence which was painful and extreme
They discoursed of gnome and kelpie and the imp that steals the cream
And of pornographic poems (which the same he never knew)
And they bade him chaunt a rondel—Mister Haggard then withdrew.

His subsequent adventures form no part of this concern—
It is to the other person Mister Rangard Hang we turn;
Our sunward-gazing nation fell upon him in a mass
Demanding little stories of his friend Umsloppogas.[1]

Baxter, DeLancey Ferguson and Marshall Waingrow, eds. (1956), p. 151].
Harte's work had made a deep impression on the young Kipling [*Something*,
p. 35], and in 1889, during his travels in the American West, Kipling was
delighted one morning when he awoke in an overheated Pullman sleeper
to find that he was in Bret Harte country [*From Sea to Sea, Works*, XVI,
84–85]. Harte and Kipling met at the dinner given by William Waldorf
Astor (1848–1919) on May 3, 1893, to inaugurate the *Pall Mall Magazine*.
But Harte found the company of a military man (Frederick Sleigh, Lord
Roberts, 1832–1914) more congenial than Kipling's, "for we [writers] are a
conceited lot." [Geoffrey Bret Harte, ed., *The Letters of Bret Harte* (1926),
p. 386]

[1] Haggard's spelling of his African hero's name is Umslopogaas.

The Prohibition Party made him lecture on the fate
Of the female Cleopatra[1] who imbibed her poison straight
While the Theosophic centres were revolving round his knees
And suggesting further volumes on some forty further "Shes."

But the straw that broke that camel was Chicago's mild request
For a Zulu dance in character—appropriately dressed
And vain is approbation when the path to glory leads
Through a wilderness of war-whoops and a wardrobeful of beads.

In the "Iroquois" at Buffalo[2] that partnership broke up
To the melancholy music of a six-shot boudoir Krupp
And the waiters on the staircase counted pistol shot and oath
While the partners argued hotly if the States could hold 'em both.

They collaborate in Yarrup where men know them who from which
And by latest information they are striking of it rich
But when evening lamps are lighted and the evening paper rustles
Still they pick forgotten bullets from each other's gluteal muscles.

Yours very penitently,

Rudyard Kipling.[3]

---

[1] The allusion is to Haggard's *Cleopatra* (1889; see pp. 9–10 above).

[2] The Iroquois Hotel was, when Kipling wrote, the newest hotel in down-town Buffalo. It had cost a million dollars to build, stood eight stories high, had handsome upper balconies and a billiards hall on the ground floor. The hotel opened for business on August 13, 1889, a mere two months before Kipling writes this letter, and he may have seen it on his visit to Buffalo earlier in the year. His report on Buffalo in *American Notes* indicates that he found much to interest him there and that he thought it "more like an English country town" than most American communities. He was, however, "horri-fied" to see two young couples "indubitably drunk." [W. E. J. Martin, "Kipling View of Buffalo as Pre-Kim," *Buffalo Courier*, CXVI (January 14, 1961), Section D, pp. 7–8; "Lakefront Enchanted Kipling on Visit to Buffalo in 1889," *Buffalo Evening News*, CXXXI (April 10, 1946), 39]

[3] Haggard visited the United States three times (1891, 1905, and 1916); Lang never. In 1889 "The Lounger," an American columnist writing in the *Critic*, publicly invited Lang to "come and see" America. Lang replied in his regular literary column in *Longman's Magazine* ["At the Sign of the Ship," XXXII (June, 1898), 186]: "Alas, the spirit is willing, but the flesh is weak. Like this hospitable author, I make a real distinction between visitors who come to make money by talking, 'and visitors who come for human pleasure.' I could

The first letter from Kipling to Haggard is undated, but it is early and could even have been written before the letter in verse to Andrew Lang.

Embankment Chambers,
Villiers Street, Strand

Dear Mr. Haggard,

Forgive a junior's impertinence but this thing was picked up the other day across some drinks and it seemed—but of course you know it.

There was first one Englishman and one mummy. They met in Egypt and the live man bought the dead, for it was a fine dead. Then the dead was unrolled and in the last layers of cloth that malignant Egyptian had tucked away a commination service of the most awful kind to the address of any man who disturbed him. He should die horribly in the open as a beast dies at the hand of a beast and there should not be enough of him to put into a matchbox, much less a mummy case. Whereat they laughed and of course later the English-man went to your country and became "fey" insomuch that he was weak enough to fire a shot gun into an elephant's trunk. Then he was dealt with after the manner of elephants till he was black-currant jam. But the rest of the camp would have taken what remained to the sea. So they cachéd it with great care and put a watcher on it. And there came in the night a Beast, such a Hyaena as never was and raked out that corpse and gave tongue to all the other beasts and—nothing remained, or it might have been that (as happened not long since in India) the elephant returned to find her dead and battered the corpse afresh into the earth. These things the native watcher told when the camp returned with the coffin.

Were the mummy not in it I could and would take the thing and

---

not pretend to regard my 'talk' as an equivalent for dollars, and the American public might take the same view, above all if, as is too probable, they could not hear the talk, the talker being 'roopy,' as Steerforth said about David Copper-field." To which "The Lounger" replied [*Critic*, XXIX (N.S.) (June 25, 1898), 417], "It is not necessary to talk, my dear Mr. Lang, come and let us look at you—we will do the talking." And to that, another columnist added: "How little the 'Lounger' knows Mr. Lang. America's talking powers are just what he dreads." ["News and Notes," *Academy*, LIV (July 9, 1898), 37. For more information about the literary partnership between Lang and Haggard, see Roger Lancelyn Green, *Andrew Lang* (1946), pp. 124–38; and *Rider Haggard*, pp. 184–86]

play with it. But there is a King in Egypt already and so I bring the body to his feet—for what it is worth.[1]

Yours sincerely,

Rudyard Kipling.[2]

The early years of the acquaintance did not produce many letters. The correspondence began in earnest only after the turn of the century, when both men had settled on their country estates or when one or both were travelling. Between 1889 and 1892, they were much in London, meeting frequently, with no reason for exchanging letters. The Savile was their favourite gathering place, they must have met at the homes of common friends, and they entertained each other. Thinking back to the early days of the friendship, Haggard remembered a dinner party "which I gave at my house . . . to some literary friends. I remember that Kipling arrived late and explained the reason by pointing to a cut upon his temple. Whilst he was driving towards my house his hansom collided with a van in Piccadilly, and there was a smash in which he had a narrow escape."[3]

We know too that in 1890, at two of Edmund Gosse's famous Sunday afternoon parties,[4] which attracted some of the most distinguished people of the time, Rider Haggard and his wife were present with members of the Balestier family: on April 13, with a Mr. Balestier, undoubtedly Wolcott, Kipling's friend and collaborator, and Josephine, Wolcott's younger sister, visiting London from Vermont; and on November 23, with Caroline Balestier, soon to become Kipling's bride.

The next letter from Kipling to Haggard, although also lacking a date, was written in the spring, 1891. Kipling here acknowledges a gift of Haggard's saga, *Eric Brighteyes*, a dark, forceful tale of an Icelandic Achilles, published on May 13 of that year.

---

[1] That Haggard never used the plot Kipling offered him is extraordinary, for he seldom let good plots about favourite subjects like Egyptian mummies get away from him. He had already used a mummy in *Cleopatra* (1889, pp. 183 ff.), and he would later use more mummies (see, for example, *Queen Sheba's Ring* [1910] and *Smith and the Pharaohs* [1920]). But when he received Kipling's suggestion, Haggard was in much demand, and the mummy plot may have come to nothing simply because he was so busy.

[2] The owner of this letter is Mr. H. Dunscombe Colt of New York City.

[3] *Days*, II, 26–27.

[4] For more about Edmund Gosse's Sunday afternoon parties, see Philip Gosse, "Introduction," *A Catalogue of the Gosse Correspondence in the Brotherton Collection* (1950), pp. vii–xiv; and *Rider Haggard*, pp. 214–15.

101 Earl's Court Road[1]

Dear Haggard,

Very many thanks for Eric which the Club waiter man handed to me only a day or two ago. Give me war anyway. That's why I like the clearing of the galley by Eric and the festive Lambstail[2] who got drunk afterwards. But it's all as strong as wire rope and 'twere impertinent of me to criticize.

Sincerely,

Rudyard Kipling.

The late 'eighties and early 'nineties were busy years for both men. For Haggard, they were the years of his greatest fame. *King Solomon's Mines* (1885) and *She* (1887) had established him as one of the best storytellers of the day, and he was to win wide audiences with the books that followed, particularly with *The World's Desire* (1890), the tale he wrote with Andrew Lang, and *Nada the Lily* (1892), his first all-Zulu story. But in his private life, Haggard suffered serious reversals. At the end of 1889 his mother died and in the spring of 1892, his father. The sharpest blow of all was the death of his only son, "Jock," aged nine, whom he had left with the Edmund Gosses when he and his wife went off on a reckless search for Aztec treasure in Mexico. Haggard was to live sixty-nine years; yet no greater tragedy would befall him in that long life than the death of this boy. The shock aged him and altered the course of his life.

For Kipling these were the years of early success. In 1890 *The Soldiers Three* and *Wee Willie Winkie* had appeared for the first time in an English book edition, and *Barrack-room* ballads were appearing regularly in the London press. Editors and readers alike marvelled at this new genius and at the constant flow from his pen, and each succeeding piece caused a greater Kipling boom than the last. By the end of 1890 Kipling was easily the most talked-about figure on the London literary scene, and his forthcoming novel, *The Light That Failed*, promised to be the sensation of the new year. But Kipling's private affairs were also unsettled, and he was not entirely a happy man, at least during the two years after his return from India. He thought London "a vile place,"[3]

---

[1] 101 Earl's Court Road is the address of Kipling's parents, who had arrived from India in May, 1890. This address was within easy walking distance of Haggard's town house, at 24 Redcliffe Square.

[2] Lambstail is Eric's servant.

[3] Carrington, p. 108.

"strange and disconcerting . . ., foreign with a close and foggy foreignness that jarred upon him and made him homesick for India."[1] Worst of all, he had suffered within a short time two successive disappointments in love. A sadness overcame him, and when he found that the only escape from his depressions was through his work, he wrote constantly, until he became seriously ill.

Time, fame, and new friends, however, helped cure his spiritual and physical malaise. He became attached to Wolcott Balestier, a dashing American entrepreneur living in London, with whom he wrote *The Naulakha*, a novel, and when Wolcott suddenly died, he cut short a worldwide journey to return to London and marry Wolcott's sister Caroline. They were wed in January, 1892, and within the month bride and groom crossed the Atlantic to make their home near Brattleboro, Vermont, where "Carrie" had grown up. England remained in their affections, however, and they returned for long visits during the summers of 1894 and 1895. Kipling and Haggard met during these visits, and the next letter we have comes from Vermont, soon after the Kiplings returned there at the end of the summer, 1895.

Waite, Windham Co.[2]
October 20, 1895

Dear Haggard,

Watt[3] has just forwarded me a letter addressed to you from a beekeeping man who wanted to quote something of a Jungle-tale of mine.[4] I daresay it didn't amuse you but it made me chuckle a little and reminded me, incidentally, that the man was nearer the mark than he knew: for it was a chance sentence of yours in *Nada the Lily* that started me off on a track that ended in my writing a lot of wolf-stories. You remember in your tale where the wolves leaped up at the feet of a dead man sitting on a rock ? Somewhere on that page I got the

---

[1] Roger Lancelyn Green, "Rudyard Kipling in London: 1889–91," *English*, VI (Summer 1946), 55.

[2] Waite, Windham County, was Kipling's Vermont post office address.

[3] Alexander Pollock Watt (1837–1914) originated literary agentry and was the first to practice the profession. He served as agent to both Kipling and Haggard.

[4] See the letter dated November 12, 1899, below (p. 41), for another instance of a correspondent confusing Kipling and Haggard.

notion.[1] It's curious how things come back again, isn't it? I meant to tell you when we met: but I don't remember that I ever did.

Yours always sincerely,

Rudyard Kipling.

In Vermont the Kiplings had a falling out with Carrie's brother, Beatty, and when the quarrel was dragged into the local court and through the Boston and New York newspapers, life in New England became unbearable. They left their American home and sailed in August, 1896, for England. They spent almost a year in a house on the coast near Torquay, where Kipling became acquainted with the officers of the training ship *Britannia* at Dartmouth, grew interested in nautical matters, and wrote poems and stories about the sea and the navy. Then, in June, 1897, the family moved to Rottingdean, where they lived for the summer in "North End House," the Burne-Joneses' summer house.

Increasing tension in world affairs was, at this time, a great concern to Kipling, and he deplored his countrymen's complacency (they "never look . . . further than their annual seaside resorts"[2]). War with the United States over the Venezuela–British Guiana border had been narrowly averted, the Jameson Raid had damaged the English position

[1] Kipling refers to p. 103 of *Nada the Lily*. In *Something of Myself*, he gives a more detailed account of how he wrote *The Jungle Books*: "My workroom in the Bliss Cottage [Vermont] was seven feet by eight, and from December to April the snow lay level with its window-sill. It chanced that I had written a tale about Indian Forestry work ["In the Rukh," first published in *Many Inventions* (1893)] which included a boy who had been brought up by the wolves. In the stillness, and suspense, of the winter of '92 some memory of the Masonic Lions of my childhood's magazine, and a phrase in Haggard's *Nada the Lily*, combined with the echo of this tale. After blocking out the main idea in my head, the pen took charge, and I watched it begin to write stories about Mowgli and animals, which later grew into the *Jungle Books*." [*Something*, p. 113. For Kipling's childhood reading and the identity of the Masonic Lions, see Roger Lancelyn Green, "Kipling's Early Reading," *Kipling Journal*, XXIII (July, 1956), 4–7.] Kipling's works contain at least five direct references to Haggard's works: to *She* in "Among the Railway Folk" (*The Pioneer*, August 1, 1888; *From Sea to Sea*, II, 295 [Uniform and Pocket edns.]) and in *Letters of Travel* (1920; see p. 78 below); to *Cleopatra* in "Her Little Responsibility," (1909; see p. 9 above); to *King Solomon's Mines* in "A Flight of Fact" (1918; *Works*, XXXV, 120); and to *Allan Quatermain* in "The Last of the Stories" (*Abaft the Funnel* [New York: Dodge, 1909], p. 344).

[2] *Something*, p. 147.

in South Africa, and the steady fighting along India's borders was a source of anxiety. Germany was already a menace to England. She was supporting Turkey in the Greco–Turkish war, and Admiral Tirpitz threatened to build a navy that would challenge Britain's. "Altogether," wrote Kipling, "one had a sense of 'a sound of a going in the tops of the mulberry trees'—of things moving into position as troops move."[1]

Britain had to do something to boost morale, and although both the third Colonial Conference and Victoria's Diamond Jubilee in 1897 were disappointingly dim affairs, they served to display Empire solidarity and England's force.

Kipling had promised the editor of *The Times* a poem to honour the Queen's Jubilee, and on Jubilee Day, June 22, he sat down at his desk in Rottingdean to write it. But the poem would not take shape easily, and he wrote many drafts, made many fresh starts. While still struggling with the verses, he sent off an early copy to Haggard, to get his friend's reaction to something that did not yet fully satisfy him. Haggard's comments on "Recessional" are lost, but we have Kipling's reply to them, written six days before he put the finishing touches on the poem that was to become the nation's hymn.

July 10, 1897

Dear Haggard,

Your note did me much good—and thank you for it.

I've just come off a fortnight with the Channel Squadron off the North Coast of Ireland—rather a jolly time. Now, any nation save ourselves, with such a fleet as we have at present, would go out swiftly to trample the guts out of the rest of the world; and the fact that we do not seems to show that even if we aren't very civilized, we're about the one power with a glimmering of civilization in us.[2] As you say, we've always had it somewhere in our composition. But my objection to that hymn is that it may be quoted as an excuse for lying down abjectly at all times and seasons and taking what any other

---

[1] *Something*, p. 147.

[2] Kipling repeats some of this sentence almost exactly in *A Fleet in Being* (first published on November 8, 1898): "Any other breed with this engine at their disposal would have used it savagely long ago. In our hands it lay as harmless as the levin-rods of the Vril-Ya." [*Works*, Sussex Edition, XXVI, 423] Haggard had also read Bulwer Lytton's *The Coming Race* (1871); in fact, he noted it as one of the two books he re-read most frequently. ["Books Which Have Influenced Me," *British Weekly Extra*, No. 1 (1887), p. 67]

country may think fit to give us. What I wanted to say was:—"Don't gas but be ready to give people snuff"—and I only covered the first part of the notion.

I'm very much afraid that we shan't be able to accept your invitation for the autumn—much as we'd like it as we shall probably be going out of England.

By the way, do you know any one who could give me a hint (a) as to the size and rent of houses for the winter in Wynberg, or near Constantia; (b) the methods and manners of housekeeping down there. I want to see South Africa again—badly—to stay for six months and it's domestic information I need.

Ever yours sincerely,
Rudyard Kipling.[1]

In later years, Kipling recalled that "it was . . . [an] uneasiness of mine ['based on things that men were telling me about affairs outside England'] which led us down to the Cape in the winter of '97."[2] Quite naturally he turned to Haggard for advice about South Africa. Haggard had lived five of the most exciting years of his life there and, although fourteen years had passed since his return, Africa exercised a powerful force on him. In England he had written, spoken, and fought by every means he could for a hard-headed, enlightened colonial policy. He had become an authority on South Africa, and could also answer practical questions about life in and around Cape Town.

The Kiplings left England in January, 1898, to winter in South Africa, and did in fact settle in Wynberg, a fashionable suburb on the eastern side of Table Mountain, about eight miles from Cape Town. "There," Kipling was to remember, "we lived in a boarding-house . . . kept by an Irishwoman, who faithfully followed the instincts of her race and spread miseries and discomforts round her in return for good monies. But the children [the Kiplings' third child had been born in the preceding

---

[1] I have not found the original of this letter. The present copy is from a typescript in the Bambridge Collection. Two notes appear on the letter. The first, on the face, reads "Kipling on Recessional," the second, on the back, reads "Re Recessional. K told me he wrote a 2nd part to the poem but tore it up. H.R.H." We have no other evidence that a "second part" was ever written, but Professor Carrington indicates that "Recessional" was a seven-stanza poem before Kipling reduced it to five. Haggard may have had the longer version in mind. [Carrington, pp. 204–209]

[2] *Something*, p. 147.

August] throve, and the colour, light, and half-oriental manners of the land bound chains round our hearts for years to come."[1]

Kipling himself had stayed at Cape Town for almost two months in 1892, as part of a journey that took him round the world. At that time, his fame was still fresh and had not spread far. But by 1898, his name was known in every corner of the Empire, and when he and his family arrived, they were immediately taken up by Cape Town society. Before long he was a friend of both Milner and Rhodes. In response to an invitation from the latter, he travelled up-country to Rhodesia and explored the area on bicycle. Soon he was at home in South Africa and fond of the country and the people. When he sailed back to England in April, he left behind a wide circle of acquaintances and even a few close friends.

He returned, furthermore, with strong feelings about the state of affairs in Africa, feelings that paralleled Haggard's, and he was prepared to speak out about them. Soon after his arrival he happily accepted an invitation, probably extended by Haggard himself, to speak at a dinner of the Anglo–African Writers' Club, which Haggard had helped to found. We are fortunate to have a detailed account of the proceedings at the Grand Hotel on May 20, 1898.[2] Haggard was in the chair, and he introduced Kipling to "an unusually large number of guests," some of whom "had to dine at an overflow feast in another room." Among those present were Sir Henry Bulwer, former Lieutenant-Governor of Natal and High Commissioner of Cyprus; Sir Walter Peace, Agent-General of Natal; B. W. Greenacre, Mayor of Durban; and Sir Marshal Clarke, Resident Commissioner of Rhodesia. Haggard proposed Kipling's health, and read a telegram from Cecil Rhodes expressing his regret at being absent. Then, "having told some stories of his early associations with Mr. Kipling that excited much amusement," Haggard hailed Kipling as a "true watchman of our Empire."

I do not believe in the divine right of kings, [Haggard said,] but I do believe . . . in a divine right of a great civilising people—that is, in their divine mission. Yes, it is the voice of those true watchmen [like Kipling] of whom I speak that warns, that stirs the blood and braces the minds of peoples, awakening them from the depth of sloth and self-seeking. . . . They it is who, having the golden gift of words, embody in fitting language the aspirations of thousands, and awake and encourage in them the love of country. (Cheers.) . . . [After

[1] *Something*, pp. 147–48.
[2] "Mr. Rudyard Kipling," *African Review*, XV (May 21, 1898), 311–13.

mentioning Kipling's "The Song of the English" and "The Flag of England" as examples of poems that can instil patriotism and give strength, Haggard continued,] I say, that these two poems were written by a man who has visions, a man who has the imagination to understand as well as the power to express. Their writer has communed with the very Spirit of our race . . . . His fame is sure, and his name will be one of the few that in future ages will be found written in living letters upon the books of this generation. (Cheers.) . . . [And turning to Kipling,] Sir, we welcome in you one who has used the great gifts given to you for no small or mean or unworthy purpose, but rather to advance the interests of your country, and to stir your fellows to a truer and loftier patriotism. We welcome in you a poet, a patriot, an Englishman of whom we are proud—(cheers)—and what, perhaps, is best of all, one of whom we may say in every relation of private and public life, Here is a man whose heart is in the right place. (Loud cheers.)

Then followed, as the newspaper reporter observed, "a thoughtful, suggestive, and Kiplingesque oration from the master in their craft," one feature of the speech having been "the rapidity with which it was delivered. . . . The creator of Mulvaney [the reporter continued] has a light, clear voice, and an utterance singularly free from the affectations of modern oratory. His diction is plain and curt, he has no airs or graces, and he talks rather than orates. 'Look here!' he says, with a jerk of the arm, when he introduces his arguments. He pauses in the full flood of adjectives to hope he does not bore his audience. And he acknowledges a cheer with a smart salute."

At the outset, Kipling praised the men who were bringing civilization and all its benefits to South Africa, the men who "are carrying out our work [there]." He explained how difficult it was to work against the tide of ignorance so prevalent in Africa. The Dutch in the Cape Colony, he said, often objected to the "elementary rudiments of civilisation" such as "precautions against the spread of disease." They also "objected more or less to railways; and they objected to 'roads' of all kinds." They fought against "little things like compulsory education and compulsory innoculation." Conditions were so bad, he continued, that merely observing them had made him "violently unwell for a week." Never before had he seen "his own countrymen 'squashed,' disarmed, and domineered over, with the great guns of forts looking into their back gardens, while foreigners from all parts of the world rode around with revolvers and other firearms sticking about all over them."

He went on to explain why the English and the Dutch had such different interests and pointed out that patience was the only cure for the troublesome circumstances. "We must try by example and precept," he said, "to coax them along the road to the material development of the land. It was no use getting angry with the unprogressive settlers. Our people have to live with these people. The Colonials and Dutch had married and inter-married until you could hardly tell the one from the other. There was room in the land for both, and it was time to stop jabbering about 'anti-Dutch,' 'anti-English,' and so on. Be quiet; stop prating about that loaded rifle, and work. Simply sit down and work. That was the opinion of most of the men he had talked with."

Turning to the Transvaal, Kipling confessed that he could not see a way out of the troubles there. He could not advocate claiming "our rights by force," and insisted that here too there was a need for patience. Only if the Boers should "rise and give trouble," would the English be justified in taking up arms. "In conclusion, Mr. Kipling said he could not tell them how grateful he was for what Mr. Haggard had said, and also for the way he was treated in South Africa. He hoped he had not done any mischief by what he had said that night. (Cheers)." And the usual toasts and replies followed.

Accompanying the report in the *African Review* is an anonymous poem:

A Humble Tribute

'I am but a 'umble waiter, Mr. Kiplin', that is all,
But I'm 'uman tho' I'm 'umble, an' I've got a 'eart an' brain;
An' I does a bit o' readin' of a evenin' off an' on,
An' on Sundays, for a instance, when I'm kept indoors by rain.

'I'm acquainted with your stories, an' by Gom, sir, they're A1!
I've laughed, an' I've cried, *an'* felt as creepy as can be.
There's Mulvaney, why, Lor' bless yer! 'e's a reg'lar pal o' mine,
So are Ortheris an' Learoyd, they are real live pals to me.

'I am not much 'and at poetry, but I 'ear as you're a poet:
(Once I 'eard a chap recitin' somethin' called "The Bolivar,"
But I can't say I remember what the verses was about),
Still they say that you're a poet, sir, an' I'll take my oath you are.

'I've always said, "Now Kiplin', 'e's a genius out an' out,
There's no bloomin' doubt about it, an' I'd say so to 'is face!

But o' course they're ain't no chanst o' that, cos why? well 'e's a gent,
While I'm a 'umble waiter, which I 'opes I knows my place."

'At the "Grand" on Monday evenin' I was fairly took aback,
An' I got no end excited when they said as you'd be there;
But you might 'ave knocked me backwards when they all flocked in
    to dine,
An' I found you at my table an' a-sittin' next the Chair.

'Oh! I waited on yer proper from the soup right to the end,
There was nothin' as yer wanted but you got in 'arf a mo.,
You'd the nicest cup o' saddle, you'd the pick o' the *menoo*,
An' I kep' yer glass a-brimmin'—tho' you takes yer liquor slow.

'Then I listened to yer speakin' (I was 'id behind the screen),
An' I said, "Well, this 'ere Kiplin', 'e's a *man*, an' no mistake";
An' I said, "Oh —— this waitin', chuck it, let's go out an' fight,
I should like to punch some fellow's 'ead for good old England's sake!"

'Now the Chairman, Mr. 'Aggard, 'e's a hauthor I admires,
I 'ave read 'is stories many times, I fairly dotes on *She*,
All the same—an' Mr. 'Aggard, 'e'll agree with this, I know—
For a general good all-rounder you're a greater man than 'e.

'Mr. Kiplin', Mr. Kiplin' ah! you little knew that night
'Ow I wanted just to speak to you an' tell you what I thinks,
I'd 'ave given my night's earnin's to 'ave 'ad a word with you,
I'd 'ave given up my week's, sir, to 'ave treated you to drinks.

'I am but a 'umble waiter, Mr. Kiplin', that is all,
But I'm 'uman tho' I'm 'umble, an' I've got a 'eart an' brain;
An' you've got one constant reader who can swear that you're a brick,
An' I'll say so to your face, sir, if I waits on you again!'

Kipling soon agreed to serve as vice-president of the Anglo–African
Writers' Club. Because of the death of his "Uncle Ned," Edward
Burne-Jones, he could not be on hand at the following month's meeting,
when John G. Kotzé, the African jurist under whom Haggard had
worked in the Transvaal, was guest of the evening. To compensate for
his absence, he wrote some verses about Kotzé, and gave them to
Haggard, who quoted two of the lines in public:

Will there be moaning at the Bar
When I put out Kotzé.

Not much time passed before the " 'umble waiter" of the anonymous poem could "punch some fellow's 'ead for good old England's sake": the old hatred among Zulu, Boer, and Briton over South Africa found its voice on the battlefield again. By winning the Battle of Ulundi (1879) and capturing Chief Cetywayo, the British had subdued the Zulu, but the Boer remained, a constant threat to England's hopes for a colonized or confederated South Africa. His ingrained independence together with Whitehall's vacillation and the discovery of gold and diamonds in the Transvaal—all inevitably produced, during the last quarter of the nineteenth century, ever-increasing Boer–British conflict. Majuba Hill and the Jameson Raid found their way into English school-boys' history texts. But the last straw was the Boer's insistence on taxing the English Uitlanders in the Transvaal without giving them a vote. Negotiations reached an impasse, and the Boers demanded that Britain withdraw virtually all her troops from South Africa. The British Government refused to leave her nationals to the mercy of the Dutch, and when, on October 11, 1899, the Dutch ultimatum expired, the Boer War became a reality.

Haggard was, of course, much concerned with events in South Africa. He had gone to Africa as an untried youth of nineteen to work at his first job, on the staff of the colonial government. There, as the violent history of the following six months unfolded, he developed into a strong, reliable, self-confident man of action and imagination. He had gone up-country to negotiate with Zulu chiefs on ground never before trod by white men; he had himself been the first to raise the Union Jack over Pretoria when Shepstone annexed the Transvaal to the Crown; he had, as Adjutant of the Pretoria Horse, taken up arms against the Boer in the uprising of 1879; and later, with his young bride, he had lived through some harrowing days within earshot of Majuba Hill. Finally, he had sat by helpless while a humiliating peace treaty between the British and the Dutch was framed in his own home near Newcastle.

Haggard's concern for South Africa did not stem solely from the memories of his youth. He was a political realist who believed that history required England to play an important role in the future of the Dark Continent, and that decency required Whitehall to behave responsibly toward the English colonists there. But as a result of the Convention of Pretoria (1880) and because of the humiliating concessions that the English Government had made to the Boers in the years that followed, Haggard had seen England's foothold in South Africa seriously weakened and the battleground for the Boer War made ready.

Haggard's strong opinions about the South African events that he had witnessed at first hand in the late 'seventies and early 'eighties were a matter of record. So incensed was he when he returned from Africa in 1881 to find his countrymen misinformed, ignorant, or complacent about African affairs that he wrote a book, his first, which he hoped, by supplying the essential facts, would fill their hearts with the necessary compassion and fire their statesmen with the will to act responsibly and intelligently in colonial affairs. *Cetywayo and His White Neighbours*, a candid on-the-scene report of conditions at a significant time in South Africa's history, an analysis of the forces operating to shape its future, is today a valuable document for historians. But in 1882, when it first appeared, it was largely ignored, particularly by Whitehall, where Haggard sought most of all to exert influence. Haggard's hard reasoning and (as we now know) startlingly accurate prophecies did nothing to change colonial policy in the 'eighties. During the fifteen years after the book appeared, the Colonial Office pursued a course that was as unrealistic as it was ultimately disastrous to English interests in South Africa.

The Boer War was not, however, Haggard's sole concern in the closing days of the century. He was already involved in another cause, and he considered it no less important for the health of England than the satisfactory management of African affairs. His new cause was the plight of the English farmer.

Earlier, in 1891, when Haggard lost his son, he retreated to his house in Norfolk and spent three years in semi-retirement, seldom going up to London or seeing friends. He had always felt a strong attachment to the land and, to alleviate the pain he felt over his personal tragedy, he turned now to his own gardens and farms and worked them diligently, building greenhouses, experimenting with orchids, growing everything from figs to oranges. He looked after an orchard containing over three hundred fruit trees, he bought outlying fields to add to those his wife had inherited, he carefully supervised his gardeners, tenants, and labourers, and, all in all, he turned his house and land into a model farming estate.

At first he saw himself in his father's image, doing this work as a gentleman farmer—certainly not as a reformer or crusader. It was the experience he gained on his land, and in writing a chatty journal, that transformed the country squire into an aggressive reformer. He began to write his farmer's journal at the outset of 1898, intending to produce a homespun record of the thought and doings of a landowner and farmer through a single calendar year. Like Thomas Tusser's *Five Hundred good pointes of husbandrie* (1557) and Gilbert White's *Natural History ... of Selborne* (1798), it is a charming work, actually one of Haggard's highest achievements, through which one can look at the face of the country as well as into the heart of a man in love with it.

Before Haggard had done, however, the work became more than a journal. For one thing, because he sought to note events accurately, he kept careful financial records. For another, he carried out researches into the life of the farming community. The facts assembled themselves before his eyes, and by the end of the year he concluded that the state of English agriculture was even more appalling than he had imagined. Haggard's journal becomes, at least in part, a record of the plight of the man on the land and a plea for a vanishing way of life. He published it as *A Farmer's Year* in October, 1899, and sent off a copy to his friend Kipling, who, in turn, commented on it in two letters, written three days apart, both alluding to the war.

> The Elms, Rottingdean, Nr. Brighton[1]
> November 12, 1899

Dear Haggard,

The enclosed seems to have come to me by mistake—so I send it on.[2] I suppose she means sending the troop horses out without slings.[3]

I wish you knew how much the wife and I have enjoyed your "Farmer's Year." In our tiny way we also have made experiments with land: and your figures made us groan sympathetically over and

---

[1] After their son, John, was born (August 17, 1897), the Kiplings moved into another house in Rottingdean, The Elms, and lived there while searching for a suitable home in the country.

[2] See letter dated October 20, 1895 (p. 31), for another instance where a correspondent confuses Kipling with Haggard.

[3] Someone, it would appear, is writing to Haggard (who had himself once been shipwrecked [p. 109 below]) about the difficulty that the troopship *Rapidan* had encountered during a gale on November 3. "All the horses were enclosed in stall boards on the main deck, while the men were quartered in the 'tween deck. On Friday evening, when the *Rapidan* was about 30 miles past Milford, a heavy storm was experienced. The wind blew at terrific strength, and the steamer laboured painfully, giving a serious roll to one side which caused the horses to fall or to come violently into contact with the fittings. The timbers broke away, and the frightened animals floundered about the deck." The troop commander directed the ship's captain to make for the nearest port. More than 140 horses were killed, and others died later of injuries. [*The Times*, November 7, 1899, p. 10]

above the cruel facts. I don't think there has ever been a better book of the sane, common (which is uncommon) quiet humourous real country life of England. I've been going back and rereading it slowly and leisurely: for the mere taste of it—same as Gilbert White.[1]

Ever yours sincerely,
Rudyard Kipling.

The Elms, Rottingdean, Nr. Brighton
November 15, 1899

Dear Haggard,
A beautiful notion, but it seems to my low and brutal mind that if there is anyone available to look after anything on the battlefield he might better look after the men first.[2] I did get a very kindly letter from you when I was sick but, as you may guess, I wasn't in any shape to answer it.[3]
I think the Year book will last—as a study of certain facts and conditions at a certain date in our history—like Tusser.[4]

Ever yours sincerely,
Rudyard Kipling.

[1] Both Kipling and Haggard responded warmly to the work of Gilbert White. Kipling had read his *Natural History and Antiquities of Selborne* (1789; see p. 49 below) and alluded once to a motor trip he made to Gilbert White country. [R. Thurston Hopkins, *Rudyard Kipling: A Literary Appreciation* (1915), p. 237]

[2] With the *Rapidan* disaster in mind, Haggard may have proposed sending more grooms to South Africa to care for troop horses.

[3] Kipling had a "lifelong tendency to fever," dating back to his days in India. In 1899, when he and his family were staying at the Hotel Grenoble in New York, a bout of serious illness overcame them. Carrie recovered quickly, but his fever and "inflammation in one lung" put his life in serious jeopardy. Worst of all, on March 6, their eldest child, Josephine, died of a fever. The shock was great and Kipling's physical and spiritual recovery was slow.

[4] Though lacking in literary distinction, Thomas Tusser's work appealed to Kipling for its hard-headed agricultural advice. In 1907, Tusser comes readily to Kipling's mind when, visiting Canada, he encounters a glib farmer who argues that the prairie dwellers should give over wheat for "mixed farming." ["The Fortunate Towns," *Letters of Travel*] Kipling took from Tusser the title and six lines of verse at the head of "An Habitation Enforced" (1905), and he parodied Tusser's proverbial verse in "The Four Points" [*Poems, 1886–1929*

Kipling was not the only one to admire *A Farmer's Year*: the Press in general hailed it, and overnight Haggard found a new reading public, one that either knew from first-hand experience the sad conditions set forth in the journal or sympathized with the description of them. Letters from readers poured on to his breakfast table in Norfolk "almost without number,"[1] convincing him that he would be performing a genuine service to his country if he succeeded in opening Englishmen's eyes to existing rural conditions. Haggard was aware, as few men were, of the facts and statistics. He knew that between 1871 and 1901 English agricultural labourers decreased by over one-third while the general population increased by 43 per cent; that between 1871 and 1881 nearly a million persons had emigrated in search of a better life. During the 'eighties and 'nineties, as a matter of fact, "the only chance for any young or enterprising person on the countryside was to get out of it."[2] English agriculture, formerly the nation's major industry, employing more people than any other, had been reduced to a mere by-product of English life.[3] *Service* was the watchword of Haggard's character, and he did not hesitate: he became a champion of the English farmer. After *A Farmer's Year* appeared, he was in much demand as a speaker at agricultural meetings and country fêtes, as an authority to testify before Chambers of Agriculture, and generally as a lively observer of the rural scene.

Because Haggard could not bring himself to surrender his campaign on behalf of rural England, he declined an invitation from Moberly Bell, editor of *The Times*, to go to South Africa as a war correspondent. Instead, he remained at home, working for agricultural reform and doing what he could to keep England informed on South African affairs. On

---

(1929)]. In later life, he persuaded E. V. Lucas to re-issue Tusser's major work, and he himself wrote a Benediction for the volume. [Thomas Tusser, *Five Hundred Good Points of Husbandry*, with an Introduction by Sir Walter Scott and a Benediction by Rudyard Kipling incorporated in a Foreword by E. V. Lucas (1931)] Haggard was no less an admirer. The opening sentence of *A Farmer's Year* reads: "It is with very real humility that I take up my pen to write of farming, following the excellent example of Thomas Tusser, who, more than three hundred years ago, as I do, tilled the land in Norfolk," (p. 1) and he quotes liberally from Tusser throughout.

[1] *Days*, II, 132.

[2] R. C. K. Ensor, *England, 1870–1914*, p. 118.

[3] See Ensor, pp. 115–19, 284–86; William Ashworth, *An Economic History of England, 1870–1939* (1960), Chapter 3; and H. Rider Haggard, *Rural England* (1906), II, 565.

the eve of the war, he published an abbreviated version of *Cetywayo and His White Neighbours* (he called it *The Last Boer War*), and he filled columns of *The Times* with letters on the war and its causes. At one point he took on no less a contender than Commandant-General Piet Joubert, the commander of the Boer forces, in an exchange of letters in the Press.[1]

When war broke out, the Kiplings were in Rottingdean. Rudyard lent his efforts to forming a volunteer company, and later to building a drill hall. He also wrote "The Absent-minded Beggar," verses which, when set to music by Arthur Sullivan, were "guaranteed to pull teeth out of barrel organs." Anyone could use the verses and the tune by contributing to the Absent-minded Beggar Club, which collected over a quarter of a million pounds for the men away at war.[2]

The Kiplings sailed for South Africa in January, 1900. They intended primarily to escape the European winter, but Kipling's interests kept focusing on the war, and as soon as his family was comfortably settled in Cape Town, he moved up closer to the battlefield. He visited hospitals, talked to English soldiers wherever he went, recited his ballads, and gave the men tobacco, pyjamas, and other luxuries made available by the Absent-minded Beggar Fund. In March he accepted an invitation from Lord Roberts, Commander-in-Chief of the English forces, to join the staff of the *Friend*, a makeshift army newspaper that the General had set up in Bloemfontein, and during the following weeks he worked happily away as a newspaper man once more, helping to write, edit, and print a lively journal that kept the troops informed and fighting.

Kipling wanted to see a real battle before returning to England, and at the end of March he went up to the engagement at Karee Siding. Then in April, he was back home, eager to share his first-hand information with the men of the Rottingdean volunteer company and anyone else who could benefit from it.

The political flavour of his verse increased measurably and steadily during the war years. He had written "nationalist" stories and verse before, but he had avoided political pronouncements. His experience in South Africa, however, had given him new insights into the reasons for Britain's repeated losses on the battlefield, and when he returned to England he had an axe to grind. His verse of the next two years would alienate relatives, friends, and readers, and his reputation as an artist

[1] See Scott, p. 174.
[2] *Something*, p. 150; Carrington, pp. 235–36.

would suffer considerably; but Kipling's sense of duty outweighed all other considerations, and he spoke his mind freely and frankly, even, at times, intemperately.

In South Africa he had seen the English soldier in all his glory—and ignominy. For though the English lads had a large share of fighting spirit, they had not been adequately trained and could not, in many cases, even fire a rifle properly. Kipling was incensed when he realized that the Government had sent forth an army of amateurs unfit to fight a war, and the pieces he wrote and published after he returned to England often alternated between biting irony and frank derision.

The Kiplings returned to South Africa for each of the two remaining winters of the war, and there they lived as guests of Cecil Rhodes at The Woolsack, a cottage that Rhodes had built for visiting artists on his Groote Schuur estate on the outskirts of Cape Town. Carrie had actually helped select the site of the house, and in 1901 the Kiplings were the first to occupy it. Here they received the many eminent newspaper men, generals and statesmen who passed through Cape Town, and here Kipling kept in touch with events, using his pen and influence in whatever way he thought would aid the British cause.

During the milder seasons, when he was in England, he worked with equal enthusiasm. Before he left for South Africa for the winter, 1901–1902, he sent a hard-hitting poem to *The Times*. "The Islanders" tried to awaken the English at home to the needs of Greater England and to the realities of the South African battlefields. It minces no words and attributes Britain's colonial disasters to inadequate military planning and training at home. At the outset, Kipling accuses his fellow-countrymen of having lived the easy life

> Till ye made a sport of your shrunken hosts and a toy of your armed men.
> Yet stopped your ears to the warning—ye would neither look nor heed—
> Ye set your leisure before their toil and your lusts above their need.

The Islanders neglected both the art of soldiering and their soldiers:

> Sons of the sheltered city—unmade, unhandled, unmeet—
> Ye pushed them raw to the battle as ye picked them raw from the street.

And

> Then ye returned to your trinkets; then ye contented your souls
> With the flannelled fools at the wicket or the muddied oafs at the goals.

He reminds his readers that their good, calm life had been hard won and must be cherished and defended if it was to last. It is as important to learn to play the game of war as it is to learn cricket. Both must be

Weighed and pondered and worshipped, and practised day and day.

Kipling intended "The Islanders" to incite reaction, and it did. His principal concern was to goad the British into training professional soldiers, through military conscription for example, as well as they trained their professional cricketers.

Certainly Haggard understood Kipling's position, and he wrote him on the day the poem appeared in *The Times*. By then, the Kiplings were on their way to South Africa, and the letter took a while to catch up. Kipling's reply comes from Cape Town at the end of the month.

> The Woolsack, Cape Town
> January 28, 1902

Dear Haggard,

I was glad to get your letter of the 4th and to learn that you approved of operations as conducted on my flank of the attack.

It was delicious to see the *Times* backing and filling—and those d—d hired pros. taking cover behind the names of good men, who happened to be cricketers, dead at the front as some excuse for their three day £1000-gate performances. I ought to have written *hired* fools instead of flannelled. That might have made my meaning clearer. But as usual people have gone off on a side issue.[1]

---

[1] On the day the poem appeared, *The Times* supported Kipling in principle in an editorial, but took issue with his view that the country was not in fact well prepared to fight its wars, emphasizing the importance of British naval power. *The Times* continued to oppose conscription, but agreed with Kipling that there should be some sort of effective training for Britain's youth. "The interest displayed in the Australian cricket matches is intelligible," *The Times* wrote, "but it is surely out of proportion to the importance of the matter at stake. We admire pluck and sport, but Mr. Kipling's scornful language is excusable when we see the streets filled with placards about these athletic contests as if issues depended upon them as vital to our race as those decided at Trafalgar and Waterloo." [p. 9] Two days later *The Times* began publishing letters which the poem had elicited from its readers. Twenty-seven appeared by January 21, and only six of these opposed Kipling's position. One of the letters that Kipling has particularly in mind came from W. J. Ford, a noted commentator on cricket. He objects to the phrase "flannelled fools" as "applied by Mr. Kipling . . . to those who happen to play cricket," and he names distinguished cricketers "all of whom have laid down their lives" and

I was talking to Chesham[1] just before he went home. He says that the Yeomanry are all right—*when* they have been taught. They don't of course know anything but De Wet & Co.[2] teach 'em and the taxpayer pays for the instruction.

Your side of the attack—the question of Food supply[3]—is as you say *the* vital one. You have the figures and facts and the influence: and for goodness sake keep on hammering at it. What makes me sick is what makes you sick—the way, to wit, in which the responsible politician admits the cold truth of one's contention and then explicitly says that he doesn't dare "go in advance of public opinion" and so on.

Well here's luck! We need it.

Ever yours,
Rudyard Kipling.

---

many others "who have not only the 'folly' to be cricketers, but to serve their country as well."[January 6, 1902, p. 4] Some letters missed Kipling's main point, assuming that he opposed cricket generally, when, as he indicates in this letter, he was really opposed only to professional cricket in wartime. As *The Times* leader indicated, test matches were in progress in Australia when the poem appeared; in fact the English team had won a three-day match on December 13, 14, and 16.

[1] Charles Compton William Cavendish (1850–1907), 3d Baron of Chesham, commanded the Imperial Yeomanry during the Boer War.

[2] Christian Rudolf De Wet (1854–1922), the "fierce-eyed, stern-faced" Boer guerilla general, commanded the Orange Free State forces in the war. The Imperial Yeomanry frequently suffered at his hands. Just before Pretoria fell, De Wet took five hundred Yeomanry prisoners in the town of Lindley; in December, 1900, he attacked the Yeomanry camp at Tweefontein, "killing, wounding or taking prisoner all its occupants and carrying off its entire contents." [Edgar Holt, *The Boer War* (1958), pp. 100, 233–34, 274]

[3] Haggard was very much concerned about the ability of England to feed itself, especially in time of war. In *Rural England*, parts of which had appeared serially in 1901, he wrote: "I am convinced that the risk of starvation which might strike our Country in the event of a European war, is no mere spectre of the alarmist. It should be remembered that fleets of battleships, even if they could keep the great seas as open as is cheerfully supposed, could never control the operations of the foreign, and indeed of the home speculators in foodstuffs. Within a fortnight of the declaration of such a war—which we must expect some day—corn would, I believe, stand at or near 100s. a quarter. If we could think that the War Office was ready to meet such an emergency—to supply food, allay panic, &c., perhaps there would not be so much cause for alarm. But what intelligent person who has studied the action of that Department during our recent troubles—in the matter of the supply of horses, for instance—can conscientiously expect anything of the sort?" [II, 560; Scott, pp. 94–95]

For Haggard, the war and England's defunct agriculture had become one: the nation could not feed itself and an army across the seas adequately. To send troops to Africa and not know where the necessary food and supplies were to come from was the greatest folly of all. The Government, shortsighted and motivated by political expediency, had turned its back on the English farmer. Plead and reason as he might, Haggard could not stir the officials. But he was not to be put off. His confidence in the English people remained: they, he was sure, would respond to the truth. In 1900, during the first year of the Boer War, Haggard devised a scheme for assembling the facts and for putting them before the people: he set out to emulate Arthur Young, who, more than a century earlier, had surveyed the English counties and written a series of books on the conditions of agriculture in his day. For Haggard this plan resulted in a labour of love, a massive tome entitled *Rural England, Being an Account of the Agricultural and Social Researches Carried Out in the Years 1901 & 1902*, and published in two volumes in 1903. To produce it, Haggard spent almost two years travelling up and down the English countryside, going from one farm to another, through one county after another, by horse, train, and ship, asking questions of labourers, tenants, public officials, land agents, and landowners. He amassed a mountain of notebooks, all crammed with facts and figures, and on the basis of these wrote his report. *Rural England* is an immense document that, as Kipling suggests, takes its place beside the most important agricultural histories in the language. The facts that Haggard accumulated present a picture of rural exodus, neglect, and decay, so shocking that they were bound ultimately to help reshape English rural life and agriculture.

Kipling's keen interest in England's welfare also caused him great concern over the agricultural crisis. But that interest was sharpened and personalized for him when, in 1902, he bought a home in Sussex. Bateman's is a seventeenth-century stone house near Burwash, surrounded by fertile land. In this handsome dwelling at the end of an "enlarged rabbit-hole of a lane,"[1] with its study as its centre, he was to live out his remaining thirty-four years in seclusion and comfort.[2] It was here that he was able, for the first time, to indulge fully his own interest in gardening and farming. He gradually enlarged his land holdings, surrounded his lawns with yew hedges, and planned and maintained a vast formal garden.

Rider Haggard, with his hard-headed agricultural knowledge and

[1] *Something*, p. 178.
[2] Carrie Kipling left Bateman's to the National Trust.

long experience in managing a Norfolk estate, was the person Kipling could tell his troubles to. He "would visit us from time to time," Kipling later wrote, "and give us of his ample land wisdom. I remember I planted some new apple trees in an old orchard, then rented by an Irishman, who at once put in an agile and hungry goat. Haggard met the combination suddenly one morning. He had gifts of speech and said very clearly that one 'might as well put Satan in an orchard as a goat.' I forget what he said about the tenants, but I know I acted on it."[1] The men met frequently in the early years of the new century, and their talk, while undoubtedly animated, was, one rather suspects, seldom about literature.

The first letter we have from Bateman's was written a little over three months after the Kiplings moved in and less than a month after *Rural England* was published.

> Bateman's, Burwash, Sussex
> December 22, 1902

Dear Cobbett–Young–Haggard,[2]

For the last week or more the wife and I have been reading *Rural England*, with deep joy (I don't mean on account of the state of things revealed) and admiration. I bought it lawfully in market overt and it stands with your Farmer's Year between Young's Agriculture of Sussex and [White's] Selborne. I take off my hat to you deeply and profoundly because it's a magnum opus and altogether fascinating and warning and chock full of instruction.

I—alas!—hold land now which I trust you will see next summer. An old house and a 25 acre farm of good hop land and fruit and a mill (water) that dates from 1196. The farm is let down and neglected: the tenant is a glib-tongued imposter and the buildings are disgraceful. I shall probably lose much in getting the farm into shape because if I grub out the hops no one will take it and if I don't I might as well keep a small Monte Carlo for hops are a demoralizing gamble. Now you see why your book touches me nearly. I shall have to put up at least two decent cottages in the place (I don't enter into possession of the

---

[1] *Something*, p. 193.

[2] Both Kipling and Haggard had read Cobbett, and Arthur Young (1741–1820) was another agricultural hero, especially for Haggard, who quotes liberally from Young in *Rural England*. [See *Days*, particularly II, 135–37; *Rider Haggard*, p. 167; R. Thurston Hopkins, *Rudyard Kipling: A Literary Appreciation* (n.d.), p. 237.]

farm till March) and I *do* want to make it possible to rear clean and healthy men on my fraction of England. That is why I want to see you when we come back from the Cape whither we go on the 27th. Of course, like all the other people who have written to you from other counties, I am exceedingly disappointed and wrath and all the rest of it that you did not devote at least 200 pp. to my own county. Sussex, Sir, has been badly treated by you. You have neglected the fattening grounds of the Ouse and the meetings of the curious old river-leet or whatever they call it, which apportions the rental of these pastures once a year I think. Likewise you haven't made enough of our down shepherds nor of our fruit: nor of our most primitive peasantry. N.B.

    Vol. 1, p. 115, l. 26

    "Cookmere" Haven should be Cuckmere

l. 27 (*ibid.*)

    "Chantenbury" Ring is Chanctonbury Ring

Elsewhere the printer speaks of a Hornsley or Horley oil Engine which should be Hornsby–Ackroyd I fancy. I have one for my electric light and sawing.[1]

I am going to have my Rural England bound in pigskin for real use.[2] Have you thought of selling each county separately for a shilling with an appendix consisting of letters and information which have

---

[1] Haggard made the corrections that Kipling suggested in the second edition (1906).

[2] Kipling did not have *Rural England* bound in pigskin, but he made real use of it and entered numerous notations in the margins of his copy, which, to this day, can be found in the outer hall of Bateman's. Two examples of marginalia will suffice. In volume I, page 129, where Haggard writes about the cultivation of hops, Kipling notes: "Hops are humbug." At the end of the chapter on Sussex (I, 136), where Haggard concludes that without the fowl industry and the purchase of farm produce by landed gentry from London both landlords and tenants would suffer terribly, Kipling adds the following note: "I think things are looking up in the last nine years. The landlord of course gets nothing, but the tenant makes a bit. My rents have not risen since 1903 but what the landlord feels most is the skinning of his land by the tenant. I don't mind not making one per cent on my money but I confess I find it very hard to watch the land being let down year by year. I reckon that seven years is the maximum land can be let to an average tenant before the landlord has to take it in hand and bring it up again." Then follows an addition on a new line preceded by the date *1911* when Kipling undoubtedly re-read the chapter and his earlier comment: "As proof that large farmers make money see how many of them are now buying their own farms."

reached you later from men explaining industries and situations which you may have overlooked. I think it might be rather a success.[1]

With all good wishes for a happy and lucky New Year and with renewed admiration (it's an immense book in every way).

Believe me
Ever yours
Rudyard Kipling.[2]

Haggard must have answered immediately, giving more farm advice, and Kipling wrote again before he set sail for South Africa.

(Received December 27, 1902[3])

Bateman's, Burwash, Sussex

Dear Haggard,

Yours is advice of gold. Apples, as you say, are likely to be the game. I have 335 trees bearing already mostly good sorts but grievously in need of oil and limewash and salt and soap and scraping which they will get this spring.

But it's difficult about the tenant. You see there's that blessed mill which is a convenience for grinding pig food and any man who takes that wants a few acres of land. However I will lay my woes before you in the spring. Meantime I have to spend £239! (two thirty-nine pounds!) on making neglected cottages habitable! Dog kennels aren't in it with their present state of filth.

Your suggestion about the Rural Muse appeals to me mightily. I am slowly discovering England which is the most wonderful foreign land I have ever been in. As you say it has no grub and no trained men except a few days' supply of each and it spends its time telling ornate velvet-plush lies. But the man-question is serious. I entirely agree with you about the town-bred person. He has to spend half his time keeping fit outside his employment which ought to be making him fit while he works. If there is any way in which my Agricultural Muse may be

---

[1] Haggard did not publish the counties of *Rural England* separately, but about a quarter of the work appeared serially in the *Daily Express* and the *Yorkshire Post* before book publication.

[2] I have not found the original of this letter. The present copy is from a typescript in the Bambridge Collection.

[3] In Haggard's hand.

of service later, why then as Virgil says "Come on, oh (young) husbandman" and command me.[1]

Ever sincerely,

Rudyard Kipling.[2]

P.S. I think the Goth will choose his own time to do his own job. He knows what he wants and he goes methodically to get it. Meantime we go out of our way to destroy what good feeling exists between us and America. It isn't as much as people make out but it is worth keeping.[3]

Moral When a Kaiser cuts about firing Brodricks and Lansdownes Red or Black Eagles—look out![4]

---

[1] Because of his close ties with India, Kipling may actually have known Arthur Delaval Younghusband (1854–1931), who spent his entire professional life in the Indian Civil Service.

[2] The envelope bears the following note: "P.S. The game has just come. Ever so many thanks." At this time, shooting parties were frequent at Ditchingham, and Haggard quite often sent part of the bag to his friends. Thomas Hardy was another recipient [*Rider Haggard*, p. 175 n.].

[3] At the close of the old century, Germany was building up her fleet; challenging England's monopoly of the seas; constructing a railroad across Asia Minor; and increasing her population, industry, and military strength. In the face of these potential dangers to British policy, Joseph Chamberlain sought a formal alliance with Germany. After several rebuffs, he did sign a treaty with her in 1898, in which Germany renounced any claims to the Transvaal. Chamberlain also cooperated with Germany in the Yangtse Agreement to keep foreign interests out of China and to maintain the "open door." At the end of 1902, England joined with Germany in blockading Venezuela, both to stop outrages against shipping and to force the Venezuelan government to pay some overdue debts. An incensed United States, led by Kipling's friend, Theodore Roosevelt, opposed this violation of the Monroe Doctrine, and insisted that the matter go to arbitration. The arbitration agreement was announced on December 19, just one week before Kipling writes this letter. [Ensor, pp. 258–62, 351–52, 365–66]

[4] Henry Charles Keith Petty-Fitzmaurice (1845–1927), 5th Marquess of Lansdowne, Foreign Secretary in Balfour's Cabinet since July, 1902; and William St. John Freemantle Brodrick (1856–1942), Secretary of War, were both house guests at Sandringham when, in early November, Germany's William II came for a week's shooting holiday with the King. The Emperor awarded a number of German Eagle medals on this visit, but I have not been able to find evidence that he actually presented them to members of the Cabinet. Kipling is probably writing metaphorically: Lansdowne and Brodrick would be the two members of the Cabinet with whom the Kaiser would most want to ingratiate himself, and Kipling doubtless felt that they were not taking the German menace as seriously as they should.

Haggard's letters of the period reflect his unremitting efforts to combat England's agricultural depression. Stanley Weyman, the contemporary storyteller, also a landowner and gentleman farmer, shared Haggard's views, and they corresponded about the subject. But by now Haggard was discouraged. For years he had worked hard for rural England, and he could not see that his efforts had had the slightest effect. "You will understand," he writes to Weyman, "what labour all this [has meant] ..., and I have to write novels in the cracks. (For 2 years past there have been *no* cracks.) A man with a family must think of his living and theirs and one does not make a fortune out of books like *Rural England* or *A Farmer's Year*." The suggestion that he should lead a campaign to establish a Land Commission he countered with: "Now what I mean is that I am in most hearty sympathy with what you propose, but to undertake its inauguration is beyond me. Why don't *you*, my dear Weyman? I'd help you all I could and so would Kipling, who writes to me just the same as you do—almost identical words—only it's *Rural England* has stirred him up. . . . You see, we have not the money to found a Parliamentary Party: we must fight with our own weapons, our brains and our pens."[1]

The next letter we have gives us Haggard's impressions of Bateman's on his first of many visits there. He writes to his wife.

Bateman's, Burwash, Sussex
Tuesday, November 22, 1904

My dearest Lou,

I got down here all right and was whirled off by R.K's motor (which I find however he don't drive himself) to this place about 4 miles from the Station. This is a most charming old house which K has bought. The front part including hall in which I am writing about 1600, the rest older. All panelled, with old stone arched doorways, and he has furnished it according. Indeed some of the things were always in the house, for instance the old Elizabethan bed in which I am sleeping. They have 3 of the draw out oak tables of various design but smaller than ours. The Kiplings are very kind and of course very interesting. With Mr. Allen,[2] a friend of theirs who was staying here, we had a

[1] The letter is dated February 13, 1903; the quotation is from a transcript I made in 1955 with the kind permission of the Weyman family, who then owned the letter.

[2] Sir George Berney Allen (1862–1917), founder of the *Pioneer* at Allahabad, had been a good friend of Kipling's parents and had given Rudyard work on

very pleasant evening discussing the affairs of the Nation. Even the drawing room here is panelled with open-work and the ceiling. They have done the place up charmingly and with much taste.

The weather has set in rather awful—strong gale and snow; but we are going to have a walk in it.

I expect to go to Town tomorrow morning and to go to Mrs. Edwards[1] if she can take me in.

The Kiplings are shortly off to winter at the Cape.

With best love to all, dearest.

Your loving husband,

H. Rider Haggard.[2]

Kipling and his family continued to winter in South Africa, but when they were at home in England, he and Haggard met frequently. In his autobiography, Kipling tells of a meeting at Bateman's with his neighbour and friend, Colonel Wemyss Feilden (1838–1921), a world traveller who had run the blockade in the U.S. Civil War and then became one of General Lee's aides-de-camp: "When Rider Haggard heard . . . [about Feilden's adventures,] he rested not till he had made the Colonel's acquaintance. They cottoned to each other on sight and sound; South Africa in the early days being their bond. One evening, Haggard told us how his son had been born on the edge of Zulu, I think, territory, the first white child in those parts. 'Yes,' said the Colonel, quietly out of his corner, 'I and'—he named two men—'rode twenty-seven miles to look at him. We hadn't seen a white baby for some time.' Then Haggard remembered that visit of strangers."[3]

Kipling enlarged his land holdings and farmed his Bateman's acres, from time to time consulting Haggard on problems that arose. Haggard's visits were, moreover, returned: Kipling "often came to our house," Haggard's daughter writes.[4] And one of Haggard's nephews has written of some of these visits:

---

his Indian newspapers. Now Allen was a retired Sussex neighbor. [Carrington, pp. 37, 314, 320]

[1] Unidentified.

[2] This letter is part of the Haggard collection in the University Library, University of California, Los Angeles.

[3] *Something*, pp. 193–95.

[4] Lilias Rider Haggard and Henry Williamson, *Norfolk Life* (1943), p. 19.

I met Kipling several times when I was a boy at Ditchingham. He gave me half-a-crown on one occasion which was riches to me—I think he knew it, but small boys in those days did not seek the company of their seniors who were on a plane apart and I do not remember ever having much conversation with him.

I recollect . . . Kipling telling an Indian ghost-story over the port after dinner and holding me spell-bound. Nor shall I forget H.R.H., thinking that such stories were not for the young, telling me to "cut along" just as the climax was coming. I think that that was the occasion when Rudyard Kipling forgot to pack his pumps and came down to dinner in a pair of pale blue bedroom-slippers. . . .

Somewhere, but alas! I cannot find it, I have a large sheet of paper on which H.R.H. and R.K. had written, probably as an after-dinner amusement, alternate paragraphs of a short story. It was not complete and of no particular interest I suppose, but I value it and hope it is not irretrievably lost.[1]

In 1904, when the Kiplings were again at Cape Town, Haggard went with Angela, his eldest daughter, to Egypt, whose mysteries always fascinated him. When he returned to England the following summer, he wrote a serious novel based on "the reflections which occurred to me among the Egyptian sands and the empty cells of long-departed anchorites." For Haggard this was a departure from the swashbuckling adventure stories his public had grown to expect, a tale of a mystical love affair, a "Platonic experiment,"[2] between a repentant English hero and a beautiful Egyptian princess. Haggard discussed the story with Kipling, who in turn expressed keen interest and read it in manuscript.

Bateman's, Burwash, Sussex
December 2, 1904

Dear Haggard,
I've been up in town or I should have written when I returned "Renunciation." The only criticism I venture to make is that it should end on the words "her Lord's bed." I don't think Lady De Vene's text at the end strengthens an already immensely strong situation.[3] For the rest I did as I have done with a many of your books

1 Andrew Haggard to Morton Cohen, December 17, 1962.

2 *The Way of the Spirit* (1906), p. 9.

3 Haggard followed the spirit of Kipling's suggestion about the ending, though he allowed himself to add a short descriptive passage after "her lord's

—simply surrendered myself to the joy of reading and read on. That's better than any criticism.

I hope the S. African idea[1] will work out all right though there seem to be an infernal lot of wheels within wheels in those brooders.

Meantime, when you are next in town I wish you could look in on H. A. Gwynne,[2] the new Editor of the Standard. He's a friend of mine and he wants signed articles out of you, so he says, on small holdings and agricultural works. Here I think he shows his sense. If you have time for such things I think it would be a help for the cause and moreover it wouldn't be taken for nothing.

On your advice we are taking steps to get Naboth's vineyard but—oh Lord, how one has to be bled for it![3]

If I don't see you at the Cape[4] which I hope I may here's to our meeting next year if we live.

Ever sincerely yours,
Rudyard Kipling.

---

bed." But Lady Devene (the correct spelling) does not speak again. Haggard discovered that his title, "Renunciation," had already been used. On a visit to Bateman's, he and Kipling set about searching for an appropriate passage from the Bible for an epigraph. They found it in Ecclesiastes xi. 9, and from it they drew the title The Way of the Spirit. [Days, II, 159]

[1] In November 1904 South Africa was galvanized into political activity by the proposed "Lyttelton Constitution" for the Transvaal. This document, which was supposed to come into force in 1905, was designed to promote self-government in the colony through an elective Assembly.

[2] Howell Arthur Gwynne (1865–1950), for many years war correspondent for The Times and Reuters, became editor of the Standard in 1904, and then from 1911 to 1937 was editor of the Conservative paper the Morning Post. Kipling met Gwynne when Kipling arrived at Cape Town during the first year of the Boer War, and they later worked together as fellow-editors of the Friend (see above p. 44). Gwynne became a close friend and was a pallbearer when Kipling was buried in Westminster Abbey.

[3] On Haggard's advice Kipling was negotiating for a neighbour's vineyard. "And it came to pass . . . that Naboth . . . had a vineyard. . . . And Ahab spake unto Naboth, saying, Give me thy vineyard . . . because it is near unto my house; and . . . I will give thee the worth of it in money." [I Kings xxi. 1–3]

[4] Haggard did not go to South Africa in 1905. The Kiplings continued their yearly winter voyage to Cape Town until 1908.

Bateman's, Rudyard Kipling's home in Sussex

Ditchingham House, Rider Haggard's home in Norfolk

Kipling's sketch of Murgh (1908)

Murgh as he appeared in the 1910 serial
publication of *Red Eve*

The derivation of Murgh's name
(in Kipling's hand) for Haggard's *Red Eve*

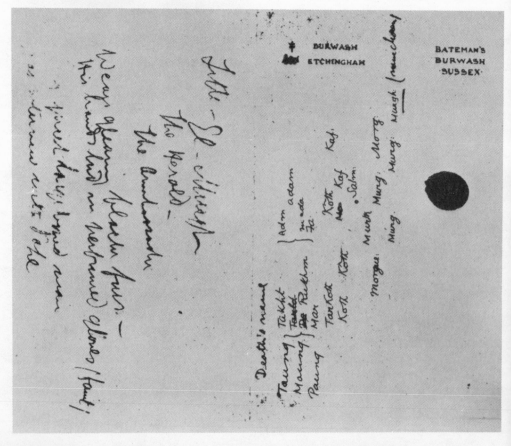

The study at Bateman's

Rudyard, Carrie, and Elsie Kipling arriving at
Westminster Abbey, 1923

Bateman's, Burwash, Sussex
December 5, 1904

My dear Haggard,

I knew you'd take my criticism (such as it was) in good part. It's only a question of what note you end on—her love for her Lord or the moral of the whole tale and *that* (i.e. that there is a God who punishes etc.) is so strongly pointed out throughout that it seemed to me better perhaps to end on the simple human sexual Love!

I think if Time wasn't an object I'd let the book lie till I could get it taken serially.[1] How would McClure do in America? It looks to me like a tale that serially would suit him.

I don't know whether the *Bystander* in England goes in for serial stuff but I think Cassells was a fool not to take it.

Anyhow I'd devote six months to investigations and then if it didn't do I'd sell outright as a book. But have a try with Sam McClure for U.S. serial rights first? F. N. Doubleday ought to take it in America in book form.[2]

You were dead right about Naboth's Vineyard. I believe I've got it now—but the chap is so wonky he may swivel round at the last minute. He left me under no illusions. If he didn't actual[ly] enclose a sample of your Kessingham[3] fishmanure in his letters he hinted it pretty strongly. So I e'en agreed with mine adversary while he was in the way.[4] Thank goodness most of the land is pasture and as such in

---

[1] *The Way of the Spirit* was one of the few Haggard tales that did not run serially, either in England or the United States, before it appeared as a book—presumably because of its strong spiritual theme and lack of conventional adventure. It was published in England in March, 1906, but failed to find a publisher in the United States.

[2] Both Samuel Sidney McClure (1857–1949), founder of *McClure's Magazine*, and Frank Nelson Doubleday (1862–1934) were close friends and publishers of Kipling's. In 1889 McClure had serialized Haggard's *Cleopatra* in the United States. He thought highly of Haggard's work in general and said that *King Solomon's Mines* had sounded "the new note in English fiction which was to make itself heard above anything else for years to come." [S. S. McClure, *My Autobiography* (1914), p. 202]

[3] In 1900 Haggard had bought a summer house at Kessingland, on the east coast of Suffolk, near Lowestoft. Here, in his garden, he carried on more of his agricultural experiments and grew interested in sea erosion. He actually found a marram grass that stopped erosion where concrete walls had failed. The Kiplings were to spend a summer at the Grange, as Haggard called his Kessingland house. (See below p. 79.)

[4] Matt. v. 25.

demand. I've just rented 12 acres round the house for £18 for next year. It's new laid grass (only two years old) and needs treading down badly.

Sorry you don't feel like writing for the *Standard*[1] but perhaps the spoken word is better for getting through the skins of this perverse generation.

We ought to sail on the 10th all being well. So good luck be with you and yours till we meet again.

Ever sincerely,
Rudyard Kipling.

They did sail for South Africa, and at the end of January of the new year, Kipling wrote from Cape Town to acknowledge receipt of a copy of Haggard's *A Gardener's Year*, published earlier in the month in London. The book, a companion to *A Farmer's Year*, but without political or social overtones, is rather an account of Haggard's experiences in the elaborate gardens around Ditchingham House, and describes his experiments in orchid growing.

Also at the very beginning of 1905 the Colonial Office induced Haggard to go as a Commissioner to the United States to inspect the Salvation Army Labor Colonies, a network of camps for rehabilitating indigents from the large cities. Balfour's Government had grown concerned over the increased number of urban poor in England and, in sending Haggard to the United States, hoped to find a remedy for their plight. A possible solution was establishing work settlements for the poor in England's overseas colonies, in which case the American Salvation Army settlements could perhaps serve as models.

The Woolsack, Rosebank, Cape Town
January 31, 1905

(8.45 p.m. A South Easter blowing after a hot day. Guinea fowl and pheasants going to bed in the garden under the loquats. Temp. 73°.)

Dear Haggard,

I write under disabilities. The wife has collared your gardening book which came this morning and is reading me excerpts. She says she doesn't believe you *could* run your garden on three men—even with a

---

[1] Although Haggard did not write for the *Standard* at this time, he did later. [Scott, pp. 165, 184, 199, 200, 476]

labourer to do heavy digging. I've been skimming through it all afternoon reading bits aloud to her. Nett result. You've played havoc with our mail day.

Everything in the book delights my sympathetic soul except your orchids. These leave me cold. I want to know more about the new lawns, A's weaknesses;[1] tree cutting and orchard works and you waste whole pages on *Muscisimilifloribunda Venezuelianinis* and such like. But I suppose you have fellow maniacs in this ploy.[2]

Glad to hear that Longman thinks of taking *Renunciation*. Shouldn't wonder if quite a few people bought Longmans in consequence. What is the telegram about your going out to America to study Salvation Army methods of planting folk on the land with a view to applying 'em to this part of the world. If it's true, hurry up and turn the current this way. We want *picked* men badly, and breeding women worse. Let's hear how the Pearson agricultural paper comes on. There's room for it under an able Editor for P. ain't what you might call rural himself.[3]

Now the wife starts reading aloud again and I must listen and argue and lay out new schemes for our own little Bateman's.

Wishing you all luck.

Ever sincerely yours,
Rudyard Kipling.[4]

What foul illustrations to "Ayesha." Pity one can't sprinkle lime over illustrators—same as slugs.[5]

---

[1] Haggard discusses his lawns on pp. 38–42 and 396 n. of *A Gardener's Year* (1905). "A." was Haggard's gardener for some twenty years, "a curious character" who "afforded . . . much amusement." He disapproved of flower shows and judges, and when Haggard began sending orchids to shows, he said, "Well, I dare say, like other gentlemen, *yew would like to see your name in print for once*," unaware, as Haggard put it, "that my name had appeared in print— occasionally." [*A Gardener's Year*, pp. 223–27]

[2] Haggard later won Kipling over to orchids. See below, p. 68.

[3] Cyril Arthur Pearson (1866–1921) was a newspaper proprietor and some- time owner of *Pearson's Weekly*, the *Daily Express*, and the *Standard*. In 1900 Haggard had agreed to go to South Africa when the Boer War ended to write a series of articles on "The New South Africa" for the *Daily Express*. But the war dragged on and the English reading public had quite enough of South Africa altogether; so Pearson and Haggard agreed to modify their contract

Haggard spent two months early in 1905 inspecting Salvation Army Colonies in California, Colorado, and Ohio. He also went to Canada and induced Governor-General Earl Grey to make available 240,000 acres of land for English labour settlements. In June Haggard's report was published as a Blue Book, and later that same year it appeared as a trade book entitled *The Poor and the Land*. In the report, Haggard concludes that the American Salvation Army installations were remarkably efficacious, and he sets forth a plan for English equivalents. The report got an excellent Press. Balfour and his Government, however, blanched at bills that called for "State interference," and they were suspicious of the religious overtones of the Salvation Army. Whitehall decided to look the other way. In June, when Haggard's report came up in Parliament, it was voted into Committee to die a lingering death.

The year 1905 was a busy one for Kipling, also. The winter months found him in South Africa again, this time planning a memorial to Cecil Rhodes. Later in the year, when both Kipling and Haggard were back in England, they met often in London. If they wrote one another, their letters of this period have not turned up. We find instead indications of visits, both at Ditchingham House and at Bateman's. On August 13 Haggard writes his wife from the Grange, Kessingland, a touching letter on the occasion of their silver wedding anniversary. In it he adds, "I shall get back tomorrow by the early train in case the Kiplings should turn up before they are expected. . . . I am looking forward to a talk with Kipling."[1] And in Haggard's pocket diary for the year, one finds scribbled: "Kipling, Bateman's, Burwash, Sussex. Charing X, 4.50 for Etchingham, 6.29."[2]

Late in the year, Haggard entered a London nursing home "for a month or five weeks . . . to undergo an operation." It was a depressing experience, and he was eager to leave the place. "When I escaped from that nursing home," he later wrote, "very feeble and with much

---

and, instead of printing articles on South Africa, Pearson ran a series of pieces from Haggard's *Rural England* before the book appeared.

[4] I have not found the original of this letter. The present copy is from a typescript in the Bambridge Collection.

[5] *Ayesha, The Return of She* began running in the *Windsor Magazine* in December, 1904, and Kipling had undoubtedly seen the first instalment. The illustrations were by Maurice Greiffenhagen (1862–1931).

[1] *Cloak*, p. 194.

[2] Norwich Library Collection.

shattered nerves, I went to stay with . . . [a friend] to recuperate, and thence for a day or two to the Kiplings'."[1] By now, Haggard had become a frequent visitor to Bateman's and a favourite of the small family. Kipling himself was later to write that "his comings were always a joy to us and the children, who followed him like hounds in the hope of 'more South African stories.'"[2] Haggard now enjoyed the "freedom" of Bateman's, and it was undoubtedly about this time that, as Kipling later recalled, "we found by accident that each could work at ease in the other's company. So he would visit me, and I him, with work in hand; and between us we could even hatch out tales together—a most exacting test of sympathy."[3] No other human being had the privilege of working with Kipling in his study, and as the letters and diaries show, in later years, this is where the two men often retreated, spending long afternoons working on their individual stories, helping each other where they could, and, when not working, engaged in long, intimate conversations on subjects which touched them deeply and which they did not talk about easily with others.

The study is a large room on the first floor of Bateman's that remains to this day as it was when Kipling worked there. From its windows facing east and south, he had an excellent view of his Sussex fields and gardens. The room itself is lined on two walls with books, and on the floor lie Indian rugs that Kipling had had specially made. The furnishings are modest, a number of unupholstered walnut chairs, a single, uninviting *chaise longue*, and a huge, wooden table. Over the fireplace hangs Philip Burne-Jones's portrait of Carrie, and against some of the books in the bookcases lean framed portraits of Socrates, General Lord Roberts, who had commanded the troops in the Boer War and for whom Kipling had worked on the Bloemfontein *Friend*, and Dr. L. S. Jameson, whom Kipling had also known in South Africa. A glazed showcase contains bunting and other relics from *The Victory* and, beside them, an ironwork pencase of ancient Chinese design that recalls an incident in *Kim*. On the floor stand two huge globes and an immense, woven wastebasket into which Kipling threw the early drafts of his work. And on the far side of the door, near the east window, is the table at which Kipling worked. It is long and oblong, and it offered him wide, open surfaces for pushing papers in different directions and for piling things. We have Kipling's

[1] *Days*, II, 204.
[2] *Something*, p. 193.
[3] *Ibid.*

own description of the items he collected to keep within reach: "I always kept certain gadgets on my work-table, which was ten feet long from North to South and badly congested. One was a long, lacquer, canoe-shaped pen-tray full of brushes and dead 'fountains'; a wooden box held clips and bands; another, a tin one, pins; yet another, a bottle-slider, kept all manner of unneeded essentials from emery-paper to small screwdrivers; a paper-weight, said to have been Warren Hastings'; a tiny, weighted fur-seal and a leather crocodile sat on some of the papers; an inky foot-rule and a Father of the Penwipers which a much-loved housemaid of ours presented yearly, made up the main-guard of these little fetishes."[1]

It was in this study, sitting at Kipling's ten-foot table, that the two friends, during an afternoon in the autumn, 1905, worked together on the idea for a story that Haggard was to write. "Here I remember," Haggard could later recall, "we compounded the plot of 'The Ghost Kings' together, writing down our ideas in alternate sentences upon the same sheet of foolscap."[2] This document—in actuality, *three* sheets of foolscap—survives,[3] a visible, moving reminder of the deepening sympathies that enabled Kipling and Haggard to work in the same room, not only on their own writings, but on each other's. They sat face to face at the long table, discussing, accepting, and rejecting the notions they freely exchanged. One of them would write down the incidents they both fancied and pass the paper across the table to the other, who took up the pen and developed the outline further. Soon, they had three pages of plot outline, the skeleton on which Haggard would build the tale.

The folio sheets bearing the outline repay close examination. Page one begins in Kipling's microscopic hand: "Two children of early Natal colonists," it reads, and carries the plot for seventeen lines. Then Haggard's hand, bold and less disciplined, takes up and carries the plot for the rest of the first page, for all of page two, and on to the top of page three, where, in the middle of a sentence, Kipling takes over and brings the outline to the end, finishing with the word *Curtain* and a flourish of the pen. The book needed a title, and they must have talked about it, for at the top of the first page, in Kipling's hand, are two titles.

[1] *Something*, p. 231.

[2] *Days*, II, 204.

[3] As part of the James McGregor Stewart Kipling Collection, Dalhousie University Library, Halifax, Nova Scotia.

The first, "The Shapes," has numerous deliberate strokes running through it. Above it, Kipling wrote "The Ghost-Kings," a title that satisfied them both. On the back of page two Haggard added a few plot afterthoughts, perhaps on the train returning to Ditchingham, for although the actual outline is in ink, these notes are in pencil.[1]

In March, 1906, *The Way of the Spirit*, which Haggard had previously discussed with Kipling, appeared with this dedication:

My dear Kipling—Both of us believe that there are higher aims in life than the weaving of stories well or ill, and according to our separate occasions strive to fulfil this faith.

Still, when we talked together of the plan of this tale, and when you read the written book, your judgement thereof was such as all of us hope for from an honest and instructed friend—generally in vain.

So, as you found interest in it, I offer it to you, in token of much I cannot write. But you will understand.

In May Kipling takes up the subject of the plot again.

> Bateman's, Burwash, Sussex
> May 28, 1906

Dear Haggard,

I've been reading over The Way of the Spirit again—it's a book that stands re-reading—and it has just occurred to me that the Woman of the West wouldn't have been impressed by the Woman of the East to the extent of admitting her *moral* superiority. Do you think I'm right? I mean admitting it at once, as she practically does. Question is, wouldn't she have made a bigger fight against the idea than she did?

I'm a little curious on the subject.

Summer is a long time coming up our way and if the grey weather holds on we shall have blight.

An intelligent tenant of mine has just gone and let die twenty good apple-trees that I put in for him—through pure asinine neglect.

But why do I vex *you* on these matters.

Drop me a line if you have nothing better to do some day and say when you may be coming south. I am up to my eyes in work.

> Ever yours,
> Rudyard Kipling.

Have you done anything to your tree yarn?[2]

---

[1] See appendix for a transcript of the plot outline.
[2] The tree yarn is Haggard's *The Ghost Kings*. It ran serially in *Pearson's*

On October 1, 1908, when Haggard was visiting Bateman's, he and Kipling again retreated to the study and planned a tale that Haggard later wrote. *Red Eve* (1911), Haggard's best historical romance, is a mysterious tale of the Black Death and of Murgh, an allegorical figure come from the East to infect and destroy Christendom. A surviving sheet of Bateman's stationery[1] reveals that Kipling took a hand in creating Murgh and helped to select his name. On one half of the sheet we find in Kipling's hand what seems, at first glance, to be a genealogical table but is instead the evolution of Murgh's name. Haggard and Kipling try to capture a sense of foreboding in the name, and as they throw out new suggestions and develop variations on earlier ones, Kipling writes them down. Eventually they get to the word *morgue*, and by taking this word through *murth*, *murg*, and *morg*, they arrive at *murgh* and agree that that is what they have been searching for. Kipling underlines it and writes "name chosen" in parentheses. In addition to the name chart, we have a pencil sketch of Murgh drawn by Kipling and certainly the model for the description of Murgh in the book.[2] And on the same side as the word chart, we have a series of notes in Haggard's hand:

Magazine from October, 1907, to June, 1908, and Cassell's published it as a book in September, 1908. Kipling liked the tale Haggard had built from their plot outline, and Haggard valued his friend's opinion. Three years later, Haggard wrote in his autobiography: "When . . . Mr. Kipling, who as a rule goes to bed early, told me that he had sat up to I know not what hour and got chilled through reading 'The Ghost Kings' because he could not lay it down, it gave me a higher opinion of that work than I could boast before." [*Days*, II, 92]

[1] In the James McGregor Stewart Kipling Collection, Dalhousie University Library, Halifax, Nova Scotia.

[2] "Truly he was worth seeing. Hugh noted his garments first, and particularly the head-dress, which caught his glance and held it, for never had he known such a one before. It was a cap fitting tight to the skull, only running across the crown of it was a stiff raised ridge, of leather perhaps, jagged and pointed something like the comb of a cock. This comb, of a brilliant red, was surmounted at its highest point by a ball of black of the size of a small apple. The cap itself was yellow, except its lowest band, which stood out from it and was also black. In the centre of this band upon the forehead glowed a stone like a ruby.... On his brow, which was prominent, smooth black hair parted in the middle, was plastered back as that of women sometimes is, making hard lines against the yellow skin below. He had very thick eyebrows that ran upward on either side of a bow-shaped wrinkle in the centre of his forehead. The eyes beneath were small and pale ... yet their glance was like the points of thrusting

Title—El Murgh
    The Herald
    The Ambassador

Wears gleaming black furs
His hands hid in perfumed gloves (faint)
Big quiet large boned man
Has interview with Pope

And alongside Kipling's drawing of Murgh, Haggard has written:

Bateman's
Kipling's idea of Murgh
5.10.08

Winter holidays on the Continent had replaced for the Kiplings the earlier journeys to South Africa. From 1909 to the beginning of the war they travelled annually to Engelberg or St. Moritz, and frequently to Vernet-les-Bains, where Carrie "took the cure."[1] Jerome K. Jerome recalls a winter when he was at Engelberg with the Kiplings:

> [Rudyard] was in the elementary stage as regards both skating and ski-ing; and wherever he went the Kodak fiends followed him in their hundreds. He must have felt like a comet trying to lose its own tail.
>
> I took him one morning to a ski-ing ground I had discovered some mile or more away: an ideal spot for the beginner. We started early and thought we had escaped them. But some fool had seen us, and had given the halloa; and before we had got on our skis, half Engelberg was pouring down the road.
>
> Kipling is not the meekest of men and I marvelled at his patience.
>
> "They might give me a start," he sighed; "I would like to have had them on, just once."
>
> Engelberg is too low to be a good sports centre. We had some

---

swords. With those little eyes alone he seemed to smile, for the rest of his countenance did not move. The nose was long and broad at the end with wide spreading nostrils and a deep furrow on either side. The mouth was thin-lipped and turned downwards at the corners, and the chin was like a piece of iron, quite hairless, and lean as that of a man long dead." [*Red Eve* (1911), pp. 184–85]

[1] Carrington, p. 322.

muggy weather, and to kill time I got up some private theatricals. Kipling's boy and girl were there. They were jolly children. Young Kipling was a suffragette and little Miss Kipling played a coster-monger's Donah. Kipling himself combined the parts of scene-shifter and call boy. It was the first time I had met Mrs. Kipling since her marriage. She was still a beautiful woman, but her hair was white. ...

It was election time in England, and the hotel crowd used to encourage Kipling and myself to political argument in the great hall. ... Kipling himself was always courteous.[1]

Politics always interested both Kipling and Haggard, and frequently entered into their correspondence, even when one of them was abroad. Earlier, in December, 1905, the Radicals under Campbell-Bannerman had dislodged Balfour, and when Haggard read that the new Government was to form a Royal Commission on Coast Erosion, he wrote to Lloyd George, then President of the Board of Trade, about his success in his summer house in Kessingland in arresting erosion with marram grass. The inevitable happened: Haggard was asked to serve on the Commission, and he did so for the next five years. In 1907 the Commission chairman and Haggard suggested to Lloyd George that the Commission look into the question of afforestation as well, and immediately "Afforestation" was tacked on to the Commission title, a few more experts were added to its membership, and, as Haggard put it, "we investigated that great subject with much zeal,"[2] concluding that England's forests were in danger of extinction. The Commission report suggested that the nation undertake to reclaim and reforest its land systematically, a proposal especially dear to Haggard and Kipling because it would give employment to a large number of people on land which now used little labour. But the timber needs of future generations were a less urgent issue than the Government's Budget. Reforestation would be costly, and, though economical in the long run, of little immediate political value to the Radical Party. In a letter that Kipling wrote to Haggard from Engelberg at the time of the Commission report, he foresaw that the Government would ignore the Commission's recommendations.

[1] *My Life and Times* (1926), pp. 232–33.
[2] *Days*, II, 211.

Hotels Cattani, Engelberg
January 28, 1909

My dear Haggard,

Ever so many thanks for the copy of the Afforestation Committee and your letter.[1] You must have had a devil of a time over it and, I should imagine, the lion's share of the work.

I am as you know *not* a lover of the present Govt and I wish I could believe they would handle your recommendations in anything approaching a broad and statesmanlike way. But my own sad conviction is that they will use your report simply to show their zeal in behalf of the unemployed and when the time comes for them to be chased off the scene of their misdeeds, neither you nor we shall hear anything more about the work. And indeed, the only thing in the Report which I mistrust is its constant reference to the "unemployed" and its tributes (which I hope are true) to the value of their labours.

Me and a local idiot of Burwash (an aged bird of 80+) planted about a hundred odd larches this autumn (and the damned little rabbits ate 'em chiefly) but at no time was either of us impressed with the idea that tree planting was any job for the idle or disorderly-minded. Also it was uncommon like hard-work.

But *what* an England we could make if we could only get ½ of your programme put through. Forgive me if I seem a pessimist. They are all such a set of flagrant and persistent liars that I *can't* believe in their rectitude over anything. I shall be enormously pleased tho' if they develop any sparks of decency or gratitude towards you.

Now let's have Murgh put in going order? I'm living a queer life amid snow and sports and a new brand of the English but I am as ever

Yours sincerely,
Rudyard Kipling.

Bateman's, Burwash, Sussex
December 14, 1909

Dear Haggard,

Ever so many thanks for the report and the speech[2] (which

[1] The Royal Commission, whose reports Kipling refers to here and in the first sentence of the following letter, published its findings between 1907 and 1911. [Scott, p. 123]

[2] Haggard was a natural speech maker. Tall, attractive, with a ready phraie and a dramatic flourish, he was much in demand as an after-dinner speaker.

interested me a great deal). You've got a long and a hard, but a very good row to hoe. Only remember that sooner or later you will be let down and given away and generally repudiated by the Beasts with whom you do now associate. They are only united on one thing and that is lying.

I send you with this a photo of mine which is about the best that there is. It is taken from my cousin's painting of me and is rather like the animal.[1]

The flowers have just come and the plants are expected. When they come the wife will write you her thanks. The orchid flowers are superb. They are now ornamenting the dining-room.

Well, good luck and bless you.

> Ever yours,
> Rudyard Kipling.

In 1911, after Haggard turned fifty-five, he began writing his auto-biography, which, when completed in September 1912, he had sealed and placed in his publisher's vault, to be opened after he died. In this two-volume work, he writes affectionately about Kipling and remin-isces over the hours they had spent together.

Among my pleasantest recollections during the last few years are those of my visits to the Kiplings, and the one they paid me here, during which we discussed everything in heaven above and earth beneath. It is, I think, good for a man of rather solitary habits now and again to have the opportunity of familiar converse with a brilliant and creative mind. Also we do not fidget each other. Thus only last year Kipling informed me that he could work as well when I was sitting in the room as though he were alone, whereas generally the

---

During 1909 he made his fair share of public speeches, and no fewer than ten of them were reported in the Press. His various subjects included small holdings, afforestation, a call for army recruits, and an appeal for Dr. Barnardo's Homes, but the speech that Kipling refers to is probably one on agriculture that he had made nearly three weeks earlier at the annual dinner of the Bungay and District Farmer's Club. [Scott, p. 202]

[1] Philip Burne-Jones (1861–1926), son of Edward Burne-Jones. Kipling sat for him in 1899 and, pleased with the result, wrote to his friend Charles Eliot Norton about it: "Phil's portrait of me is a Regular Stunner and shows specially well in the reproduction. I resent the sleek baldness of my head, but the intellectual air and the tummy are beyond dispute." The original now hangs in the National Portrait Gallery. [Carrington, pp. 228–29]

presence of another person while he was writing would drive him almost mad. He added that he supposed the explanation to be that we were both of a trade, and I dare say he is right. I imagine, however, that sympathy has much to do with the matter.

Of late years Kipling has been much attacked, a fate with which I was once most familiar, since at one time or the other it overtakes the majority of those who have met with any measure of literary, or indeed of any other success. . . . No man is continually at his best, and the writer of "Recessional" and other noble and beautiful things should be spared these scourgings. However, I have no doubt it will all come right in the end, and I hope that when this book is published he may be wearing the Order of Merit.[1]

Besides writing the story of his life, Haggard wrote regularly in a diary. In the autumn of 1911 he records a visit to Bateman's:

September 30, 1911: Went to Kipling's. At Bateman's till Monday.
Found him very well. Mrs. K. not so well. Elsie almost grown up.[2] We talked a great deal on many subjects—making plots for books, etc. He read me 2 of his plays—and we discussed others, especially one that would deal with the fall of the British Empire.[3] He remarked to me

[1] *Days*, II, 208–209.

[2] Elsie, born in 1896, was now fifteen.

[3] Elsewhere Kipling styles himself an "envious dramatist" (p. 80 below, letter from Kessingland, Summer 1914) because his efforts at writing plays were not successful. Either he himself destroyed most of his play manuscripts or he transferred the best material in them to his poems and stories. The two plays that Haggard alludes to cannot be identified with any assurance. But there is evidence that Kipling was working with plays of one sort or another at this time. In 1935 Messrs. Hodgson & Co. sold at auction the manuscript of a three-act play adapted by F. Kinsey Peile from Kipling's "The Man Who Would Be King," containing "about 300 alterations (some extending to whole sentences in the dialogue), additions or suggestions in Kipling's own hand." Accompanying the manuscript were two autograph letters and a card (all written in 1910 and 1911) from Kipling about the play ("It seems that the play will be a middling strong one and the last two acts ought to go well"). The sales catalogue refers to Kipling's role in adapting the story for the stage by describing the play as "an interesting attempt, in which, as profuse alterations attest, Kipling himself took a considerable part, to dramatise . . . one of . . . [his] finest short stories." [*Book Prices Current*, L (1936), 417] Because the catalogue attributes Kipling's additions and emendations to 1911, a date that seems to be borne out by (as well as based on) the accompanying letters and card, this may be one of the plays that Kipling read to Haggard. "Gow's Watch" is another

on what he called my remarkable power of "sustained imagination" asking me if anybody had made a study of it. I said that to the best of my belief nobody had ever thought it worth while. He replied that "it ought to be done." Afterwards apropos of some passage I came across in a history of the Eastern Empire he said words to the effect that in decaying civilizations it was always the case that real gifts were ignored. They devoted themselves to the criticism of style and other details. They had no longer the mind to appreciate mind.

I went through the plot of *The Mahatma and the Hare*[1] with him. He thought it a fine thing but said that I should have carried it further. I answered the arguments of the hare with the instance of the sufferings of mankind at the hands of a power as superior to it as we are to the hare. I replied that such things have a limit: we should hunt in the

---

work which Kipling must have written as a verse play. Four fragments exist today, scattered in Kipling's verse. The characters in the fragments are the same, the plot more or less develops as one reads the successive fragments, and Kipling retains act and scene designations as part of the fragment titles. Other Kipling works that were adapted for the stage before Haggard made this entry in his diary are *The Naulakha* (1891), *The Light That Failed* (1898 and 1903), and "The Man Who Was" (1903). One Kipling play that we can easily identify he wrote in 1913, too late for it to apply to Haggard's diary entry here. It is *The Harbour Watch*, a one-acter he composed in collaboration with his daughter Elsie. Pyecroft is the hero and it tells of a sailor's intended desertion from the Navy. It was produced twice at the Royalty in 1913, but, according to Mrs. Bambridge, "it was not a great success." [Typescripts of *The Harbour Watch* are in the British Museum and the Library of Congress. The available fragments of "Gow's Watch" are: "From Leyden's 'Irenius,'" Act III. Scene 2 (*Traffics and Discoveries*, 1904); "Gow's Watch," Act II. Scene 2 (*Songs From Books*, 1912, a few lines having appeared as a chapter [X] heading in *Kim* as early as 1901); "Gow's Watch," Act IV. Scene 4, and "Gow's Watch," Act V. Scene 3 (both in *Debits and Credits*, 1926). In the *Inclusive Edition* of his verse (1927), Kipling brought together Act II. Scene 2; Act IV. Scene 4; and Act V. Scene 3. Elsie Bambridge, "Epilogue," Carrington, p. 399; Chandler, pp. 106–107; R(oger). L(ancelyn). G(reen)., "Kipling and the Stage," *Kipling Journal*, XXX (March 1963), 4; L. Whitbread, "Kipling and the Stage," *Notes and Queries*, CLXXXIV (January 16, 1943), 37–39]

[1] Haggard took a serious interest in supernaturalism and psychical phenomena. In July, 1904, because of an unusual dream that correctly informed him of the accidental death of his retriever dog, Haggard foreswore blood sports. *The Mahatma and the Hare* is a mystical tale based on another dream. A kindly old mahatma with supernatural powers meets, on the road to the gates of heaven, first a hare, then the hunter who killed him, and hears their tales in turn. Thomas Hardy thought it a "strangely attractive book" and was "much moved by it." [*Days*, II, 159–67; *Rider Haggard*, pp. 175 n., 274 n.]

nowhere. I asked K. if his work was ever discussed in his own family. He said it was never mentioned, although he talked over things privately with his wife. His boy Jack had said to him the other day on his going to school at Wellington: "Thank heaven, father. I hope that there I shall hear no more of 'Recessional.'" I said it was the same in my own circle. He told me that his children showed no signs of imagination and that he was thankful for it. I said *ditto*—ditto.

On Sunday and Monday I sat in the study while he worked and after a while he got up and remarked to me that it was odd but that my presence did not bother him a bit—he supposed because we were two of a trade but that when the other day some friend of his, Jameson[1] or another—I forget who, had been in the room with him it had upset him altogether. With me present he could work as well as though he were alone. He told me that I was the only literary man with whom he cared to associate at all. He knew no others, though Conan Doyle, who lives somewhere near,[2] sometimes came to call, but he "got

---

[1] Sir Leander Starr Jameson (1853–1917), from whom the Jameson Raid took its name.

[2] Both Kipling and Haggard were well acquainted with Conan Doyle. Doyle tells us that when he read some of Kipling's critical remarks about the United States, he wrote to him "to remonstrate." As a result, when Doyle himself visited America in 1894, he spent Thanksgiving with the Kiplings in Vermont. "I had two great days," Doyle later wrote, ". . . and have a grateful remembrance of Mrs. Kipling's hospitality. The poet read me 'McAndrew's Hymn,' which he had just done, and surprised me by his dramatic power which enabled him to sustain the Glasgow accent throughout. . . . I had brought my golf clubs and gave him lessons in a field while the New England rustics watched from afar, wondering what on earth we were at, for golf was unknown in America at that time. We parted good friends, and the visit was an oasis in my rather dreary pilgrimage as a lecturer." In 1896, Conan Doyle sent Kipling a pair of Norwegian skis, which also stirred much curiosity among the local Brattleboro citizens when Kipling tried them out because they were "probably the first pair of skis in Vermont." Conan Doyle thought highly of Kipling's work and included "The Drums of the Fore and Aft" and "The Man Who Would Be King" in his list of the great masterpieces of all time. Conan Doyle's home, Windlesham, at Crowborough, Sussex, is about twenty miles from Bateman's. [Carrington, pp. 159, 165, 179; Arthur Conan Doyle, *Memories and Adventures* (1924), pp. 215, 245–46; Arthur Conan Doyle, *Through the Magic Door* (1908), pp. 121–22, 241] Haggard and Doyle probably met in the mid-1890's. On November 25, 1898, Haggard wrote Conan Doyle to say "what an excellent vivid tale I thought 'The Tragedy of the Korosko' especially to anyone who has been in Egypt." On April 24 of the following year, Haggard, as Chairman of the Anglo-African Writers Club, invited

nothing from him." His opinions on reviewers were similar to my own: "they do not understand."

He told me he had dined recently with—or [gone] to meet—Balfour[1] and had expressed his views. B. said, "Let us talk of something less distressing." "Yes," answered K., "let us talk of golf." On the ratting of the peers[2] we feel the same. We made—or rather he made—

Conan Doyle to take over as the Club's Chairman. On September 22, 1900, and again on July 28, 1902, Haggard was Chairman and Conan Doyle Guest of the Evening at dinners of the Authors' Club. Their names occasionally appeared together on behalf of worthy causes, and when Haggard was principal speaker of the bicentenary celebration honouring the publishers Longmans, Green & Co. (November 5, 1924), Conan Doyle was present. See also p. 73 below. [Scott, pp. 193, 195, 215; letters from H. Rider Haggard to Arthur Conan Doyle in the Sir Arthur Conan Doyle Estates Collection, reproduced in a letter (August 2, 1958) to me from Professor Pierre Weil-Nordon; *Rider Haggard*, p. 245]

[1] Arthur Balfour thought highly of Kipling's work, and he sought to have the Laureateship go to him on Tennyson's death. In 1903, Balfour, as Prime Minister, offered Kipling a K.C.M.G., and Kipling, who had already refused the K.C.B. that Lord Salisbury had offered four years earlier, replied:

> Bateman's, Burwash, Sussex
> November 7, 1903

My dear Mr Balfour,

I have to thank you for your letter of yesterday and to assure you of my entire appreciation of the honour you propose, as well as of the more than flattering terms in which you propose it.

But I find that my position has not changed since '99 when Lord Salisbury was kind enough to offer me a somewhat similar distinction, and that such honours must continue outside my scheme of things.

> Yours very sincerely,
> Rudyard Kipling.

Kipling did not agree with Balfour's politics and was relieved when, in 1905, Balfour resigned. [Carrington, pp. 203, 301–302, 305, 318; the letter to Balfour is the property of the Kipling Society] Andrew Lang introduced Haggard to Balfour in the late 1880's, hoping that Balfour would be able to help Haggard return to Government service. Later Haggard too became disenchanted with Balfour's politics. In 1905 Balfour was instrumental in killing Haggard's Report on the U.S. Salvation Army colonies. [See p. 60 above (January 31, 1905); *Days*, II, 24–25, 107, 190–94; *Rider Haggard*, p. 243.]

[2] On August 10, 1911, the House of Lords allowed the Parliament Act to pass, stripping itself of almost all its power rather than risk "a large and prompt creation of peers," with which Asquith and his Liberal Government threatened them. [Ensor, p. 430]

a poem about it.[1] His readiness is very wonderful and so is his memory. He repeated to me a long poem he had written, "The Female of the Species,"[2] without an error—very true and amusing.

Both Kipling and Haggard were acquaintances and admirers of General William Booth. In 1910, when John Manson published an unjustified attack upon the "General" and his organization,[3] Booth asked Haggard to write an impartial history of his Army. Haggard was reluctant because he was too busy with his other burning interests, but when Arthur Conan Doyle suggested that in writing the book Haggard would be lending his "honoured name to . . . [induce] many people to support . . . an evil organization," Haggard hesitated no longer. He wrote the book and refused payment for it, turning the copyright over to the Salvation Army. He called it *Regeneration*.[4]

October 12, 1911

Dear Haggard,

Many thanks for Regeneration, and for what you say about the "Empire" play and the possibility of using your Queen of Sheba's ring setting. I'd like to have a try some day.[5]

We're all filled with colds here and are dripping like eaves on a south roof.

Your coming—even if you did bring the cold—was a great comfort and joy to me.

Ever yours,
Rudyard Kipling.

P.S. I'll think about that foul field but—Lor!—it do look awful. Water grass like being cultivated.[6]

[1] The poem seems not to have survived.

[2] Kipling finished "The Female of the Species" on August 20, 1911. It first appeared in the *London Morning Post* on October 20, 1911 [Chandler, p. 81]. For an amusing account of the first American publication of the poem, see Edward Bok, *Twice Thirty* (1925), pp. 373–74; and *The Americanization of Edward Bok* (1923), pp. 306–307.

[3] John Manson, *The Salvation Army and the Public* (1910).

[4] *Rider Haggard*, pp. 245–47.

[5] Haggard's *Queen Sheba's Ring*, which had been published a year before Kipling writes, is set in North Central Africa and has an allegorical application to England and the Empire under Liberal rule.

[6] Haggard, an expert on field draining, who had even devised new and

Hotels Cattani, Engelberg
January 3, 1912

Dear Haggard,

The English papers are just in, with the New Year honours, and I make haste to send you all our heartiest congratulations on your Knighthood.[1] It's the most sensible thing that this alleged Government has ever done and if they had souls I might be tempted to believe that there was some good in 'em. You've done such good work for the State, for so long that in this case the State truly honours itself in honouring you. It's a banal phrase but you know what I mean and you will know too, that no one is more pleased than we are.

Ever sincerely yours,
Rudyard Kipling.

Later in the year Haggard visited Bateman's again, taking along the proofs for *Child of Storm*, the second part of his trilogy about the rise and fall of the Zulu dynasty. While at Bateman's, Haggard read the tale aloud to Kipling, and then he left the proofs behind for Kipling to read on his own. The book would be published two months later.

(Received, 9 November, 1912[2])   Bateman's, Burwash, Sussex

Dear Haggard,

The proofs of "Child of Storm" go to you today. I've read it; re-read it and re-reread it and I don't think you're wrong when you say it's the best you've done. *I* can't see where it needs anything being done to it. It marches straight off from the first and holds like a drug! I'm especially pleased with the characterisation of Mameena, who is a nice little bitch though dusky.[3]

---

efficient methods for the purpose, had very likely suggested that Kipling drain one of his fields. Haggard discusses land drainage both in *A Farmer's Year* and *Rural England*.

[1] Haggard was awarded a knighthood for service to his country, not for his literary accomplishments. He could not have been more pleased. "It was Recognition," he wrote, "for which I felt grateful." [*Days*, II, 226]

[2] In Haggard's hand.

[3] Mameena, a Zulu Helen, is the villain of the piece. Her charms and diabolical craftiness cause dissension between Umbelazi and Cetywayo, Chaka's grandsons, who, for love of her, lead their tribes into battle. Ultimately she meets a tragic end.

I feel better for your visit. Incidentally, you brought me luck, for my tenant, a big grazier, has taken 75 acres of extra fields on my terms, 34/-. That ain't so bad even if he wants a few new gates. Take good care of yourself and return a Wild Tariff Reformer.[1]

Ever sincerely,
Rudyard Kipling.

On the back page of the letter, Haggard adds the following in his own hand:

I read from this "Child of Storm" to Kipling till I could read no more and he would not let me stop. At the end, when my throat had given out, he said to the effect, There you see: what book is there of our day to which I could have listened like that all this time. He expressed himself of the work in very strong terms indeed, almost overpowering terms: "as terse and strong as a Greek play, not a word that could be improved on or cut out," etc.

The only thing he had to suggest was the removal of the last 2 lines where A.Q. tries to explain away the laughter above the hut, but this he abandoned.[2]

I was very pleased at his enthusiasm as he is a severe critic of his own and other people's stuff; also because it agrees so thoroughly with my own judgment. But no one else will understand. It takes big men to recognize big work and such are scarce.

November 9, 1912   H. Rider Haggard.

[1] Haggard had agreed to be one of six to serve on a Royal Dominions Commission that would travel to the Dominions, inquiring into the state of imperial trade, economic and social conditions, and the use of natural resources. He was to leave on the first leg of his mission, to Australia and New Zealand, on November 29. [*Rider Haggard*, pp. 255–63]

[2] Kipling and Haggard were quite right not to delete the last two lines of *Child of Storm*, which, with the penultimate paragraph, give the reader a final shudder:

I [Allan Quatermain] made no answer, for at that moment I heard a very curious sound, which seemed to me to proceed from somewhere above the hut. Of what did it remind me? Ah! I know. It was like the sound of the dreadful laughter of Zikali [the Zulu magician], Opener-of-Roads—Zikali, the "Thing-that-should-never-have-been-born."

Doubtless, however, it was only the cry of some storm-driven night bird. Or perhaps it was an hyena that laughed—an hyena that scented death. [P. 348]

Haggard made a copy of his reply, and it is one of his two surviving letters to Kipling:

Ditchingham House, Norfolk
November 10, 1912

(Copy)

My dear Kipling,

I am so glad that on reading "Child of Storm" through you find your judgment thereof confirmed.

I am no particular admirer of my own work but in this case it came home to me that things were well:—I saw that it was good!—Why are some things good and others out of the same factory—not so? The same pains are taken: the conditions are identical: but the results are often very different. Now "C. of S." was written quite easily, dictated straightaway, and except for a few Zulu details not altered at all—also more or less invented as I went along. It was the same thing with "She" which I did with my own hand in six weeks, beginning to write it with no idea in my head save that of a woman who had "discovered the trick of long life."

However it's no matter since reviewers—eight out of ten of them—either cannot or will not discriminate, and most readers don't know. Only high minds can sense high work and high minds don't grow on blackberry bushes!

You will see "C. of S." described as a boys' story "as usual too bloody for most tastes" ("Piff! What is blood in Zululand?"). I believe there is a class of journalist who would have described the Odyssey as a boys' story—too bloody for most tastes!

I enjoyed my stay with you very much indeed and wished it had been longer, which perhaps you didn't. There were matters of which I had no time to talk!

Ever yours,
H. Rider Haggard.[1]

Egypt continued to be one of Haggard's enthusiasms. He studied the ancient culture and became an authority on its history. When he was able to travel there, he explored its monuments and museums. On hands and knees, he crawled into newly opened tombs, and he often brought back

[1] The copy of this letter is in the Huntington Library, San Marino, California.

to England with him trunks full of souvenirs. His excitement sparked his imagination, and he invented new tales about Egypt. By 1913 he had already written *Cleopatra* (1889), *The World's Desire* (the collaboration with Andrew Lang that appeared in 1890), *The Way of the Spirit* (1906), and more recently *Morning Star* (1910). Haggard's enthusiasm might have been one of the reasons for the Kiplings' journey to Egypt in the spring, 1913, when Haggard himself was doing some Royal Commission work in Australia and New Zealand and visiting for the first time Kipling's own India. The two kept in touch as they travelled, and we have a letter that Kipling wrote on the Nile when his boat was stuck in the sand.[1]

s.s. "Prince Abbas,"
March 3, 1913
On a sand bar between Assouan and
Luxor—apparently well stuck.

Dear Haggard,

I'm glad to learn from yours of the 21st Jan: that you were stuck too. We've been hung up on our 3' 6" draft for the last two hours: and by the look of things may be here for another two.

I was awfully glad to get your letter and to have your impressions of the Shiny.[2] Well, whose fault is it that the Babu is what he is? *We* did it. We began in Macaulay's time: we have worked without intermission for three generations to make this Caliban. Every step and thought on the road is directly traceable to England and English influence. Twenty smitten years ago I... but no matter.[3]

I'd have given a month's pay to have heard you convert your

---

[1] Both Haggard and Kipling wrote travel pieces about their visits to Egypt. Haggard's appeared in the *Daily Mail* in 1904; Kipling's in *Nash's Magazine* and *Cosmopolitan* in 1914, later collected in *Letters of Travel*. [Scott, p. 164; Stewart, pp. 352–54]

[2] *Shiny* is Regular Army slang for "the East, especially India." [Eric Partridge, *A Dictionary of Slang and Unconventional English* (1951), p. 757]

[3] Macaulay was a member of the Supreme Council of India from 1834 to 1838 and spoke out strongly in favour of an English, rather than an oriental, type of education for India. In 1853, under his leadership, competitive examinations were substituted for patronage as the basis for recruiting the Indian Civil Service; Macaulay in fact headed a committee charged to draw up detailed plans for the competitive system that the Act authorized. ["Report on the Selection and Examination of Candidates for the Indian Civil Service," xl Parl. Papers, 1854–55]

Radical friend. Question is, will he *stay* converted. Remember the more advanced forms of Radicalism are a disease—not a set of ideas.

You are dead right about simultaneous exams. We fought 'em in India a generation ago but Evil is immortal.[1]

I have been seeing your name under various dates in various dragoman's books up and down the river. No wonder you have Egypt in your blood. It's a land that lays hold of one like influenza. When I saw the sun strike those terrible Four at Abu Simbel I felt I had got it too and should never quite shake it off again.[2] The wife and I are both agreed that this trip isn't to count but that we're to come back and to get to Khartoum via Port Soudan and go down into the far South.[3] All I object to in Cook's boats is the fat and too-familiar-with-white-women dragoman.

[1] As part of a campaign to increase the numbers of Indians in the Indian Civil Service, the Congress Party in India and a small group of liberals in England urged the British Government from 1885 onwards to hold examinations for the Indian Civil Service simultaneously in England and India. In 1893 they succeeded in getting the House of Commons to pass a resolution favouring simultaneous examinations, but no action followed the resolution. [Edward Thompson, *Rise and Fulfillment of British Rule in India* (1934), pp. 537–38] The proposals for simultaneous examinations turned up again in the hearings of the Royal Commission on the Public Services in India, which was taking evidence in India in 1913. Among the questions the Commission put to witnesses, two bore on simultaneous examinations. [Questions 7 and 8, Appendix to the Report of the Commission, Vol. VI, "Minutes of Evidence . . .," p. v., 1914, Cd. 7579, XXII, 503] Simultaneous examinations were not offered, however, until 1924. [Herman Finer, *The British Civil Service* (1937), p. 116; W. H. Moreland and Stul Chandra Chatterjee, *A Short History of India* (1953), pp. 400, 423, 427, 459]

[2] The temple of Rameses II (1290–24 B.C.), the entrance to which is guarded by four seated figures more than sixty-five feet tall. Haggard described the temple in *The Way of The Spirit* (1906, pp. 152–53), and interestingly enough, when Kipling records his own impression of the temple in his *Letters of Travel*, he alludes to Haggard's famous heroine on the same page: Kipling writes of seeing the four figures at dawn "red from head to foot . . . as horribly and tensely alive yet blindly alive as pinioned men in the death-chair before the current is switched on." Then looking from the temple to the left, he sees "the statue of an Egyptian princess, whose face was the very face of 'She.'" [*Letters of Travel, 1892–1913* (Garden City, New York: Doubleday, Page & Company, 1920), pp. 285–86]

[3] The Kiplings did, in later years, return to Egypt, but their exact itinerary is lost. We know that "twice they went up the Nile as far as the First Cataract" and that Kipling did some work in Egypt for the War Graves Commission, visiting the cemeteries of the Palestine campaign and going into Sinai at least

It rained hard when we were at Cairo and we saw the pyramids under a leaden European sky with driving squalls between us and the city. Bet *you* never did that? I haven't bought any date-farms yet tho' I hear most glowing accounts of 'em.[1]

It's a bit impossible to write. Our boat sputters round first with one paddle, then with the other, like a hen in a sand bath. Now another steamer has come from the north and shows every sign of going aground too. There is also a small but voluble collection of native craft *all* of whom offer advice to our rais[2] who is sending out a boat and a hawser. Yes! The second boat has stuck. She is a stern wheeler and is now trying to go astern. The wind is getting up. The sky is grey and were I in India I should say we were going to have a dust-storm.

Lord knows where this will catch you. Probably in Australia among an unchaste and idle democracy but wherever it fetches up it carries my best wishes for your happiness. I *am* glad you're seeing India, old man.

Ever,
R. K.

During the summer of 1914, Haggard was occupied with his tasks on the Royal Dominions Commission, travelling to South Africa and Canada, and in his absence he lent his summer house near Lowestoft to the Kiplings. Kessingland Grange was a strange nautical structure that Kipling must have enjoyed. The two-storied building perched on a cliff, its many windows looking out over nine acres of land and miles of churning water. U-shaped, it had once been a coastguard station and was filled with the sounds and the smells of the North Sea. Haggard, who had given each of the cabin rooms the name of an English admiral, had

---

once. [Carrington, p. 386] In February, 1929, A. E. W. Mason, writing from the Semiramis Hotel in Cairo, notes that "Kipling and his wife are out here at this hotel." [Roger Lancelyn Green, *A. E. W. Mason* (1952), p. 192]

[1] A few months earlier, Kipling had undoubtedly read a long article by Haggard in *The Times* describing a visit to the Pyramids Estates, in which he reports in sharp and engrossing detail the operation of a large date farm, and concludes that it is a prudent and profitable business. [H. Rider Haggard, "An Egyptian Date Farm: The Financial Aspect," *The Times*, October 11, 1912, p. 5.]

[2] *Rais (rays, rayyis)*: head, chief, president, commander, captain of a ship, pilot, mate, petty officer, boss, chief [Joseph Catafago, *An English and Arabic Dictionary* (1858), p. 167; Hans Wehr, *A Dictionary of Modern Written Arabic*, J. Milton Cowan, ed. (1961), pp. 318, 371].

furnished the rooms with his private collection of souvenirs, domestic and exotic, including a treasured bust of Nelson that had ostensibly been carved out of the timbers of the *Victory*. The walls were lined with family photographs and framed illustrations from his books. Kipling, writing to a friend on August 4, just before the outbreak of the war, described Kessingland Grange as "for all practical purposes the side of a ship. The garden runs about fifteen yards to a cliff—then the sea and all the drama of the skirts of war laid out before us. Destroyers going up and coming down in twos and fours—then a gunboat or so—then a N.Y.K. (Jap. boat) all white and disinterested going to London; then a Nelson liner with a sort of 'Mike, you're wanted', look on her; then steam trawlers and the usual procession of tows and barges."[1]

Haggard returned from his South African journey in the first week of June and remained in England for about six weeks before leaving for Canada. Some of that time he spent at Ditchingham, and undoubtedly he and Kipling often traversed the fifteen miles between Ditchingham and Kessingland for visits. But one letter we have tells of a visit Kipling could not make to Ditchingham.

Kessingland Grange
Saturday

Dear Haggard,

I thought I c'd get over for Sunday lunch but find I can't 'cause a man's coming from town. Herewith the M.S.S. The Necklace I like *immensely*—it all goes with a rush and a whirl and holds like all the others of yours. Now I have had an idea of where you get your drive from I'm not so amazed as I was.[2] Don't like the play so much. That's because I'm an envious dramatist I suppose. Besides I love not Irish dramas being a low minded Englishman.[3]

Ever thine,
R. K.

[1] Carrington, p. 332.

[2] *The Wanderer's Necklace* had been published in January, 1914, and Haggard must have sent Kipling a copy of the manuscript before publication. It is a Norse tale of reincarnation, and Kipling, in saying that he now understands where Haggard gets his drive, undoubtedly draws a parallel between Haggard and the hero of the tale, attributing to Haggard the power of thinking or dreaming himself back into previous incarnations.

[3] In a letter dated March 21, 1910, Haggard wrote to his Egyptologist friend E. W. Budge: "I am amusing myself dramatising 'Morning Star.'" In two letters to Haggard, both inadequately dated, W. B. Yeats speaks of

On July 25, 1914, Haggard began to keep a "war diary," in which he recorded, almost daily, his reactions to the war news, his own activities, and whatever seemed to him at the time of any lasting value. So strong did the diary habit become that even after the war was over, he continued to keep the record. The last entry is dated April 22, 1925, about three weeks before he died. The diaries are $7\frac{1}{4}'' \times 9\frac{1}{4}''$ in size and number twenty-two volumes of about three hundred hand-written pages each, which Haggard either wrote directly or dictated to Miss Hector. They contain many allusions to Kipling, transcriptions of letters from Kipling, and detailed accounts of their meetings. Although Haggard clearly intended his diaries to be edited and published after his death, they remain unpublished.

March 23 [1915]

The total casualties among officers in the recent fighting according to last night's Globe now amount to 724. I do not know whether the names given in today's paper are included or not. As Kipling, who was here yesterday, said, "Heaven save us from more such 'victories'!"[1] The Kiplings, neither of them, look so well as they did at Kessingland. He is greyer than I am now and as he says, his stomach has shrunk, making him seem smaller. I expect that anxiety about the war is responsible. Their boy John, who is not yet 18, is an officer in the Irish Guards and one can see that they are terrified lest he should be sent to the front and killed, as has happened to nearly all the young men they knew.[2] He does not take a cheerful view of things, either as regards

---

"having kept your plays too long" and says that "neither would be possible at the Abbey." Although a number of Haggard's books were produced as plays and films, the "Irish drama" seems never to have gone beyond the manuscript stage, and the manuscript was either destroyed or lost. [The letter to Budge is in the Huntington Library, San Marino, California; the two from Yeats in the Lockwood Collection, University of Buffalo. All three are more fully quoted in Rider Haggard, p. 199 n. See Scott, pp. 224–27, for a list of play and film productions of Haggard's novels.]

[1] The battle of Neuve Chapelle had begun on March 10, when the British launched a surprise attack against the Germans. But the Germans stoutly resisted the British advance and counterattacked on March 14. Though the ultimate result was a technical victory for the British, losses on both sides were heavy.

[2] Kipling's only son, "a slim, good-looking boy . . . with quick dark eyes behind his glasses, with a great sense of fun," enlisted in the Irish Guards in September 1914. [Carrington, pp. 332, 335–36, 344]

our prospect in arms abroad or the labour question at home. When I remarked to him that it was nothing less than providential that it should have chanced to be a Liberal Government that declared this war, since had the Conservative Party been in power, all the Radical extremists would have been on its back, he replied with his usual wit, that this fact was the one thing that made him believe that we should win in the end. In it he saw the hand of the Almighty himself who had created the Radical Party and borne with it during its eight long years of rule, merely that it might be in power when the great crisis of our fate arrived and thus constrain its louder-voiced and more unpatriotic elements to silence. He does not blame the workmen so much for striking,[1] because he says they are only doing what they have been taught to do for years by the Government and its Press, who have steadily belittled patriotism, lessened and attacked the army and so on, but now are pained and surprised to find their lessons bearing fruit. Also he said that a large ship-building friend of his had told him on the previous day that Lloyd George's speech as to the public purse having no bottom to it had done an enormous amount of harm.[2] "You say that," cry the workmen, "then you are in a position to pay us anything we ask." But, added R.K., *I* am the public and *I* have a bottom. I remarked that this was the case with all of us. He declares that it is not Kitchener who is to blame about the suppression of news, but the Government who are hiding behind Kitchener and making use of him. In time to come when he has served his turn, they will declare that fate gave them this military despot for a bedfellow, forcing them into participation with his evil deeds, which all along they loathed and hated. This, he thinks, explains why Kitchener used the pronoun *I* in his minatory letter to the Liverpool strikers two days ago, instead of speaking in the name of the Government. He was told to do so that the responsibility might be on him, a burden that does

---

[1] Two thousand Liverpool and Birkenhead dock labourers had declared a weekend strike, complaining that they were not receiving each Saturday the wages they had earned up to the time they finished work. [*The Times*, March 22, 1915, p. 10]

[2] On February 15 Lloyd George spoke in the House about agreements with France and Russia for raising money for the war. His theme was England's affluence, and he referred to England and France as "two of the richest countries in the world, . . . the great bankers of the world. We could pay for our huge expenditure," he continued, ". . . out of the proceeds of our investments abroad." [*The Times*, February 16, 1915, p. 10]

not trouble him.[1] Lilias returned from Brighton yesterday and told us she had seen a letter from a friend in India to Dolly,[2] in which it was stated that there had been a mutiny, or threatened mutiny, among native troops—unfortunately she (Lilias) forgets where and what regiment or regiments were concerned—of sufficiently serious character to necessitate the laagering of the women and children in the clubhouse. Now this is an ugly item of news, one too which throws light upon what Curzon wrote to me the other day. Kipling also had heard something of the same sort, but nothing about it has been allowed to get into the Press, I suppose in the hope of keeping the truth from the Germans who no doubt stirred up the trouble through the Sultan. R.K. who of course has an intimate knowledge of Indian affairs, seems to think that if the Dardanelles are forced and Constantinople is taken, Indian disloyalty will be quelled, but that in the event of our failure there, complications may arise.[3] In the same way

[1] Horatio Herbert Kitchener (1850–1916), first Earl Kitchener, was Secretary of State for War, 1914–1916. He was attempting, at this time, to expand the British Army, over the objections of critics who disagreed with his view that the war would go on for a long time and would have to be fought on land as well as on the sea. The text of the letter to which Kipling refers appeared in *The Times* (March 22, 1915, p. 8):

Dear Mr. Sexton [Secretary of the Dock Labourers Union]:
    I am surprised to find that there is a section among the dockers of Liverpool who still refuse to work overtime during the week and on Saturday. I feel sure that these men can hardly realize that their action in thus congesting the docks and delaying munitions of war and food required by our men at the front is having a very serious and dangerous effect, and must be stopped. I hope that this message, if you communicate it to the men, will put things right for the future. At this time we look to every British man, whoever he may be, to do all in his power to help in carrying on the war to a successful conclusion, and in this your men can do their share and thus help their comrades now fighting in France. If this appeal has no effect I shall have to consider the steps that will have to be taken to ensure what is required at Liverpool being done.

[2] Haggard's second daughter, Dorothy, married to Major Reginald Cheyne.

[3] It is impossible to know precisely which events the rumours of Indian mutinies referred to; at this time both German agitation and local disaffection were troublesome. British difficulties were compounded, moreover, by the concern of Indian Moslems over the consequences of combined British and Russian military operations against Turkey, seat of Islam. The British and French fleets had launched an attack on the Dardanelles on February 19 and had renewed their attack on March 18, but bad weather and heavily mined waters prevented these operations from being successful.

both he and I are of opinion that if the Allies conquer decidedly, the African and other troubles will die away. Personally however, I am not certain that this applies to the Boers who are singularly obstinate and detached from world politics. He believes that in S. Africa we have given up attempting to do anything beyond declaring a block-ade, whatever that may be worth, and are content to try to hold our own.[1] I asked him what he was doing to occupy his mind amidst all these troubles. He answered, like myself, writing stories, adding, "I don't know what they are worth, I only know they ain't literature."[2] Like all big men Kipling is very modest as to his own productions. Only little people are vain. How anybody can be vain, amazes me. I know that in my own small way I grow humbler year by year.

June 22 [1915]
    Kipling has been making a good speech [at Southport], a report of which appears in the Morning Post.[3] It says exactly what we all think, neither more nor less, pointing out the terrible things that defeat would mean to this nation. The speech was made at a recruiting meeting and its first words were, "I am here to speak on behalf of a system in which I do not believe, . . . the system of voluntary service. It seems to me unfair and unbusinesslike that after 10 months of war we should still be raising men by the same methods as we raise money at a charity bazaar." The audience said "Hear, hear" to this, as I do very heartily.

On October 2, 1915, John Kipling was reported wounded and missing in action in France. The anxiety and frustration of the following months are reflected in Haggard's diary.

[1] General Louis Botha, having suppressed a rebellion of South African generals in February, 1915, had not yet undertaken the brilliant operations which would in July give the British mastery over German South-West Africa and unquestioned control of the long but safe route between England and India. A seemingly quiescent front in March apparently misled Kipling in assessing the strategy at the Cape.

[2] In March Kipling was working on two war stories, "Mary Postgate" (to appear in September 1915) and "Sea Constables: A Tale of '15" (to appear in October). Haggard had probably just completed Finished (1917) and begun Love Eternal (1918).

[3] The speech was also reported in The Times and other papers. See Chandler, p. 226.

October 16 [1915]

Watt sends me an extract from a letter from Mrs. Kipling about John. It seems that at the beginning of the month, according to a communication received from his colonel, "he was with his men in advance under a captain of the Scots Guards. There were 200 men and but one man returned. They were enfiladed, and John was seen to fall, get up and go into a small shed which was almost immediately surrounded." He was in advance of his men at the time and up to last Tuesday nothing more had been heard of him. Of course if the case had been one of an enemy officer surrounded by our troops and wounded, it would in all probability mean that he had been taken prisoner and was in an English hospital. But where Germans are concerned one is not so sure. Still he may be captured and alive. It is terribly anxious work for his family. If perchance he is dead, it would be better to know the worst at once. Yet he is only one of hundreds of similar cases which excites my particular interest because I happen to know him and his parents.

December 22 [1915]

I saw Kipling in town. He has heard nothing of John and evidently has practically lost hope. He says that from all accounts that he can gather that the boy made a good end in his first action, that he liked his men and was liked by them. Poor lad! He added that he was very fond of me and asked me what I had done to make his children so fond of me. I answered, I didn't know except that young people like those who like them—a fact, I think, to which I owe the affection of so many of my nieces and nephews. R.K. expressed his opinion of the Government and individual members thereof in language too strong to write down even in a private diary. His vigour on the subject is amazing.

December 27 [1915]

Today I interviewed a young wounded soldier of the Irish Guards named Bowe.[1] He was near to John Kipling (within 40 yards) when

[1] Gdsm. Michael Bowe (No. 7786) has kindly replied to my request for a first-hand account:

Shortly after the engagement described in the extract from Sir H. Rider Haggard's diary, I was wounded and sent home to a hospital in Norwich. ... Afterwards, I was moved to a hospital in Surrey, where a lady, whom I believe to have been Sir Rider's daughter, visited me and invited me to lunch.

She brought me to a big mansion where I was introduced to Sir Rider.

they entered the wood near Givenchy where they both vanished. What became of him remains a mystery. He may have rushed ahead in charging the German Maxims and been captured. If he fell it is a marvel that he was not picked up as the wood remained in our hands for days. Bowe and another man named Frankland[1] who was with him, were of opinion that he was either blown absolutely to bits by a large shell, which they had seen happen several times, or taken and murdered in the German lines during the 2 hours that elapsed before they finally rushed the wood. Or he may have been buried by the explosion of a "Jack Johnson."[2] These possibilities however I did not put down in the signed statement which I sent to R.K. There is still a faint hope that he is a prisoner. He has just vanished. Bowe said that the poor boy was much liked.

December 28 [1915]

Lilias has received a letter from Frankland, the soldier who accompanied Bowe here yesterday—a very well educated man. He writes that Bowe, who is a very nervous youth and shy, now remembers certain other things about John Kipling. "Bowe *did* see Lt. Kipling after the wood was taken, under the following circumstances. The Irish Guards had dug themselves in on the edge of the wood when they heard a loud shouting from a body of men in their rear. The Sergeant in charge thinking the Germans were making a flank or rear

---

After lunch he took me to his study and asked me if I knew Kipling. I said I did and he then asked me if I knew how he was killed.

I told him that as far as I knew he had been blown to pieces. I saw Kipling about 40 yards away from me before we went into the wood. A shell dropped near him and when the smoke cleared away in about half a minute there was no sign of him.

I did not know Kipling personally—only as a soldier. The men in his platoon had great praise for him. He was leading his platoon when he disappeared. [Letter dated November 18, 1964]

[1] Unidentified. Mr. Bowe writes: "I'm afraid my mind is almost a complete blank on Frankland. I remember that his Christian name was Joe, but I can't remember anything else about him. I could have met him in the Irish Guards, or it could have been in hospital." [*Ibid.*]

[2] A "Jack Johnson" was a heavy German shell, especially a 5.9. It was named after John Arthur "Jack" Johnson (1878–1946), the American Negro prizefighter (the first Negro to hold the heavyweight championship of the world), because the shell issued a mass of black smoke when it burst and because Johnson was also known as "The Big Smoke." [Eric Partridge, ed., *A Dictionary of Slang and Unconventional English* (1961), II, 430]

attack ordered them to retire from the wood. This they did and found the noise to be the cheers of the Grenadier Guards who had come up to support the Irish. Bowe now says that as they left this wood he saw an officer, who *he could swear* was Mr. Kipling, leaving the wood on his way to the rear and trying to fasten a field dressing round his mouth which was badly shattered by a piece of shell. Bowe would have helped him but for the fact that the officer was crying with the pain of the wound and he did not want to humiliate him by offering assistance." I shall not send this on to R.K.; it is too painful, but, I fear, true. Still it makes J.K.'s disappearance still more of a mystery. A shell must have buried him, I think.[1]

Bateman's, Burwash, Sussex
January 7, 1916

Dear Rider,

I like that! I got one really exciting letter from you telling how you had debauched Legislatures and forged a P.M.'s signature to a bill—or words to that effect—which interested us enormously.[2] (You know your letters are family possessions with us.) I then wrote back and—napoo! Got no report from you either, nor any letter covering report. But if your local post office is in the same state of disintegration as ours all is explained. We get letters, and papers—or we don't—when the G.P.O. thinks good for us. They chuck any mail bag into any train and wait for results. But it's good to get in touch with you again. You will be badly wanted down here in the spring to hear what

[1] John's body was never found.
[2] Haggard was lobbying for his plan that would simultaneously decrease unemployment in the ranks of returning servicemen and improve the state of English agriculture. He sought to have England and the Dominion Governments set aside land for returning veterans to enable them to take up farming as a profitable way of life. Although the Government was not receptive to his scheme, he found independent backers, most particularly the Royal Colonial Institute. In February, 1916, the Institute was to send him on a journey to the Dominions to determine which lands were available for resettling soldiers and sailors. The report that Kipling alludes to must be one published by the Dominions Royal Commission, on which Haggard had been serving since 1912. (See p. 75 above.) The Commission issued three reports in 1915, all part of the twenty-four volumes they would prepare and publish by 1917. [Scott, p. 134; *Cloak*, pp. 213–46; *Days*, II, 85, 121, 227–30, 232; *Rider Haggard*, pp. 255–69; Rider Haggard, *The After-War Settlement and Employment of Ex-Service Men in the Overseas Dominions: Report of the Royal Institute* (1916)]

we've tried to do in the farming line. I can tell you tales of "ladies on the Land" which beat even your "Come out, Kerswell you b——"[1]

Also about emigration as arranged by wounded men in hospitals. But *do* send on your report if you've got a spare copy.

"Oro"[2] promises well. 'Gad what an undefeated and joyous imagination you have! I want fuller details, please, of what Oro did when he re-entered upon life on the earth.

Can you send me a typed scenario. I suggest that when O. decides to finish up the world a second time, he does it by turning the sea into a line of submarine volcanoes. It's a thing that quite conceivably may end the world one of these days, same as kitchen boiler bursting— but I'd like to see you do it. There was a small attempt (by Nature) in this direction when Krakatoa erupted.[3] The sea got into a volcanic crack in the bay and blew up a few hundred square miles. But turn half the Atlantic or Pacific into a really *big* fault under ocean and you get something worth describing.

We peg along here, somehow or other and the days go by. The

---

[1] Less than a month earlier, Haggard had written to *The Times* declaring that he considered women from towns more suited for work on the land than those from the country. "In the main," Haggard writes, "country women will not work upon the land. . . . The representative from the Board of Agriculture . . . told us recently of a farmer who 'put his cook, housekeeper, and housemaid to pull mangolds,' intimating that we might do likewise. Well, most of us do not keep a housekeeper, but if we tried the experiment with the cook and the housemaid I am convinced that the day's mangold pulling would end for them at the nearest railway station." ["Women on the Land—Town Girls' Unfitness for Farm Work," *The Times*, December 9, 1915, p. 11; see also H. Rider Haggard, "Women's Work on The Land—A Palliative in Hard Times," *The Times*, November 29, 1915, p. 3.] Kipling and Haggard must have shared a private joke about an unidentifiable Kerswell, and the joke must have lived for years (see p. 168 below).

[2] "Oro" was an early name for what would later be Haggard's *When the World Shook* (1919), a science fiction tale about a highly developed civilization on a South Sea Atlantis. It would appear that he had summarized the plot in a letter to which Kipling is replying. Kipling would later see the book in manuscript (see p. 94 below).

[3] In 1883 an eruption occurred on the Indonesian island of Krakatoa (or Krakatau), between Java and Sumatra, destroying part of the island and killing many inhabitants. The explosion was so great that it carried debris from the island as far as Madagascar, and the volume of the lava and ash was such that it formed new islands.

wife is very tired but indefatigable and I've got a queer inside, due, I expect, to indigestion.[1]

We all send you our love, specially Elsie, and when Spring comes (D.V.) we'll meet and collogue and let the years go by.

I'd like to hear the gist of what Roosevelt said to you if you could dictate it.[2] Don't fuss to write with your own hand.[3] What between

[1] For details of Kipling's illness, see p. 121 below.

[2] Both Kipling and Haggard were friends of Roosevelt. The Kiplings first met him when they came down from Vermont to spend a six-week winter holiday in 1895 in Washington. He was then Under Secretary—"I never caught the name of the Upper," Kipling wrote—of the U.S. Navy. "I liked him from the first and largely believed in him." "He would come to our hotel, and thank God in a loud voice that he had not one drop of British blood in him. . . . Naturally I told him nice tales about his Uncles and Aunts in South Africa—only I called them Ooms and Tanties—who esteemed themselves the sole lawful Dutch under the canopy and dismissed Roosevelt's stock for 'Verdomder Hollanders.' Then he became really eloquent, and we would go off to the Zoo together, where he talked about grizzlies that he had met. . . . I never got over the wonder of a people who, having extirpated the aboriginals of their continent more completely than any modern race had ever done, honestly believed that they were a godly little New England community, setting examples to brutal mankind. This wonder I used to explain to . . . Roosevelt, who made the glass cases of Indian relics [at the Smithsonian Institution] shake with his rebuttals." [*Something*, pp. 121–24] Kipling and Roosevelt met only once more, in England in 1910, when Roosevelt came to give the Romanes Lecture at Oxford, but they corresponded from time to time. [W. H. Harbaugh, *Power and Responsibility: The Life of Theodore Roosevelt* (1961), p. 180] In 1898 Kipling sent a copy of "The White Man's Burden" to the then Vice President, who, in a letter to Henry Cabot Lodge, said that he thought it "rather poor poetry, but good sense from the expansionist viewpoint." [Carrington, p. 217] Writing to Roosevelt after the American forces had arrived in England in 1917, Kipling reported with delight "the almost comically good relations between the two navies. . . . All our young men speak very highly indeed of the U.S.N. and are getting on as sociable as a 'basket of kittens.'" [Carrington, p. 346.]

Haggard met Roosevelt in 1905, when inspecting Salvation Army colonies in the United States. Roosevelt was the newly elected President, and Haggard went to see him at the White House (perhaps with an introduction from Kipling, though not necessarily, for by this time Haggard's reputation was established, and Roosevelt had read and admired his books). They talked about many subjects they had in common, and a few days later Roosevelt gave a White House lunch in Haggard's honour. Haggard set down a summary of their conversation, in which the President said: "It is an odd thing that you and I, brought up in different countries and following such different pursuits, should have identical ideas and aims. I have been

Royal Commissions and Dentists your life must be hectic and harried.

Ever yours,
Rudyard.

---

reading your book, 'Rural England,' and I tell you what you think, I think, and what you want to do, I want to do. We are one man in the matter." Haggard met briefly with Roosevelt in London in June, 1910. [*Days*, II, 177–89] In 1911, when Haggard's book about the Salvation Army was published in the U.S., Roosevelt reviewed it: "There are few men now writing English whose books on vital sociological questions are of such value as [Haggard's] . . . I wish it were in my power to convey to . . . [readers] the vivid impression which this book . . . has made on me." ["Rider Haggard and the Salvation Army," *Outlook*, XCVIII(July 1, 1911), 476–77]

In a letter to Roosevelt in June, 1912, Haggard captures some of the attitudes that both men shared and that lay behind the friendship: "I take some credit to myself in that, although we have met but a few times in the flesh, I have yet been able to discern what kind of spirit is in you. I suppose the truth is that as deep calls to deep, like not only draws to but understands like. Though my powers be less, and my opportunities smaller, yet our fundamental inspiration, and the aims of our hearts are in fact the same. I too hold that the civilized world wallows in a slough worse perhaps than the primeval mud of the savage; that it is possible if not probable that it may be dragged from the slough, cleansed, and clothed in white garments. That is the bounden duty of every man, as they shall answer for it at the last, to do their honest best to bring this about, regardless of any wreaths of success, or any dust of failure, regardless of everything save the glory which, in all probability, will never crown their individual strivings." [*Cloak*, p. 188] In June, 1916, while Haggard was sailing from New Zealand to Canada, investigating the possibilities of settling ex-servicemen in the Dominions, he expressed regret in his diary over Roosevelt's loss of the Republican Presidential nomination to Charles Evans Hughes. And he took time from his Canadian tour to go south to New York, in a very hot July, to call on Roosevelt at his home at Oyster Bay, Long Island, where the two men had a three-hour conversation. "Heaven, how we talked!" Haggard later wrote. "Of all sorts of things; of the world and its affairs, of religion, of heaven and hell, of the fundamental truths, and the spirit of man; for when Roosevelt and myself meet—men who are in deep and almost mysterious sympathy with one another, there are many vital matters on which we need to know each other's mind." [*Cloak*, p. 253] Roosevelt gave Haggard a characteristic photograph of himself jumping a horse over a fence, and, the day after the visit, sent him a copy of his own book, *Fear God and Take Your Own Part*, inscribed "To Sir Rider Haggard, who has both preached and practised fealty to the things of the soul. With the regards of his friend, Theodore Roosevelt." Haggard thought the inscription "perhaps the greatest compliment that was ever paid to me," and was deeply touched by it. [*Diary*, November 1, 1916] Haggard followed American politics closely in these years, particularly as they bore upon the possibility of America's entering the war, and his diary is

Bateman's, Burwash, Sussex
January 9, 1916

Dear Haggard,
Thank you! I'd have to be pretty far gone before a book of

---

replete with reflections of how much better than Woodrow Wilson, Roosevelt, had he been President, would have managed the country. Repeatedly Haggard comments in his diary on Roosevelt's views whenever they appeared in the Press. When Roosevelt fell ill in the spring of 1917, Haggard wrote to him and Roosevelt replied, paying tribute to Haggard's prophecy in *A Farmer's Year* (1899; see p. 103 below) that there would come a day when the British Empire and the United States would fight side by side for the freedom of the world. [Diary, April 8, 1917] That year Haggard wrote in his dedication of *Finished*:

My dear Roosevelt,
You are, I know, a lover of old Allan Quatermain, one who understands and appreciates the views of life and the aspirations that underlie and inform his manifold adventures.
Therefore, since such is your kind wish, in memory of certain hours wherein both of us found true refreshment and companionship amidst the terrible anxieties of the World's journey along that bloodstained road by which alone, so it is decreed, the pure Peak of Freedom must be scaled, I dedicate to you this tale telling of the events and experiences of my youth.

Your sincere friend,
H. Rider Haggard.

Roosevelt wrote to thank Haggard: "The book has come and I am very proud of the dedication. I have already begun to read it with the delight I always experience in reading anything by you. I shall not forget your visit here. It was one of the most enjoyable afternoons I have spent with any friend. I wish I were to see you again." [Transcript supplied by Miss Lilias Rider Haggard.]
In November, the War Office almost involved Haggard in "rather curious" unofficial negotiations with Roosevelt. General Frederick Maurice, Director of Military Operations of the Imperial General Staff, asked him to write as (in Haggard's description) a "semi-demi-rank outsider-official," putting detailed questions to the former President about America's wartime military and financial capabilities—apparently in an attempt to get more information than was forthcoming in official reports. However, the Foreign Office asked that the letter be held until later, and there is no evidence that it was ever sent. The two men never met again, for soon Roosevelt was dead. [Both Kipling's and Haggard's letters to Roosevelt are in the Library of Congress; a draft of Haggard's "War Office" letter is in the Huntington Library; and transcripts of Haggard's conversations with Roosevelt and two more letters from him to Haggard are in the Houghton Library, Harvard University.]

3 Unlike Kipling, Haggard could dictate his work and correspondence. He walked up and down his study while his secretary, Ida Hector, recorded what he said directly on to a typewriter.

yours[1] didn't take me altogether out of myself. But you oughtn't to send it on a Monday morning just when a man is going to attend to his mail. It makes for shirking.

Ever,
R. K.

P.S. Have you observed in your correspondence that the percentage of d——d, vacuous, idle, unconnected idiot [letters] rises steadily with every month of the war?

Haggard's schemes for settling returning servicemen on the land found no official government support, but the Royal Colonial Institute offered him strong backing. Early in 1916, the Institute arranged to send him on a round-the-world journey that would take him to the British Dominions and enable him to ask the Dominion Governments for gifts of land to returning English war veterans. The Institute planned a farewell luncheon for Haggard at the Hotel Cecil on February 1, and on the 3rd he was to be guest of honour at an Authors' Club dinner. Haggard wrote to Kipling inviting him to the luncheon.

Bateman's, Burwash, Sussex
Tuesday, January 11, 1916

Dear Haggard,
Yes, if I can by any means get up to town on that day.

Ever,
R.K.

You're in for the deuce and all of a big job.

Bateman's,
January, 20 1916

Dear Haggard,
I have just had to wire to Wilson[2] that I can't come to the lunch on Feb. 1st.

I'm sorry for this as I should like to have seen you have your send-off: but, I have undertaken certain work[3] which I have to do when I am asked to do it and it so happens that the next call cuts into the beginning of next month.

Ever yours,
Rudyard Kipling.

[1] *The Ivory Child*, published on January 6.

[2] Sir Henry Francis (Harry) Wilson (1859–1937), Secretary of the Royal Colonial Institute (1915–21).

[3] Probably *Sea Warfare*, articles and verses that resulted from his visits to ships on active duty. The articles "were written for the Minister of Information for publication in British and American newspapers." [Stewart, p. 308; see also Carrington, p. 340; Chandler, pp. 243–45.]

On February 10th, Haggard left London on the first leg of what would be a 20,000 mile journey to twenty different lands. The war was still on and the seas he sailed were menaced by submarines. But he was intent upon his resettlement scheme, and in the months that followed he carried out his mission with great success, returning at the end of July with large commitments of land from the various governments he had visited. In spite of failing health and of warnings from his family doctor, he spent the remainder of the year explaining his scheme and enumerating the commitments he had received from the Dominion Governments to Whitehall officials, to the Press, and, in lectures, to the general public. He made time, however, to deal with other subjects as well.

Bateman's, Burwash, Sussex
January 1, 1917

Dear old man,

I see you can write to the *Times*.[1] Why the dooce can't you send me a letter? I want to know how you are first and next what chance there is of your coming down to town. Our trains and our mails are few and fragmentary but I manage to get away occasionally.

Here's luck for the new year!

Ever thine,
Rudyard.

Kipling and Haggard saw much of each other in the spring, 1917. Haggard's family actually came up to London to enable him to press for

---

[1] Haggard's letter reported that "an American correspondent personally unknown" had asked him in his next book to "let us have something about the thousands of Americans who have gone to a strange land and given their lives for liberty and humanity." Haggard observed that "public work and other reasons" prevented his acting upon the suggestion, "but [that] there are some well-qualified writers to whom it may appeal. At least I hope so." ["Mr. Wilson's Note. British Publicity," *The Times*, December 28, 1916, p. 7] Haggard's letter supplements the views of Mr. Eric Fisher Wood, who, in a long, discursive letter to *The Times* two days before, had made the point that British war aims were imperfectly understood in the United States in large part because Britain had not "organized to combat the extensive and shrewdly managed German propaganda into whose clutch the United States are falling." ["President Wilson and Peace. The Allied Cause in America. British Publicity in the United States," *The Times*, December 26, 1916, p. 7] These letters were inspired by Woodrow Wilson's Peace Note of December 18, in which the President of the still-neutral United States had asked both parties to state their war aims as a step towards reconciling their differences.

official action on his resettlement scheme. In March he was elected Vice-President of the Royal Colonial Institute, and in April the Government finally created an Empire Settlement Committee with Haggard as a member.

He visited the Kiplings at Bateman's, and we know from the following diary entry and letter that the two friends met in London as well. Haggard's *When the World Shook* would not appear in book form for another two years, but Kipling had helped with the plotting,[1] and it was natural for Haggard to ask him to read the manuscript.

March 30 [1917]

I said to Kipling at the Athenaeum today that I trusted that we should not be expected to inhabit the region in the next world which was occupied by Germans. He replied that he was quite convinced that we should find none in any hell that he and I might land in. I think so too; whatever our sins, we have not deserved that! R. K. and Martin Conway were lunching together. Afterwards Conway came into the billiard room downstairs and informed me that R. K. had been talking with admiration and amazement of the manuscript of the story *Yva*[2] which I had given to him to read, saying that it was "as full of go and imagination as though I had been 16 instead of 60." Later Rudyard hurried up and repeated this and more. He said to me that he had read the whole thing at a sitting, "interlineations and all," really read it, and its grip and "freshness" astonished him. He lay upon a sofa with those slipping sheets before him, unable to leave it, and thought it a remarkable work of imagination—really a new thing. I asked him if he had any criticism to make. He said that he would not venture to offer any—there was the work, in a way outside of criticism, as good as anything I had ever done, or words to that effect. Evidently too he meant all he said. This from such a man is complimentary, especially as he is not prodigal of compliments, but I am sure that when it appears the public, or rather the critics, will not discuss these virtues in the book. It is not their fashion to praise my work. However I am glad that the tale pleases its first reader so completely. The truth is that he (R.) has imagination, vision, and can *understand*, amongst other things, that Romance may be the vehicle of much that does not appear to the casual reader.

[1] See p. 88 above.
[2] *When the World Shook.*

Brown's Hotel,[1] London, W.1.
March 31, 1917

Dear old man,

Here's your M.S. back again and a thousand thanks for the privilege. As I told you yesterday it's as fresh and as convincing as the work of a boy of 25 and it held me like a drug. That's your d——d gift!

My only criticism is that I don't quite realize the essential clumsiness and angularity of Bastin.[2] It's indicated all right but I want it brought out more in the various situations—either by the clumsiness of his actual feet or hands (but he wasn't clumsy with the latter) or by more references to his peculiar delivery and intonation. Look out for "baretta." It's "biretta" I believe.[3]

All our sympathy to poor Lilias who could justly be reported as "wounded in action."[4] Let us know how she is coming on.

---

[1] The Kiplings usually stayed at Brown's Hotel when they went up to London, occupying a first-floor suite of rooms looking out on Albemarle Street. They could receive visitors in the large sitting room, and we know that Kipling was able to write at a desk by one of the windows. The Management of Brown's (now a Trust House hotel) value the memory of their association with Kipling, and, with the help of the Kipling Society, have furnished the "Kipling Room" with illustrations from his books and other memorabilia.

[2] The subtitle of the book is "Being an Account of the Great Adventure of Bastin, Bickley and Arbuthnot." Here is Haggard's description of Bastin:

Bastin—Basil was his Christian name—was an uncouth, shock-headed, flat-footed person of large, rugged frame and equally rugged honesty, with a mind almost incredibly simple. Nothing surprised him because he lacked the faculty of surprise. He was like that kind of fish which lies at the bottom of the sea and takes every kind of food into its great maw without distinguishing its flavour. Metaphorically speaking, heavenly manna and decayed cabbage were just the same to Bastin. He was not fastidious and both were mental pabulum—of a sort—together with whatever lay between these extremes. Yet he was good, so painfully good that one felt that without exertion to himself he had booked a first-class ticket straight to Heaven; indeed that his guardian angel had tied it round his neck at birth lest he should lose it, already numbered and dated like an identification disc. [p. 14]

[3] Haggard made the change (p. 156, l.4, in the 1st ed.).

[4] Miss Haggard has kindly explained the reason for Kipling's concern about her. She writes: "I am afraid the answer to your query is not very romantic! I had been nursing through the winter of 1917 which was bitterly cold in a hospital at Exmouth. We had a very bad epidemic among young recruits of measles and pneumonia and had lost a lot of cases. In March I left the hospital and came up to London for a holiday with my parents in a hotel, and dismayed

We hope to go back to Bateman's next week.

> Ever sincerely,
> Rudyard.[1]

> Bateman's, Burwash, Sussex
> September 1, 1917

Dear old man,

Just back from Edinburgh to find (and I've told Elsie she isn't to touch or look at it till I've done) "Finished."[2] Any book of yours takes one out of oneself more potently than any drug I know and as soon as I'm finished with a d——d pile of accumulated mail, I go to my study, curl up and enjoy myself. Thank *you*, sir.

I've been seeing ships—and ships—*and* ships at Edinburgh whereby I am a little cheered and happy.[3] So buck up and believe me

> Ever yours,
> Rudyard.

February 14 [1918]

I had an interesting letter from Rudyard Kipling this morning about the war. As his views are always able and singularly clear-sighted I copy it here for reference. Once letters are put away I never seem to find them.

> "Bateman's
> February 12, 1918

Dear old man,

I was very glad to see your handwriting again and to learn that you

---

them by developing a bad attack of German measles with a high temperature and spent my holiday in bed." [Letter from Ditchingham House, July 21, 1962]

[1] I have not found the original of this letter. This is a copy of a typescript in the Bambridge Collection.

[2] *Finished* is the concluding story of a trilogy (*Marie* [1912] and *Child of Storm* [1913] are the others) in which Haggard recreated in fiction the history of the Zulu nation. It had been published in August.

[3] Kipling's "closest contacts with fighting men were made in ships of the Royal Navy," writes his biographer. He designed crests for ships and units, he wrote songs and ballads for sailors, he sailed on the sea and under it with them. At least once he visited the Grand Fleet in Scotland. [Carrington, p. 342]

are so near to us,[1] though in these days of no motors 18 miles are as bad as 100! I think you're wise in what you've done—for every reason. The less one has to bother about these days the better. We are still stuck with the farms, the cattle, etc., and all the Government Departments make us their sport with regulations after regulations. It's a mad world. I fancy, however, that the Russian débacle[2] is by no means smooth going for Germany. One can't do much with a thousand mile front of raving lunatic asylum and—as one sees behind all the German papers—there is always the fear of political infection. Again remember that the Hun knows what the U.S.A. is capable of doing and he has a very fair idea that now the U.S.A. is launched,[3] it will be very difficult to stop the blow. This is a point we do not consider as much as the Hun does. My own notion is that the second there is any sort of armistice to discuss peace—the minute the thoughts of the German army are turned to their own land—then the real trouble will begin for Germany. Up to the present the external pressure has kept her solid. Once this is removed we may see developments.

But these are strenuous days all the same. I am sure our national

[1] The war forced the Haggards to shut down Ditchingham House, at least for the winters. They tried living in London, but found it too expensive. Instead they bought and moved into North Lodge, a small, quaint gate house in St. Leonards, where they could enjoy the mild climate of the coast. Here they were sixty-two miles from London, and Haggard could get up to town to attend to commission affairs.

[2] In December, 1917, German and Soviet authorities began the negotiations which were to culminate in the Treaty of Brest–Litovsk in March, 1918. The treaty talks were anything but smooth. They were interrupted once in late December when Soviet emissaries found that the Germans did not intend to surrender control over the Baltic states and Russian Poland. When the talks resumed in January, 1918, with Trotsky heading the Russian delegation, the Soviet delegates engaged in inflammatory political speeches. The Germans meanwhile were conducting separate talks with non-Communist Ukrainian separatists, with whom they signed a treaty on February 8. This move, implying that Germany would recognize the Ukraine as a separate state not under Soviet authority, seriously imperilled the shipping of food and undermined Soviet prestige. Trotsky, confronted with a *fait accompli*, adopted his "no war, no peace" formula, broke off the peace talks (February 10), and went home with his delegation, maintaining that the Soviets would neither fight nor make peace. The Germans resumed hostilities on February 18 and continued their advance into Russian territory until the Russians were prepared to come to terms.

[3] The United States declared war on Germany on April 6, 1917.

unimaginativeness is going to be our salvation in the long run and, between ourselves, I look for peace by the end of the year—a bad peace for Germany too.

I would say that I am coming down to see you except there seems no means of turning a wheel in that, or any other, direction; so I'll e'en have to take my chance of it and send you a wire if by any happy accident it is possible. I hope to goodness the milder air is keeping your bronchitis[1] under. I have a small collection of petty diseases in my interior but nothing that makes one ill. You know the difference. The wife is *very* nervy and very tired, the daughter is well and we all send you our love and blessings. Affectionately ever, Rudyard."

I've no doubt but that he is right as to the external pressure keeping the Germans quiet, also as I have written to him, I too feel that the war will end this year, one way or another. My views about America I have often expressed in these pages. Their appearance on the field will win the war—*and the Germans know it,* or at any rate their leaders do. Hence their anxiety for Peace before the American strength develops, especially their air strength. My fear, as I have also written to Rudyard is that our food position may be profoundly unsatisfactory and that our people may refuse to bear the privation and discomfort which it will entail. But, at bottom, I cannot believe that; surely we are made of better stuff. By the way it appears from an official statement that we are compelled to rely upon the U.S. and Canada for no less than 65 per cent of our essential foodstuffs!

[May] 22, [1918]

Still no news. Last night I was kept awake till 2.30 by mysterious explosions which rattled my door violently ending with a fearful noise about 2.15. I thought that another air raid was in progress but no one knows whence they came or what was their meaning. The heat has been very great; I do not remember anything like it in May, but tonight thunder is growling. Most of the day I have spent with the Kiplings at Bateman's. Rudyard is not well. I thought him looking better when I arrived but when he came to see me off at the gate I noticed how thin and aged and worn he is. Elsie says that he varies much. He suffers from fits of pain in his inside but he told me that although there is "something" there, X-ray examinations show that there is no cancer or tumour or anything of that sort. I hope and pray

---

[1] All his adult life, Haggard suffered periodically from a weak lung condition variously diagnosed as "bronchitis" and "influenza."

that this is so. Seated together in his study in the old house at Bateman's, we had a most interesting few hours together while he fiddled about with fishing tackle with which he tries to catch trout in the brook. There are two men left living in the world with whom I am in supreme sympathy, Theodore Roosevelt and Rudyard Kipling. The rest, such as Theophilus Shepstone[1] and Andrew Lang[2] have gone. What did we talk of? So many things that it is difficult to summarise them. Chiefly they had to do with the soul and the fate of man. Rudyard, apparently, cannot make up his mind about these things. On one point, however, he is perfectly clear. I happened to remark that I thought that this world was one of the hells. He replied that he did not *think*, he was *certain* of it. He went on to show that it had every attribute of a hell, doubt, fear, pain, struggle, bereavement, almost irresistible temptations springing from the nature with which we are clothed, physical and mental suffering, etc., etc., ending in the worst fate that man can devise for man, Execution! As for the future he is inclined to let the matter drift. He said, what he has often said to me before, that what he wants is a "good long rest." I asked him if he wished for extinction and could contemplate without dismay, separation eternal from all he loved—John, for instance. He replied that he was never happier than when he knew that as a child his boy was asleep in the next room. Why therefore should he mind it in the grave, or words to that effect. I pushed the subject and found that he does not really want to go out—only to *rest*. I pointed out that his notion was futile since if he "rested" for a million years or for a minute, it would make no difference to him in a state of unconsciousness, should he awake after all. Here he agreed. The upshot of it is that he is no unbeliever, only like the rest of us, one who knows nothing and therefore cannot understand. Like myself he has an active faith in the existence of a personal devil and thinks (I gathered) that much which is set down to God, is really attributable to the personality who

[1] Theophilus Shepstone (1843–1907), as Lord Carnarvon's special commissioner to Natal, marched into Pretoria in January, 1877, and annexed the Transvaal. Haggard, a youth of twenty-one, was one of the ten or twelve men to make up Shepstone's official party, and when Shepstone's secretary read the Annexation Proclamation in Market Square, Haggard held the document from which he read. [*Days*, pp. lxxvi, 286–87; John Kotzé, *Biographical Memoirs and Reminiscences* (n.d.), p. 238; Manfred Nathan, *Paul Kruger: His Life and Times* (1942), p. 118; *Rider Haggard*, pp. 33–39]

[2] Lang died in 1912.

at present cannot be controlled *even* by God, at least not altogether. He holds that the story of Pharaoh is being repeated in the case of the Germans. God is "hardening" their heart, to their ultimate destruction. His humility is very striking. We were talking of our failings. I said that what grew on me from day to day was a sense of my own utter insufficiency, of complete humiliation both in the case of those things that I had done and left undone and of the knowledge of sin ingrained in my nature which became more and more apparent to me as I approached the end of my days. He answered that it was absolutely the same with himself in every sense and detail, and proceeded to speak very strongly on the matter, pointing out how we were subject to different weaknesses and temptations at the various periods of life. I commented on the fact that he had wide fame and was known as "the great Mr. Kipling," which should be a consolation to him. He thrust the idea aside with a gesture of disgust. "What is it worth— what *is* it all worth?" he answered. Moreover he went on to show that anything which any of us did *well* was no credit to us: that it came from somewhere else: "We are only telephone wires." As example he instanced (I *think*) "Recessional" in his own case and "She" in mine. "*You* didn't write 'She' you know," he said; "something wrote it through you!" or some such words. On general matters, he was caustic about President Wilson[1] to whom he thinks the world owes much tribulation because he delayed so long in coming into the war— as I do. As for the Irish he thinks that they should have been conscripted long ago, but now he would leave them severely alone that they may suffer the undying scorn of the rest of the Empire and the Allies. He repeated to me a really remarkable and most bitter poem he has written on the conduct of the Pope, called, I think, "When the Cock Crew."[2] Of course he compares him to Peter, to Peter's infinite

[1] Kipling had grown bitter about Wilson's policy of non-involvement in the War, and, in a letter to Roosevelt, he vented his spleen about "Wilson's idiotic Fourteen Points." When Wilson was in England in December, 1918, Kipling was one of the guests summoned to Buckingham Palace to meet the American President, but he was not impressed: for him Wilson was "arid— first, last, and all the time a schoolmaster." Wilson, on the other hand, admired Kipling and sought to acquire an autographed copy of "If—," which, Kipling's biographer reports, "had been a constant inspiration to him." [Carrington, pp. 346, 348].

[2] "A Song at Cockcrow," composed in 1918, appeared in *The Years Between* and in *Rudyard Kipling's Verse, Inclusive Edition*, both in 1919. It is a

advantage. He says he means to publish it as he has nothing to gain or lose from anyone. I hope he may for it will certainly make a hubbub. I trust that the Pope will enjoy its perusal.

Also he read me a quaint story about Death and St. Peter,[1] written in modern language, almost in slang, which his wife would not let him publish. It would have been caviare to the General if he had, because the keynote of it is infinite mercy extending even to the case of Judas.

He opines in his amusing way, that if the present taxation, etc., goes much further, he and I shall be seen on opposite sides of the Strand selling "Recessional" and "She" for our daily bread. How interesting it would be to have a shorthand report of such a 3-hours' conversation as ours, especially upon the nature of the Divinity, the destiny of man, the quality and consequences of sin, etc., etc., of which I can only recall a point here and there, especially as I write when I am very tired after a long, hot day. I believe honestly that outside of his own family, there is no one living to whom R. opens his heart except to myself. Practically he lacks intimate friends; it is not in his nature to make them; he said he could count those he had cared for "on my fingers" although all mankind interested him. I remarked that nowadays, although with the exception of himself and one or two others all my friends were gone, I still made acquaintances. "I *don't*," he replied grimly. He parted from me with much affection and said how delighted he was to have had the opportunity of a good mental and spiritual clean out. So was I. How he hates politicians! Worse than I do, even. . . .

P.S. R. asked me how much older I was than himself exactly. I told him—ten years. "Then you have the less time left in which to suffer," he answered, or words to that effect. I think he was alluding chiefly to the great loss which has overtaken both of us in life.

---

denunciation of Pope Benedict XV, who appealed to the belligerents on July 30, 1915, and August 1, 1917, urging them to negotiate their differences. Kipling and Haggard considered the Pope's initiative to be pro-German.

[1] "On the Gate: A Tale of '16" is a fantasy set in heaven about the administrative problems created by the vast increase in the number of deaths that have resulted from the war. Kipling did in fact delay its publication until years after the war was over; written no later than 1918, it did not appear in print until 1926 (in *McCall's Magazine* in June, and as the last story in *Debits and Credits*).

May 23 [1918]

I write this in bed before rising for my journey.[1] I've slept well and it has been a blessing for a night to go by without the sounds of bursting bombs or mines or other hellish explosions. Last night there were only thunder and lightning which seemed quite innocent by comparison. Wherever one goes—St. Leonards or London or Ditchingham where the distant guns growl continually, one is pursued by these voices of war and death.[2] What then must it be at the Front! The more I think of that poem of Rudyard's—"When the Cock Crew"—the more I feel the terrible nature of the indictment it conveys. When he had repeated it to me, amongst other things, with the marvellous memory which he has, I said what a great gift was his of being able to express in terse rhyme exactly what other men like myself were thinking. He answered that this was the great object and power of verse, to put things in a form in which people would not only read but *remember* them. Doubtless what most of us lack is the power of *expression*. For instance there is not a thought in the poem which has not been in my own mind, only alas! I could never clothe them as he can. He is convinced that Rome is working all she knows to regain the temporal Power—that this is to be her fee if Germany wins, in reward for her support throughout the world and her condonation of the frightful crimes of the Kaiser and his armies. Also he is convinced that if she regained this coveted power, soon the Inquisition and other religious methods, supposed to be obsolete, would be at work again in the world. I daresay. We agreed that the enormous power of the R.C.

---

[1] To Ditchingham, where he would spend the summer. [*Cloak*, pp. 261–62]

[2] On September 3, 1916, Haggard wrote in his diary: "We had a terrible time last night. . . . During the evening we got news that the Zeppelins were about. . . . Lilias . . . had gone to bed. I sat down to smoke in the old Study. A little after 11 Lilias called to me from the top floor, 'Dad, I hear a zeppelin!' I called down to her at once to come down to the cellar, but instead of doing so, she . . . looked out of the window for the Zeppelin, which . . . [she] saw approaching from Earsham way. Louie also saw it out of the bathroom window. . . . A bomb exploded quite near, about 200 yards from the house and 60 or so feet from the stockyard pond, where it has made a huge hole, but by some miracle did not kill the horses. . . . Then followed a veritable rain of . . . [bombs], the idea being that the guns at the Pulham sheds had hit this machine and it was lightening itself. . . . By the goodness of God, they missed both this house [Ditchingham] and the cottages, etc., near the gate. It was hellish, the whine of the machine above the fearful boom of the bombs and the cracking of glass in the greenhouses."

religion lies in its support of the individual—whereby his spiritual cares are lifted from his shoulders. He "touches the button," his church does "the rest," whereas the English Church for the most part does nothing, but tells him to worry through with his doubts and sins and troubles as best he can. I said that I did believe that, as a result of much spiritual labour, occasionally there is born in one a knowledge of the nearness of God and of His personal, embracing Love. He replied that occasionally this had happened to him also, but that the difficulty was to "*hold*" the mystic sense of this communion—that it passes. Now strangely enough this is exactly my own experience. *Occasionally* one sees the eternal Light, one touches the pierced feet, one thinks that the Peace which passes understanding is gained, and then—all is gone again and with our spirits things are as they were. R's explanation of this phenomenon of the soul is that God means it to be so,—that He doesn't mean that we should get too near to Him,—that a glimpse is all that is allowed; I *think* R. added because otherwise we should become unfitted for our work in the world. Perhaps! Also we discussed the possibility (and probability) of reincarnation and agreed that every year which passes draws back a curtain as it were, and shews us to ourselves in yet completer nakedness. He was of opinion however that there are many to whom this did not happen: "little" men who are increasingly pleased with themselves and gave example which I will not record.

It is so, the small man is the vain man, the larger he grows the more clearly does he see what a *Thing* he is, and (speaking in metaphor as well as in what some of us believe to be fact) how needful it was that Christ should die for *him*. Thus of all the men I know I think that Roosevelt and Kipling are the humblest. I know that in my own small example, now in my age I feel—well, I cannot express how *stripped* I feel of all merit and value. Perhaps it is well to be thus and then we may be clothed again and in other garments which *we* did not weave!

R. is much impressed with the prophecy about America and England fighting for the liberty of the World on p. 380 of "A Farmer's Year"! He copied it or rather I dictated it to him from the book (of which I have no copy here) and gave it to me in an envelope endorsed "prophecy by H.R.H."[1] He thinks such things are pure *vision*,

[1] Haggard wrote the passage on November 2, 1898, when some friends had reported to him that there had been a war scare and that the Coastguard had been mobilized at Harwich: "The spectacle of the Empire defending itself against a combination of Powers, and putting out all its strength in men and

coming whence he knows not. He tells me that when first the Americans came under the fire of high explosives they retired with more rapidity than grace. We agreed that this occurrence has no particular meaning. The same thing has happened to sundry of our own divisions under pressure of this first fearful experience. Doubtless the Americans will fight like heroes when they come to understand the horrible game. The only fear about them is not whether they will stand high explosives but whether they can bear a Flanders winter. It is true that they have severe cold in their own country but *their* winter is "steam-heated." They all live in very warm houses.

Brown's Hotel, London, W.1.
November 6, 1918

Dear old man,

Your letter came on here where we have been held up for a fortnight while Elsie has been having influenza. It was a sharp go but she is better now and we are thinking of returning in a few days.

Meantime I've been reading The Moon of Israel[1]—E. bagged it first tho' I got it for myself. What *is* your secret, old man? It goes, and it grips and it moves with all the first freshness of youth and—I got into a row with the wife because I had to finish it in bed with the electrics turned on. It's *ripping* good and I'm d——d jealous. You've got a new type in Ana—which you know as well as I do. Also, you've developed [that] which Scripture makes plain but which no one else dwells on—the essential turbulence and unaccommodativeness of the Israelites in their captivity.

---

money, would be the most tremendous that the world has ever seen. But although, doubtless, we should meet reverses, for my part I should be sorry for the Powers, as I believe that within a year they would scarcely have a ship left between them, and not much British territory by way of consolation. One day, the rest of the world, or most of it, I suppose, will fling itself at the throats of America and ourselves. That will be the day of Armageddon, after which may come the long peace. But the British Empire and the United States will dictate the terms of that peace." The foolscap sheet that Kipling copied survives (in the Stewart Kipling Collection, Dalhousie University). At the top of the page, Kipling wrote: "Farmer's Year: 1899: Nov. 2. 1898." Below, in Haggard's hand, appears this note: "Copied from *A Farmer's Year* by Rudyard Kipling one day at Batemans (in the Spring of 1919—I think) and given by him to me when I was visiting him there. H. Rider Haggard. 21. June, 1920."

[1] *Moon of Israel*, a tale about Moses and the Exodus, appeared on October 31, 1918.

I don't know what to think of these amazing days. We're back in the 8th Century after the Holy Roman Empire turned in its hand: and there was only a welter of small powers left. Next time you come along bring your diary with you. I want to see how it struck you day by day.

With all love and special thanks from Elsie for "The Moon."

Ever,
Rudyard.

They've tidied away your letter, so this goes to your publisher in default of address.[1]

R.[2]

November 15 [1918]

I have been spending the day at Bateman's with the Kiplings. Rudyard is much better than when I last saw him at the beginning of April. I think fatter also—he puts it down to the war news. So I think is Mrs. Kipling. Elsie has had influenza and is a bit peaky but recovering and in good spirits. As usual we discussed all things in heaven and earth—especially the great dangers we have escaped. I took this diary over, as R. had asked me to do, and read him passages out of it till I was tired. These interested him *greatly*. He thinks that it must be a very important work some day—of much value indeed to the generations to come. His chief anxiety is as to its preservation, concerning which he made various suggestions:—that I should hand it over to the British Museum in a packet not to be opened for 50 years—(which is the time he thinks should go by before its publication:) that I should deposit it with one of the "Safe Deposit" Companies: that I should

---

[1] Haggard must have gone up to London and was probably staying in a hotel.

[2] Haggard's diary for November 8 reads: "Today I have received a very charming letter from Kipling about my new book, Moon of Israel, which I did not send him fearing it might bore him. [Here he quotes the second and third paragraphs of the letter.] This opinion is worth a ton of professional criticism, because it comes from a great writer who knows what creation is and its difficulties. But as I wrote to Rudyard to-day it makes me laugh to hear him say that he is jealous of *me* who am written down as the deadest of dead letters. [Haggard's popularity had, for some years, been declining, and since the beginning of the war he found it increasingly difficult to place his tales with publishers.] Also I wish that I could rise to his high opinion of my work."

put it in an iron box enclosed in a lump of concrete and bury it, and so forth.

I told him what I am doing, namely depositing one typed copy with Longmans and keeping the other, also the original, myself in different places. Of course I recognize the danger, i.e. that when I have been gone a few years, and someone may get hold of it and publish a highly bowdlerized version of it as the whole "war-diary." Well, it must take its chance.[1] After the reading I happened to say to him that I wished I were a poet as so many things occurred to me of which I should like to make poems. R. answered—in these words as nearly as I can remember them: "Don't you see, Rider, that much of what you write in your reflections etc., *is* poetry and very *fine* poetry? Only the rhyme is lacking; the fall of the sentences and the essentials of poetry are all there, also the poetic imagination. You do not chance to have the gift of rhyme as I have, and I'm glad of it, as I should not like your competition!" (This he said jokingly.) "The foolish critics" he went on, "and the ordinary readers think that poetry consists of rhyme but it is not so. The matter is or is not poetry." Also much more of the same sort that I cannot recollect well enough to write down.

He and the others were full of *Moon of Israel*, which they seem to know much better than I do myself. No single point in the tale has escaped R's piercing attention. I asked him if he really thought it a great piece of fiction. He replied: "What does one understand by 'great'? *I* call a book which can hold a man in a vice in the midst of such times as we are passing through, with his daughter in a high fever in the next room, so that he forgets everything else and is lost in the characters and the story, great." "All the same," I answered, "seeing how poorly many of the critics seem to rate me, you would not dare to say over your name that you thought me a great writer." "*Wouldn't* I just if it came my way to do so!" he exclaimed.

Well, it is pleasant to have one competent admirer left now that Andrew Lang is dead.

He described to me a dinner to which he had recently been bidden at Buckingham Palace and its appalling dullness—and then being shepherded up to speak to Royalty and the rest. It was a most amusing account. Altogether I had a very pleasant afternoon. A long talk with Kipling is now one of the greatest pleasures I have left in life—but I

[1] The original war diaries are in the Norwich Public Library; the copy he had lodged with Messrs. Longmans was probably destroyed in the bombings in World War II.

don't think he talks like this with anyone else, indeed he said as much to me. He is a very shy bird, and as he remarked, has no friends, except I think myself, for whom he has always entertained affection, and no acquaintance with literary people. "But then," he added, "I do not think that I am really 'literary'; nor are you either." I suggested that our literary sides were "by-products." "Yes," he repeated, "by-products." In one way R. is a very curious man:—when he talks he always likes to be doing something with his hands. "I must occupy my hands," he said, and went to fetch a holly-wood stick he had been drying and peeled and sandpapered it, continually asking my advice as to the process and the subsequent treatment of the stick which I told him to hang up a chimney like a ham. Last time we talked in this fashion he employed himself with a fishing rod and line.

Poor old boy, John's death has hit him very hard. He said to-day that I was lucky to have lost my son early, when I still had youth to help me to bear up against the shock and time in which to recover from it, at any rate to some extent (which I never have done really). "If he had lived to see this war," he added, "he would now have been dead or mutilated, perhaps leaving a family behind him." Mayhap he is right: often I think so myself. I pointed out that this love of ours for our lost sons was a case of what is called "inordinate affection" in the Prayer Book which somehow is always bereaved. "Perhaps," he answered, "but I don't care for 'ordinate' affection and nor do you." He thinks that imagination such as mine is the sign and expression of unusual virility, a queer theory that may have something in it. . . .

Rudyard told me that he had been approached during the war and asked to give his active support to and identify himself with the interests of certain political persons—as to whom, although he mentioned no names, one can hazard a guess—and to write them up; in short to give them the weight of his name which is, of course, considerable. In return, he was informed, he could get "anything he wanted." His answer, practically was—"Go to Hell!" He added that his experiences during the war had not raised his opinion of the Press! He rejoices over the Republican victory in the States,[1] which he thinks

---

[1] On October 25, President Wilson, eager to have solid Congressional support at the ensuing peace conference, appealed to the American voters to return a strong Democratic majority to both Houses of Congress in the coming election. On November 5, the American people elected a Republican Congress, the Republicans winning the House by twenty-one seats and the Senate by two.

will save us trouble with Pres. Wilson over such matters as "Freedom of the Seas."[1] (Of President Wilson he is no admirer—remembering those two long years of inaction—as I do.) He has been writing to Roosevelt[2] to congratulate him and says I should do the same. I think I will.

The year 1919 began with a mixture of good and bad news. On New Year's Day Haggard's name again appeared on the Honours List. This time he was awarded a K.B.E. for his services during the war on the Dominions Commission and the Empire Settlement Committee. But the satisfaction that he and Kipling must have felt with the new distinction was quickly tempered by the sudden death of Theodore Roosevelt on January 6. The news hit both Kipling and Haggard hard, and each responded to it with his own public tribute. Kipling wrote the poem "Great Heart" (it would soon appear in the *London Daily Telegraph*, the *Boston Post*, the *Philadelphia Ledger*, and the *New York Tribune*). Haggard wrote a letter to *The Times*: "I enclose copy of a letter written exactly a month before his death by Mr. Roosevelt in answer to one from myself, in which he expresses his latest opinion as to a matter whereon, perhaps, hang the future safety and happiness of civilization. I take this responsibility because I know that great and good man, in whom the world has lost one of its purest and most intrepid spirits, would wish that his view should be put on record at this time of crisis. I do not publish the two names which occur in the first sentence of the letter, as I have no permission to do so, and to seek it would take too long. I am, Sir, your obedient servant, H. Rider Haggard. North Lodge, St. Leonards-on-Sea, January 7.

New York
December 6, 1918

My dear Rider Haggard,

In a moment of pessimism the other day, I said I never wished to hear from any Englishmen, excepting ———— and ————. But that was because I had forgotten you. I doubt if I ever again go back

---

[1] Kipling and Haggard believed that the second of Wilson's Fourteen Points (free navigation of the seas in peace and war, except as the seas might be closed by international action to enforce international covenants) might interfere with the traditional freedom enjoyed by the British Navy.

[2] On October 28, 1918, Roosevelt had made a speech in Carnegie Hall "blasting Wilson's record, motives, and proposals." [W. H. Harbaugh, *Power and Responsibility: The Life and Times of Theodore Roosevelt* (1961), p. 518]

into public place. I have had to go into too much and too bitter truth telling. Like you, I am not at all sure about the future. I hope that Germany will suffer a change of heart, but I am anything but certain. I don't put much faith in the League of Nations, or any corresponding universal cure-all.

Faithfully yours,

T. Roosevelt.[1]

Many years later, Kipling, in his short autobiographical essay, wrote this of Roosevelt: "My own idea of him was that he was a much bigger man than his people understood or, at that time, knew how to use, and that he and they might have been better off had he been born twenty years later."[2]

Four days after Roosevelt's death, Haggard writes in his diary:

January 10 [1919]

I had a nice note of congratulation from Kipling to-day in which he says "Dear old man, I am glad to see you took it because if ever any one was a Knight of the Empire—by land and sea and shipwreck[3]— you're It! Like you I am awfully heavy hearted about Roosevelt. He was the best friend we had out there and I can't see who takes his place. I noticed you suppressed the two names. He sent me a long and sad (I don't wonder) letter the week before. It is curious the papers don't seem to realize that it was the wound when that crazy fool Socialist shot him, at a public meeting, which was the deferred cause of his death."[4] I did not know this either, who thought that it resulted from the fever he caught on his South American expedition.[5] I had written

---

[1] "A Great American," *The Times*, January 8, 1919, p. 4.

[2] *Something*, p. 124.

[3] In the summer of 1888, Haggard had gone to Iceland to seek out local colour for an Icelandic saga (*Eric Brighteyes*, 1891). The *Copeland*, the ship he boarded for his return to England, foundered on the rocks in a fog. Haggard and the other passengers were rescued by courageous islanders. [For a full account of the shipwreck, see *Cloak*, pp. 145–46; *Days*, I, 288–94.]

[4] Roosevelt was shot at and wounded on October 14, 1912, in Milwaukee, on his way to deliver a speech as part of his campaign against Taft. The bullet pierced Roosevelt's "overcoat, spectacles case, and folded manuscript, fracturing his fourth rib and lodging a little short of his right lung." But he insisted on giving the speech before going to the hospital for care. [Harbaugh, p. 448]

[5] In February, 1914, Roosevelt, as a member of a party of twenty-six, went to Brazil to explore the River of Doubt. "Roosevelt caught a fever, then gashed

to Rudyard and told him that his was one of the names, which I think will please him.[1]

The Russia that emerged from the war evoked disgust and horror in many Conservative Britons. And so it did in Kipling and Haggard, who saw Bolshevism as a serious threat to civilization, a menace to be opposed actively. Haggard's diary shows the concern both men felt and chronicles their anti-Bolshevist efforts.

August 25 [1919]
   In a note I have just had from Rudyard, he says, "But it is a perfectly crazy world and, like you, I don't see the end of it—or rather I see the end a little too clearly to comfort me." In my answer I have said this, "You say you see the end—I don't quite. I am not sure whether it will be of the comparatively painless boa-constrictor kind—by absorption of all accumulations, property, savings, bequests, etc.; or of the Russian back-against-the-wall kind with suitable accessories. As we are a 'constitutional people,' possibly the former. Meanwhile I have insured this place and contents against 'Riot.'"

December 4 [1919]
   Kipling who has been lunching here today, is of opinion that we owe all our Russian troubles, and many others, to the machinations of the Jews.[2] I do not know, I am sure, but personally I am inclined to think that one can insist too much on the Jew motive, the truth being that there are Jews and Jews. If, however, they are as mischievous as he believes, the evil that they do is likely to recoil on their own heads, since in extremity the world has a rough way of dealing with Jews. For my own part I should be inclined to read Trade Unions instead of

---

a leg while trying to prevent two capsized boats from being thrown against rocks; the leg became infected, malaria and dysentery set in. . . . He contemplated suicide, feeling himself too great a burden on the others." The river was later named Roosevelt River or Rio Teodoro, in his honour. [Harbaugh, p. 463]

   [1] The other name was that of Arthur Hamilton Lee (1868–1947), 1st Viscount Lee of Fareham. During the Spanish–American War, he served as military attaché to the United States Army in Cuba. He was made an honorary member of the Rough Riders, and he and Roosevelt became intimate friends.

   [2] For a discussion of Kipling and anti-Semitism, see: Lionel Trilling, "Mr. Eliot's Kipling," Nation (New York), CLVII (October 16, 1943), 436, 440, 442; T. S. Eliot, "T. S. Eliot on Kipling's Anti-Semitism," ibid., CLVIII (January 15, 1944), 83; Lionel Trilling, "Mr. Trilling Replies," ibid.

Jews, for surely they are the root of most of our embarrassments and perplexities. I suggested to R.K. that perhaps it might do good if two or three of us, say he and Inge[1] and I, sent a letter to the Times setting out this Bolshevist business clearly and trying to arouse the country to a sense of all its horror. He is going to think the matter over but is rather afraid that if we did so, it would be set down as a "Northcliffe Stunt." As a matter of fact neither he nor I nor Inge (if the last would bear a hand) have anything to do with Northcliffe and I think that the world knows this.[2] Kipling believes also that the worst thing that is happening to us as an Empire is what he calls "the handing over of India."[3] This is a matter of which he understands and I do not, therefore I shall not discuss it, but from what I have read, I have little doubt but that there is mischief afoot.

The idea of forming an anti-Bolshevist society had already taken root in other minds as well. On January 22, 1920, Haggard records in his diary that he went, by appointment, to see H. Wickham Steed, Editor of *The Times*, and that "Mr. Steed unfolded to me a mighty plan for fighting Bolshevism in this country, by means of elaborate propaganda. The idea is that a Council is to be formed which he thinks would have the blessing of the Government, with representatives of the various churches in it, and I know not who besides." Steed thought that Haggard, "being well known, trusted by the people and honest," might well be President

[1] The Very Rev. William Ralph Inge (1860–1954) met Kipling in 1914 and Haggard in 1917. His name does not appear among the organizers of the Liberty League. [W. R. Inge, *Diary of a Dean* (1949), pp. 27, 37, 142]

[2] Alfred Charles William Harmsworth (1865–1922), 1st Viscount Northcliffe, founded the *Daily Mail* in 1896 and became chief proprietor of *The Times* in 1914. In 1918 the British Government appointed him Director of Propaganda in Enemy Countries, and after the war he took personal charge of several campaigns in his newspapers, calling for immediate demobilization of troops in the field, demanding that the Kaiser be brought to trial, and insisting that Germany pay for the cost of the war. To many people, including Kipling, these journalistic "crusades" appeared to be stunts.

[3] On August 20, 1917, the British Government announced (the Montagu Declaration) that it planned to employ an increasing number of Indians in every branch of the administration in India and to develop "self-governing institutions, with a view to the progressive realisation of responsible government in India as an integral part of the Empire." The India Bill of 1919 may well have prompted Kipling's remarks, designed as it was to advance self-government. [Percival Spear, *India, A Modern History* (1961), pp. 342–43, 352]

of such a Council, even though his having a title might be a disadvantage. Haggard argued against himself, primarily on the grounds of age and previous commitments, and urged the choice of another for the Council Presidency with himself as Vice President. He raised Kipling's concern, that the Council would be regarded as a "Northcliffe stunt," because he understood that Steed was approaching him on behalf of Lord Northcliffe. Steed denied the suggestion and urged the Council's importance. The men agreed to meet again, and the fruit of their labours appeared in *The Times* on March 3, in the form of a letter, by and large as Haggard had drafted it. The letter announced the birth of the Liberty League and declared its intentions. The Liberty League would "combat the advance of Bolshevism in the United Kingdom and throughout the Empire." The first two of the seven signatures beneath the letter are Haggard's and Kipling's. On the same day, *The Times* hailed the "striking communication" from the founders of the Liberty League in a leader and urged its readers to support the venture, stating that Sir Rider Haggard was "a man whose record of unostentatious political service needs no emphasis," and calling Rudyard Kipling a "poet, seer, . . . patriot, . . . [and] national possession." On the following day, *The Times* ran a news story, outlining the purposes of the organization in detail.[1]

The Times was not alone in noting the Liberty League letter. The *Daily Herald* commented at some length and with considerable ingenuity:

> Of the making of Leagues there is no end. But the "Liberty League," launched in a manifesto in yesterday's "Times," is a League among Leagues, which promises what the showmen call "lots of fun and endless diversion." Its sponsors are none other than H. Rider Haggard and Mr. Kipling and Lord Sydenham, and a number of major generals and other important folk, and it lives somewhere in Mayfair. It is appealing to "all right-minded men and women throughout the Empire, and to all who profess any form of religious faith" (no questions asked about practising it, apparently). And it is out to squash the Bolsh and those evil-hearted folk over here who are "influenced by secret funds and hope to fish in blood-stained waters."
>
> Sir Rider and the rest have discovered that Bolshevism is "the

---

[1] "The Liberty League. A Campaign against Bolshevism," *The Times*, March 3, 1920, p. 12; "The Defence of Liberty," *The Times*, March 3, 1920, p. 17; "The Bolshevist Peril," *The Times*, March 4, 1920. See also Haggard's letter to *The Times* of a year earlier: "Shut the Door," March 10, 1919, p. 8.

Sermon on the Mount read backwards: that it leads to bloodshed and torture, raping and destruction; that it repudiates God, and would build its own throne upon the basest passions of mankind." 'Sawful, ain't it? But all is well. The Leaguers will fight the plague—"in a clean and open fashion." Lenin and Trotsky shall never see the day when, as the poet put it,

> "The Rudyards cease from Kipling,
> And the Haggards Ride no more."

"Light is to be let in on dark places." "The Truth is great and shall prevail." And lots more to the same effect. Meanwhile, money is needed, and they ask you to help. You won't, "Then, sir, I perceive you are a vile Bolshevik."

Two Hearts that Beat as One . . .

> "Every Bolsh is a blackguard,"
> Said Kipling to Haggard
> —"And given to tippling,"
> Said Haggard to Kipling.

> "And a blooming outsider,"
> Said Rudyard to Rider.
> —"Their domain is blood-yard,"
> Said Rider to Rudyard.

> "That's just what I say,"
> Said the author of "They."
> —"I agree; I agree,"
> Said the author of "She."[1]

Haggard in fact became President of the Liberty League and devoted considerable time to it. His diary records frequent visits to its offices and shows that he was in the forefront of the organized anti-Bolshevist movement. By April 21, however, the League was in financial difficulties. It lacked no funds, but, as Haggard confided in his diary, "all men are not honest"; one of the League founders, it appears, had mishandled funds. "It looked to me," Haggard wrote, "as though we had become involved in a veritable romance of fraud, if fraud can be romantic. . . .

[1] G. G., "Way of the World," *Daily Herald*, March 4, 1920, p. 4.

One's natural impulse would be to return the subscriptions and wash one's hands of the whole affair, but that would be almost a National catastrophe and cause Bolshevists everywhere to rejoice."

Haggard spent much of April 23 with his associates working over the League's finances. That evening, however, he took time to attend the Festival Dinner of the Royal Society of St. George, at which Kipling spoke:[1]

April 24 [1920]

Kipling's address was very learned, very profound, and very analytical, but it took no hold of the large audience, much of which, I think, could not hear him. Evidently he had learned it by heart in his usual fashion and its polished periods smelt of the lamp. However it reads well in the papers, to which, I imagine, it had been furnished beforehand. I do not know whether the possession of such a marvellous memory is a blessing or a curse. During the dinner, which was en-livened by the presence of enormous Beefeaters and Yeoman of the Guard dressed in their quaint uniforms and by a procession in which 4 white robed *chefs* bore a huge baron of beef around the great hall of the Connaught Rooms, which they nearly managed to upset on Kipling's head, I became a Life Member of the Society. Afterwards the Kiplings and I, after a furious hunt for a taxi, returned to their rooms at Brown's Hotel and there I set out all the melancholy facts concerning our Liberty League imbroglio, which, as he remarked, gave him "something to think about." He is coming to the meeting next Thursday. Then I walked home dog-tired. The Kiplings, who have just returned from France, say that the feeling there against the English is very bitter. Nor, after going through the devastated areas, do they wonder at it. I have had plenty more Liberty League business today, including two hours at the Lawyers'. . . . I am sick of it, and it tires me very much, especially, as I am not in the least responsible for anything.

On April 29 Haggard was in the chair at a meeting of a League com-mittee and, as promised, Kipling was present. "I set out all the circum-stances of the disastrous conspiracy of which we have been the victims," Haggard wrote in his diary. The members present set up a Finance Committee and adjourned the meeting for several days "to allow Mr.

[1] The speech, "England and the English," was collected in *A Book of Words* (1928).

Wickham Steed to see Lord Northcliffe and ascertain what he is prepared to do." On May 7 Haggard records that "the Liberty League worries are overpowering. I spend most of my days trying to deal with them, but without much result. We seem plunged in an atmosphere of deception or worse. Today I have been talking to Mr. Wickham Steed on the telephone and told him straight out that if Lord Northcliffe makes up his mind that he will not help, we must wind up the League. He stated that the Times 'acted in good faith.' I announced that so did we all, but that would not prevent attack and scandal. He agreed. Now I have suggested by letter that . . . I should see Lord Northcliffe. I think the best thing would be to wind up." Haggard did not get to see Northcliffe, who, it became quite clear, would not help solve the League's problems. At another meeting (May 14), with Kipling again present, the members decided that the Liberty League should end its independent existence.

Bateman's, Burwash, Sussex
November 26, 1920

Dear old man,

Like a fool I wrote you my thanks for "Smith & the Pharaohs"[1] and—posted it under a blotter on my dunghill of a table! Well, *you* know what my table is like: so I won't even attempt to apologize.

Best of all—you know I'm no Egyptologist—I like Little Flower[2] for its power and justice and humanity (it's a young gem) but,—as ever, it is the amazing *freshness* of the work that always hits me between my envious eyes.

I do hope that your chest ain't troubling you in these days of raw frost and damp cold.

Let me have a line to say all is well; and *do* let me know what has happened and is going to happen, in regard to winding up the affairs of the Liberty League. I am *not* sorry about the financial side of it and most earnestly wish to be clear of that before all.

Ever affectionately,
Rudyard.

[1] *Smith and the Pharaohs and Other Tales* was published on November 4.
[2] "Little Flower" is the fourth story in the volume.

July 22 [1921]

I have just returned from London whither I went to attend the royal garden-party. It was an interesting function. Thousands of people more or less well-known, or the friends of the well-known who had obtained them invitations, including many of the most distinguished in the land, wandered about the great sun-scorched grounds of Buckingham Palace, talking to anybody they met whom they chanced to know, or squabbling over the possession of chairs. Also, if they were lucky, they had a chance of seeing the King and Queen in the distance with other royalties. Fortunately the weather was not too hot and very fine. So on the whole it was an agreeable function. The business reminded me of similar parties at Windsor many years ago when Edward was King. In those days I remember being impressed with the matchless way in which he received persons introduced to him—the bow, the lifting of the white hat, the few words of apt conversation, the renewed bow and second lifting of the white hat in dismissal. The same thing goes on in another generation. I saw it yesterday, but not I think with quite the same chic; such perfection is not easy to re-capture. All the afternoon I searched for L[ouie] who arrived later from Cecil Hildyard's wedding[1] in some remote place, resembling, as some observer remarked to me at the Athenaeum today, Orpheus hunting Hades for Eurydice. It was quite useless—I never found her, and she, too, abandoning the hunt, took refuge in coffee ices. I met a good many people whom I knew, among them the Kiplings. R. held forth about this diary, saying that he wished that I would make him my literary executor with discretion to publish such portions of it as he wished (I suppose that rightly he expects to live much longer than I shall). There is something in the idea. The work edited by Kipling would be a formidable document![2]

January 28 [1922]

Kipling, who came over to see me on Thursday, takes a most gloomy view of the Indian situation. I read to him what I had written above and asked him his opinion.[3] He answered that if Phyllis were his

[1] Cecil Hildyard and Louisa Haggard were cousins.

[2] In his will, Haggard left all his literary rights to his wife; he did not make Kipling his literary executor.

[3] Many Indians were, at this time, hostile toward Europeans. Mahatma Ghandi had appealed for non-violent revolts against British rule, but many of his followers found more direct ways of expressing their antagonism. The

daughter, simply he would not allow her to go (as though he could prevent it when she is another man's wife). Indeed he says that in answer to requests for advice on this very point, he had to reply that as he supposes the truth, as he sees it, is what is wanted from him, he thinks it right to say that he does not think that any white woman should visit or remain in India. Indeed he said that he heard from Indian correspondents that no white ladies and children are ever left alone, especially at outlying stations. If some of the officers go out on duty or pleasure, others remain to watch them. In short his opinion seems to be that there is grave risk of our being faced with another mutiny. As he knows India if any man does, his view impresses me. More disorder is reported from Calcutta and other Indian towns.

January 30 [1922]

I have just returned from spending a most interesting day with the Kiplings at Bateman's. As usual R. and I talked till we were tired about everything in heaven above and earth beneath. Incidentally, too, we hammered out the skeleton plot for a romance I propose to write under some such title as "Allan and the Ice Gods," which is to deal with the terrible advance of one of the Ice-Ages upon a little handful of the primitive inhabitants of the earth. He has a marvellously fertile mind and I never knew anyone quite so quick at seizing and developing an idea. We spent a most amusing two hours over this plot and I have brought home the results in several sheets of manuscript written by him and myself. He takes a most despondent view of the position in Ireland, Egypt and India, and even went so far as to say that it looks as

---

Moslems particularly objected to Allied support of the Greeks against the Sultan of Turkey, then regarded as head of Islam. These threats to both the Empire and the war effort disturbed Kipling and Haggard. In the diary entry that Haggard read to Kipling, he quotes the Special Correspondent of *The Times* at Bombay, who had written "a very alarming article about the state of affairs in India . . . [where British] policy is producing its inevitable fruits and . . . sooner or later it will become a question either of fighting to retain India, or of its abandonment. The history of events in Ireland suggests that if this happens, we shall not adopt the former course. How the Hindus would like being left to settle their differences with the Mohammedans is an interesting question that the future alone can elucidate, though from the little that I have seen of them, I do not think they would like it at all. For my part I am sorry that my newly married niece, Phyllis Wickham, is just starting for India with her husband, a Royal Engineer. I wish that she could remain at home for a while." [January 26, 1922]

though the Empire were going to fall to pieces.[1] The only hope he could see was in young men who may arise, but when I asked him where these young men were, he replied that he did not know. He trusts, however, that they may arise under the pressure of circumstances. So do I, but at present I discern them not.

The manuscript sheets of *Allan and the Ice-Gods* that Haggard mentions survive, and they reveal that Kipling gave Haggard extensive help on this novel. The material comprises six hand-written pages (three quarto sheets). Embossed in the upper right-hand corner of the first page is "North Lodge, St. Leonards-on-Sea"; the writing on this page is entirely Haggard's. At the top the title is underscored once. Then the beginning of the plot: "Allan inherits from Lady Ragnall who dies the chest of Taduki with a letter in which she hints at many things." The plot goes on for twenty-four lines to the bottom of the page. Page 2 continues the plot, but for the most part in Kipling's hand. He begins at the top: "The tribe conceived itself to be all of mankind, by special act of creation. They had come, or had been made 'Beyond the Throne whence the God descends.'" His writing continues for thirty-three lines, through a description of the story's terrain: "Originally the valley had been long, level, and green—about five miles long. The glacier had worked its way down it at the rate of perhaps a yard or two a year. No one noticed that it was moving quicker except Allan who had the curiosity to measure it with two sticks." Then Kipling draws a sketch of the landscape showing the descent of the glacier and labeling the parts of the sketch from left to right "bay," "last tilt," "valley," and "glacier." The sketch is followed by a single sentence in which Kipling misspells the hero's name "Alan." At the bottom of the page, Haggard's hand again takes up for five lines to continue the plot on to the third page for only a single line, where again Kipling takes over to carry the plot another twenty lines. Then Haggard resumes again for the remaining twelve lines on the page to the end.

[1] In Egypt the Wafd Party had just issued a manifesto outlining a far-reaching scheme of non-cooperation, including a boycott of British goods and British society and an incitement of government servants to insubordination and strike. The Egyptian government was itself in suspension because no Egyptian wished to assume governmental responsibility until Britain made clearer commitments about Egyptian independence. In Ireland Michael Collins of the Irish Free State and James Craig of Northern Ireland met and came to a substantial and promising settlement of most of their problems, raising real hopes for genuine Irish unity. Kipling may have feared that this agreement foreshadowed the loss of all of Ireland.

Four pages more accompany the summary. One, entirely in Kipling's hand, contains a list of the characters' names and descriptive phrases. Most of the names are followed by epithets or other identifying tags. At one point in the list, Kipling writes: "The longer the name the greater the honour of the wearer. The real name, the hunter's name; and the wife's name told only in his ear to carry to the dead as he is dying." At the top centre of the page, in neat printing, are the words *The Glacier* under-scored, and below it is a detailed aerial view of the landscape with a number of designations written in: "The Throne where the God descends," "faces and threatening figures *inside* the ice of the imprisoned Forces of Destination," and "small bay, intense blue with floating ice. The seal lie on the floes." Another page bears still another list of names with accompanying tags, but this is almost entirely in Ida Hector's hand. One is entered in Haggard's hand, and on the left margin, Miss Hector has entered "Page 37" vertically beside three names, which would seem to argue that this list was made when at least the early part of the manu-script already existed. The last page, undoubtedly the outer cover page, bears two items in Haggard's hand, one a sentence addition to the plot, the other Haggard's summary of the contents: "Synopsis of story drawn up by Rudyard K and myself at Batemans, Feb. 1922. H. Rider Haggard."[1]

Bateman's, Burwash, Sussex
February 8, 1922

Dear old man,

No. As far as I recall, that letter did *not* come to my hand. I only hope it was [not] my dam carelessness at *my* end. I think you'll find that all—"inspected" shall we say?—letters arrive at their destination *after a little delay*. I suggest Miss H.[2] keeps tab on the actual *arrivals* of some of your correspondence. I've just had a note from the P.M.G. about some delayed letters saying:—"If the P.O. is responsible it is sorry." Very cheery!

The Virgin of the Sun[3] has arrived and E.[4]—trust her!—has swiped and stands guard over it! I shan't get it till she and Carrie have done (My God! I wish I had your flaming vitality).

[1] See appendix for a transcript of the plot outline.
[2] Ida Hector.
[3] *The Virgin of the Sun* had been published on January 26.
[4] Elsie Kipling.

Your hint as to the combined stringing of the blue beads shall be duly attended to.[1]

Ever thine,
Rudyard.

July 22 [1922]

At the Athenaeum some of us who were going to the Garden Party —Sir Edward Henry,[2] Sir Mackenzie Chalmers,[3] myself, etc., old fellows, all of us—had a quite interesting competition as to which of us could boast the most antique frock-coat worn for the occasion. Henry won, at least I think it was he, because he was able to prove that his was marked 1900, but I feel sure that the honour ought to have been mine, which I am sure is Victorian and except for a few trifling moth holes, almost as good as the day it was made. The fame of the discussion spread to the party for one of the first questions that Kipling asked me was who had won, adding that if he had been there with his coat, none other would have had a chance!

September 21 [1922]

By the way Watt told me this morning that as I guessed, the Kipling "interview" was a report of a private conversation which he had in the intimacy of his own house with Mrs. Clare Sheridan whom he has known from a child. She is a daughter of Moreton Frewen with whom I had many talks at St. Leonards last year and with whom the Kiplings have been friends for years. (Poor Frewen who is very old must now be much upset.) Her mother is the sister of the late Lady Randolph Churchill and I think that she is married to an American.[4] All this

[1] On at least three winter holidays the Kiplings visited Egypt, and some of Haggard's zeal for collecting ancient Egypt keepsakes might have rubbed off on them. The beads may in fact have been from a mummy.

[2] Sir Edward Richard Henry (1850–1931), Indian civil servant, London Police Commissioner, and Equerry to the King.

[3] Sir Mackenzie Dalzell Chalmers (1847–1927), Indian civil servant, barrister, judge, and frequent commissioner.

[4] Clare Consuelo Sheridan (b. 1886) was the European correspondent for the New York *World*. Her mother, Clara (wife of Moreton Frewen [1853–1924], economist and author, a neighbour and friend of Kipling), was the daughter of Leonard Jerome of New York City, whose other daughter, Jenny, was the mother of Winston Churchill. Mrs. Sheridan was, in fact, at this time a widow. Her husband, Lieut. William Frederick (Wilfred) Sheridan, killed in France in September, 1915, was the son of Mr. and Mrs. Algernon Sheridan of Frampton Court, Dorset, the grandson of John Lothrop Motley,

WI = a "personage of predeluvian times". He preaches to Mira and Wi also disregarded him. Hence the Flood.

VININI = The Shudderer   THE   GLACIER.

AKA = a pretty woman.

He throws stones the Gods descend

MOANANGA – avaricious

PITOKITE = a churl one of the unlucky.

WHAKA = a bird of ill-omen – one who howls.

TAREN = the witch who hides up.
RAHI = the local millionaire in flesh hooks.

IOU = the unstable feather
HOTOA = the slow man   noises & cracklings
                              inside the glacier – when the
NAMES: sun shines or when
                              it freezes.
Ah = who has always afraid
URK = The old man
TAH-O = the old woman who talked:
LAN = the girl
FOH =
DOM =
PAG =
The longer the name the
greater the honour. The
names: the hunter's
name; and the wife's name
told only in his ear to carry
to the dead as he is
dying +
NGAE = The Magician:
MATOURA = Murmeena.

KOW = the fish or   Small bay
      swimmer.   unless this with
                        floating ice. the seal lie on the floes.

faces of threatening
figures inside the ice
of the unknown Powers of destruction

A page from the plot outline of Haggard's *Allan and the Ice-Gods*
(*See Appendix page 186*)

G.C.CIGOLINI, Dᵉ Gᵉ

Mar. 31:/25

Dear old man — You may be suffering from incurable diseases (I'm delighted at the victory over the Pirate Company), but you've still got a fine glow of moral wrath over the sufferings of S. Africa. And you're dead-right I believe. The evil that wt. G. planted isn't all seeded yet but (and here's the silver lining) the very mineralization of the sub-continent is acting, I think, as a buffer against the too rampant Dutch. A man the 'other day was telling me of the discovery of (and consequent gambling in) platenum discoveries that he stuff — a heavy black powder — he is out all along a reef of 40 miles and he's been traced and pegged for eighty miles! Question, of course, is whether it goes down but, anyhow, it's a huge proposition and it will draw people. By the way Hertzog has and is showing himself not equal to his job — like all Socialists — 'cause he doesn't work and doesn't know how to work. And his Pact with labour don't work, either: all that is to the Good. My own special "moan" is over the state of European affairs after the war — specially with respect to Disarmament. But I suppose, every man, looks back with a half-broken heart on the failure of all the things he has tried to bring about in his life. Even it otherwise, O Theophilus — we should be as the Gods. Which, all decent information at my disposal advises me that we are not

6. 15. p. m. It was a fine — a really fine forenoon of
still sea and hot sun and blue sky behind stone buildings.
Didn't quite know what to make of it; not having seen
sun for about a year — so ~~sat~~ it lay tenderly on the
beach and grilled. Amazing sensation! Quite like being
alive! Then, after lunch, to see a Pelota game wherein
Chiquito (champion of the world) ~~performed~~ performed. It
was all quite new to me. The great fantastic wall against
which they play their colossal fives, the
cement floor on which the server stands,
the immense size of the court — looks
like 70 yards — and the amazing
implement — the cursed basket that
on their wrists — Its wicker — &
must more hooked how lie

they shot

drawn it — and its width may be three 1/2 inches at the widest.
Anyhow they do miracles with it in the way of catching the ball,
and David's Sling was lost in it when it comes to returns. One
can hardly follow the ball as it is smashed in from the far end of
the course. It's three men aside; the rules are beyond me: but it's
fives & racquets in a ~~nightmare~~ nightmare. We sat for nigh two
hours, in a most hairbreadtching a game of 50 up. When the
men were too winded — it's a punishing game — the masker
with no trace of self-consciousness, slipped off his beret cap,
took position in the centre of the court and sang stanzas of
Basque songs — to the huge edification of the crowd. He always
broke off, snapping like a dog. You never heard anything so
stirring as a finale. I shall introduce it in all my future
verses then into Bayonne shopping. (You and I don't
feel that way when we come to a new town.) In a
~~material~~ moist-feeling & cooering of soft clouds
that made me realize that the whole nature of the
year had turned.

A page from the Candidates' Book showing Kipling's election
to the Savile Club

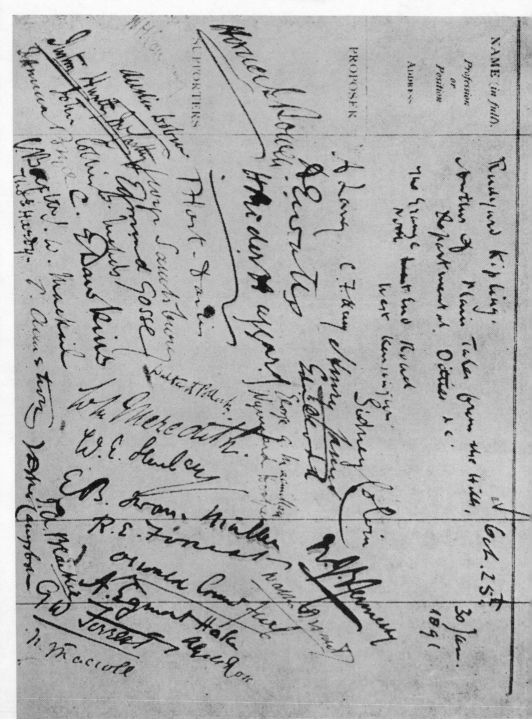

makes the business peculiarly discreditable, but why English papers should go out of their way to allege that K. could never have said such things I am sure I don't know, unless, as usual, it is due to fear of America. There was nothing improper in the opinions attributed to him, whatever may have been his exact words uttered in privacy to an old friend. Indeed everybody has heard them scores of times, not so infrequently from the lips of Americans themselves. It is the person who sent a garbled account of them to the Press who should be reprimanded.

Kipling frequently suffered from what the doctors called gastritis, which they treated "with purging and dieting." The misdiagnosed condition often caused him serious pain. In 1922 it grew so severe that an exploratory operation was ordered.[1]

November 15 [1922]

I grieve to see in a paper that Kipling has gone to a nursing home where he may have an operation, which may or may not be true. A year or two ago he complained to me of his stomach, but said the doctors told him it was nothing to worry about, and, I think, the last time I was at Bateman's, he told me it was all right again. I hope it has not reasserted itself. . . .

I went this morning to inquire after Kipling and as Mrs. Kipling had gone to see him in his nursing home, I saw Elsie and had a long talk with her, which however has not left me much the wiser as to his illness. She said it was not cancer, or so they declared, but what it was she did not seem to know. It appears that the ailment has been going on for years and is the same as that of which he spoke to me a long

---

former United States Minister in London, and the great-grandson of Richard Brinsley Sheridan. Mrs. Sheridan came to tea at Bateman's and later reported that Kipling said "that the war had not been fought to a finish, that [America] . . . had come into the war two years, seven months and four days too late . . . [and] quit the day of the armistice, without waiting to see the thing through." Speaking of the two million U.S. Civil War dead, she quoted Kipling as saying, "They . . . represented the courageous and strong. After the war, . . . America was flooded with aliens of the wrong type." [Carrington, p. 358; "America's War Record Impeached by Kipling . . . ," World, LXII (September 10, 1922), 1–2]

[1] Carrington, pp. 339, 357–59.

while ago, grown worse so that of late he has had much pain, especially after eating. I suspect some kind of growth which has necessitated some short-circuiting operation. The doctors, she added, are quite satisfied with his present condition, although he still suffers pain. But then, as he remarked to her, I think yesterday, "doctors are d——d easily pleased." I gather generally that he will probably recover from this trouble, but can scarcely hope to be the same man again. He hates his nursing home and they hope to get him out of it into the hotel as soon as possible.

March 20 [1923]

I have been spending the day at Bateman's with the Kiplings. I found Rudyard looking drawn and considerably aged. He has been and still is suffering from sundry minor consequential troubles as the result of his operation. I hope that these are not serious but they are a great worry and keep him continually thinking of his insides. It struck me that we were a pretty pair of old crocks, I lying with my leg up on the couch in his study and he bending over the fire.[1] We read bits of "Wisdom's Daughter"[2] which he was kind enough to describe as "—— good prose" (this he repeated several times making me reread passages that he might note the fall of the cadences), with other complimentary remarks. He had not yet finished the book but described it as a philosophy of life and an epitome of all the deeper part of my work. He says he will write to me about it later. We talked of many things and as usual I found that our views were practically the same. He is now convinced that the individual human being is not a mere flash in the pan, seen for a moment and lost forever, but an enduring entity that has lived elsewhere and will continue to live, though for a while memory of the past is blotted out. He does not, however, think this of all individuals but holds that for some there is no future because they have no soul to inherit it and no desire to uplift their hearts and attain to it, exemplifying this argument by the name of one brilliant and much-praised writer—"*He* won't live," he said. These were his views on this point, if I have interpreted them rightly. As to the future of our country he was despondent, not being able to see a way out of all our troubles,

[1] During the last few years of his life, Haggard suffered from gout. As for Kipling, not until 1933 did a Parisian doctor discover that for fifteen years he had been suffering from duodenal ulcers. [Elsie Bambridge, "Epilogue," Carrington, p. 399]

[2] See pp. 124–25 below.

any more than I can. The advent of a Labour Government, or even the near approach of it, would, he thought, produce a terrible financial crash,[1] and he asked whether all those that we lost in the war, his boy John and the rest, died to bring about such a state of affairs as we see today. We agreed that we were both of us out of touch with the times, but he added grimly that these clever young men who are so loud in their self-praise and air their views so freely, would learn their lesson before all was done, when in due course they found themselves face to face with forces that are banking up on every side. Altogether our talk was most interesting, for in Kipling there is more light than in any living man I know, the same sort of light that distinguished Lang when he dropped the shield of persiflage with which he hid his heart. There are three men with whom I have found myself in complete sympathy during my life—Rudyard is one of them and the other two were Andrew Lang and Theodore Roosevelt. The outlook of all four of us was and is identical—that is so far as I can judge. R.'s memory is really marvellous; he repeated to me two long unpublished satirical poems of his without a single error (these are aimed at America's post-war conduct which infuriates him especially where the debt is concerned, and if ever they are read by the citizens of that "communal country," I don't know what will happen).[2] I believe if he were put to it he could do the same with most of what he has written. To be short, we enjoyed our talk very much—in the middle of it he broke in to say, "I am *so* delighted to see you here, old man." I hope to heaven that he will get quite strong again, but I must say that I was not altogether pleased with his appearance—he looks so worn and thin. They are going to the south of France soon that he may get warmth and rest. Meanwhile he is writing some amusing stories; he says that is how it takes him just now, perhaps in mental re-action to his physical worries.[3]

[1] Labour in fact was victorious in January, 1924, but the Conservatives were back in office in November and remained there until June 4, 1929. Labour came in again at that time and was in power during the early years of the depression, until August, 1931.

[2] Kipling must have written the poems at the time of the row over Mrs. Sheridan's controversial report in the New York *World* (see p. 120 above). They appear never to have been published. He was also troubled that the United States was gradually coming to believe in reducing Germany's reparations, a policy carried out by the Dawes Plan (1924).

[3] In late February and March, Kipling was working on "The United Idolaters" (to appear in the *Strand Magazine* in June, 1924) and "The Janeites" (*Story-Teller Magazine*, May, 1924).

July 27 [1923]

Kipling and I lunched together at the Athenaeum today. He is much better than he was and as bright and amusing as ever. We were discussing the woman's vote and the advent of woman with a big W., generally as to which he told me and others stories of remarks he alleges I made in his presence in argument with the other sex that I had totally forgotten. He reproached me for not having acknowledged a long letter he wrote to me from Cannes about "Wisdom's Daughter," a work of which it seems he thinks highly and desires that I should enlarge and elaborate on certain lines. But as I never received the letter naturally I could not answer it. I have no doubt it was stolen for the autograph, probably in the French hotel. He says that he will write it again in order to develop his argument, but this I doubt. He is on the French side in the Ruhr business[1] and generally, and seems to think the Germans are cutting off their nose to spite their own face, and in short would rather ruin their own people than give up. It may be so. I confess I find it difficult to understand the business, or to find anyone who does.

Kipling kept his promise to comment on Haggard's manuscript of *Wisdom's Daughter* (1923), the last of the books about Ayesha, She-who-must-be-obeyed. After Kipling and Haggard read it together at Bateman's, long letters passed between them on the subject. Although the original letters have not come to light, we have Miss Lilias Haggard's account of them:

Kipling was . . . much impressed with *Wisdom's Daughter* [Miss Haggard writes] which Rider read to him in manuscript and at Kipling's request left with him for a more considered opinion. A week or two later he wrote to Rider suggesting revisions, much amplification and some softening of the character of She:

"The more I went through it the more I was convinced that it represented the whole sum and substance of your convictions along certain lines. That being so, it occurred to me that you might, later on, take the whole book up again for your personal satisfaction—and go

---

[1] In January, 1923, France occupied the Ruhr in an effort to force Germany to pay reparations. The French encountered passive resistance from the local population and did not succeed in getting Germany to pay up. Moreover, the occupation dislocated Germany's economy, helped depreciate its currency, and created a runaway inflation.

through it from that point of view. I am not suggesting this from the literary side—that is a matter of no importance—but as a means of restating and amplifying your ideas and convictions through the mouth of your chief character. All this on the assumption that I never hid from you, that the book is miles above the head of the reader at large. It will not come to its own for a long time, but to those to whom it is a message or a confirmation it will mean more than the rest of your work.... Damn it man—you have got the whole tragedy of the mystery of life under your hand, why not frame it in a wider setting? (This comes well from a chap who could not write a novel to save himself.) That's what I suggest for *Wisdom's Daughter* because I know that as you did it, you'd take a woman in hand and through *her* mouth speak more of what is in her heart. You are a whale at parables and allegories and one thing reflecting another. Don't cuss me. You wanted to know what I thought and so I send it to you."[1]

An extract from Haggard's reply to Kipling appears in Haggard's diary:

August 1 [1923]
    ... As usual—you see the truth which few others do—few indeed. In that book is my philosophy—or rather some of it. The Eternal War between the Flesh and Spirit, the eternal loneliness and search for unity—wrongly aimed for it is only to be found in God, the blinding of the eyes and the sealing of the soul to Light, which (I think) is the real sin unforgiveable—oh! and lots more which I hope to explain, if explanation is necessary for I feel that we both mean much the same thing even if neither of us can quite express *what* we mean.

    In these latter days—thank Heaven I do seem to be grasping the skirts of vision—though they slip from the hand like water. But to describe—to set down!—There's the rub!—

    Well—I don't think that the attempt can be made with *She*—unless I scrapped everything concerning her and began afresh, which can't be done.

    But how about that Wandering Jew idea, which I think I propounded to you? The *direct* outrage to the Divinity, the sin incarnate—wrought by whom? Pilate's adviser. The resulting separation from the all-surrounding Love and Grace, the slow upward climb through the ages, the fall through the woman, the redemption by way of the

[1] *Cloak*, pp. 271–72.

woman. Then the periods,—Egypt at the beginning of Christianity, the first I suppose. What others? I must think them out. The end in the war. I presume it would take several years, the rest of my life probably —several volumes. And what Title? And what form? Memoirs?

It would be tremendous if only one were given the grace to do it.

P.S. As regards volumes, how about the fight of the Norse Gods against the White Christ for one. The plot of Germany against the world with the rise of Bolshevism for another (the last). The Crusades for one perhaps.

I thoroughly agree with you about the Cloister and the Hearth.[1] I read it all through again a few years ago. One of the greatest novels ever written. Yet the wise arbiters of taste don't seem to think much of its author![2]

To this letter [Miss Haggard tells us] Kipling replied:

You aren't choosing any small canvas for your latter years to expiate in, are you, when you turn your mind towards the Jew? Let us be generous while we are about it. The little business might be worked out in a trilogy quite easily. Book One would deal with the origin of the man far back. He might be a composite sort of breed, a bit of an Arab, and a bit of a Sephardim; with a Roman ancestor or two in his line. A hell of a school-taught intellectual, who really was no more than politely cruel to the Lord. He did not say in so many words "Get out with you"; he just hinted to the Figure staggering beneath its Cross that it was blocking *his* way to an appointment. We can guess the appointment; and the whore comes in later too. Or, he might have told one of the soldiers to shove the malefactor out of his light; which the just-minded Latin refused to do—and here is a point, had his reward in later incarnations!

Anyhow you would have to close the first Book with the Crucifixion, but you might do it from the wholly disinterested point of view of the Jew upon whom the Doom has not begun to work. What *he* noticed was the dust storm that darkened the city, and again interfered

---

[1] In Kipling's "In the Same Boat," Nurse Blaber on a trip she had taken "buried herself in *The Cloister and the Hearth*." [*Works*, XXVI, 111] Kipling was later to write that he had "dreamed for many years" of writing a "three-decker" based on "pure research and knowledge... worthy to lie alongside *The Cloister and the Hearth*." [*Something*, p. 228]

[2] This extract appears in the diary in Ida Hector's handwriting.

with his appointment on the day of the execution, and the row that two or three low-class women made over the fellow's tomb. Book Two leaves one with the whole choice of either the Fall of the Roman Empire or the complete history of the Middle Ages, introduced by a little talk or two between the Jew, and a wandering disputatious little chap of the name of Paul, who seems to have built up some sort of sect upon the words of this Hebrew ruffian of thirty or forty years back. The Jew himself is elderly now and (still ignorant of his lot) looks to be gathered to his fathers before the times get any worse. (He is a *good* Jew remember.) Paul thinks otherwise but won't give his reasons. The Jew attends a Christian service at the very dawn of the Creed, and warns Paul that he has brought his new faith to a market where it will be bought up by the vested interests attached to the service of the Old Gods. Paul don't see. From that point you can go on. Dead easy, isn't it?

So the letter goes on [Miss Haggard tells us]. Kipling's vivid and merciless imagination painting in a few swift words scene after scene—the Crusades—the Black Death—the Inquisition—the painfully acquired wealth of the Wandering Jew which when attained worked only fresh horrors and new wars, and he ends:

> Now you won't do one little bit of this, but it will help stir you up to block out the first rough scenario, and in the intervals of answering demands of idle idiots and helpless imbeciles to which cheerful task I am now about to address myself for the next hour.

> Ever thine, R.K.[1]

Kipling was right; Haggard never wrote the story.

Between 1923 and 1925 letters did not get written, or if they did, they have got lost. Both men were busy with work and involved in their own domestic routines. Kipling, moreover, was seriously ill in late 1922 and early 1923,[2] and it is inconceivable that Haggard failed to write and visit him. By the spring, Kipling was better, and the family took their usual holiday on the Riviera. In October, 1923, Kipling was elected Lord Rector of St. Andrews University, and he was occupied throughout

[1] *Cloak*, pp. 272–73.
[2] See pp. 121–22 above.

the middle 'twenties writing stories that would be collected in *Debits and Credits.*[1]

For his part, Haggard continued to work for agricultural reforms and on his various commissions, and, his daughter tells us, was content and happy.[2] In January, 1924, the Haggards let North Lodge and spent the remainder of the winter in Egypt. In April, Haggard was back in London taking his accustomed walks through the British Museum and attending both the Garden Party at Buckingham Palace and the Prime Minister's Party at Hampton Court.

Haggard continued active through the summer, 1924, and on November 5, he attended an important luncheon in Stationer's Hall, celebrating the bicentenary of Longmans, Green and Company, for many years his publisher. Haggard gave the major address of the afternoon to a distinguished audience that included the Dean of St. Paul's, G. M. Trevelyan, Mrs. Andrew Lang, Sir Arthur Conan Doyle, and Sir Edmund Gosse, and he spoke cheerfully and humorously about the "bonds of matrimony" between authors and publishers.[3] Later that afternoon, however, he was taken ill. Here is his own account of the "catastrophe," as he recorded it in his diary:

November 6 [1924]

While I was hurrying to find a taxi in order to catch a train at Charing Cross (which didn't exist), I was seized with a most fearful attack of indigestion that almost seemed to stop my heart from beating. How I managed to get down to St. Leonards and into this room really I do not know, but it was a great struggle. Luckily Scarlyn Wilson,[4] the doctor, was in the Club and came to help me to undress, sent for remedies, etc. Today I am better but still have wind, etc. The immediate cause of this attack was, I believe, eating some oysters and then a sort of lobster stew, after which I drank a glass of champagne and a liqueur brandy. Also the heat of the room followed by the cold of the street and the excitement of speaking may have had something to do with it. The fact is however that I am no longer at all robust and I do not know how long I shall be able to undertake London enjoyments in winter.

[1] Carrington, pp. 359–60.

[2] *Cloak*, p. 267.

[3] "Two Centuries of Publishing," *The Times*, November 6, 1924, p. 17.

[4] Archibald Scarlyn Wilson of 7 Warrior Square, St. Leonards-on-Sea. His last entries in the *Medical Directory* and the *Medical Register* are for 1945.

Haggard was well enough by the 25th of the month to attend another public meeting in London and address an audience on "The Good and the Bad of the Imagination."[1] But during the meeting he suffered a relapse. He took to bed again. Here is his diary entry for Christmas:

December 27 [1924]
   Another Christmas has come and gone, a mild, open Christmas with the sun shining. (Today it is blowing a mean gale from the southwest with torrents of rain.) It has not been a pleasant Christmas for me. About a month ago, after various preliminary illnesses and symptoms at St. Leonards and indeed before I left Ditchingham (including an almost total loss of appetite), on the top of an attack of gout, I was seized with a disease which the doctors have diagnosed as infection of the bladder by germs. Certainly it is one from which I hope that my worst enemies (if I have any) may be spared. To let the details be, it has made an invalid of me and there are symptoms that I do not altogether like. I had to sit through a Christmas Day dinner at which my grandsons, as children do on these occasions, did justice to their creature cravings, and I shall not forget the experience. Well, we must suffer what it pleases God to send us with such patience as we may, but I begin to think that my active career is at an end. I wished to begin a new romance, but I cannot face it. On Christmas Day I did manage to get to the second service in a motor car, and to sit it out. I suppose it is the first time I had been able to enter a church for about six weeks!

Haggard's daughter remembers noticing that "he had changed . . . in some intangible fashion. . . . His hands had grown oddly thin, so thin that the heavy Egyptian rings which he wore almost slipped off them. Also his face had settled into . . . [a] brooding sadness."[2]
   Still, some of the old vitality was there, and one gets glimpses of Haggard dictating to Ida Hector and even writing himself. The image of his declining days is reflected in a series of sixteen letters he received from Kipling.

Bateman's, Burwash, Sussex
February 15, 1925

Dear old man,
   I heard, a day or two ago, that you are under the weather at Ditchingham; and I write at once to send you mixed condolences and con-

[1] Haggard's diary, November 28, 1924; Scott, p. 218.
[2] *Cloak*, p. 278.

gratulations. In a hell-broth of a winter like this, bed's the best and soundest place there is; and, anyhow, all England is one filthy ditch (full) at present. So lie up in peace: only send me a line when you feel like it.

We've been visiting Elsie at Brussels in her new house[1] (she charged me to send you her special love next time I saw you) and only came back a few days ago.

The young couple were giving a fancy Ball (1850 epoch) and, at the same time, were on the edge of 'flu. The ball was a great success; particularly as they introduced the esurient Belgae to sausage and mash *and* beer at 3-a.m! Then they devoted 'emselves to their colds. Elsie recovered quickly but her husband got it very thoroughly. All Brussels reeked of 'flu. (Another cause, by the way, for abiding between blankets.) But they were, and are very happy. She has a polyglot establishment which includes one Spaniard, two Welsh (a *most*

---

[1] The Kiplings often visited their daughter, Elsie, and her husband, Capt. George Louis St. Clair Bambridge (1892–1943). The couple met when Bambridge came to Bateman's after Kipling had interviewed him in connection with that immense labour, *The Irish Guards in the Great War* (1923). Bambridge was a brave officer who had been wounded several times and decorated with the Military Cross "for conspicuous gallantry and devotion to duty." [Rudyard Kipling, *The Irish Guards in the Great War*, II, 236] Elsie Kipling and he became close friends, and in 1924, when the Kiplings visited Madrid, where Bambridge was military attaché at the British Embassy, they became engaged. They were married in October in London, and went to live in Brussels, where Bambridge was then serving. Elsie has recalled that after she was married, her father's "abiding interest was now to be everything that concerned my new life. The house, furniture, domestic arrangements, friends, social doings, and above all my health, everything interested him. He wrote me long letters, demanding details of every kind, from the description of a court ball to plans for improvements in the kitchen. My parents visited us in Brussels, afterwards in Madrid (where we returned in 1926) and later in Paris. They enjoyed, I think, the parties we gave for them, as well as the more formal entertainments at the embassies, and our various homes were a constant source of interest to them. When I was asked . . . to urge my father to make a speech at a big dinner in Paris, he undertook the task to please me without a question." [Elsie Bambridge, "Epilogue," Carrington, pp. 402–403] In 1936, when Kipling died, Capt. Bambridge wrote the following entry in his diary: "My sorrow at losing R.K. is great. He was wonderfully kind to me and I shall miss him much. He was far away the greatest living Englishman to-day, wonderfully far-seeing and great-hearted, and his work will live." [Carrington, p. 393; "Obituary: Fallen Officers: Captain G. L. St. C. Bambridge," *The Times*, December 24, 1943, p. 7; "Funeral: Captain G. L. St. C. Bambridge," *The Times*, December 22, 1943, p. 7]

foreign nation), one English and a background of Belgian cook and Walloon scullion. Whereby, life is a perpetual pentecost! Oh yes, and she has launched into a spotted female spaniel-dog called "Issy," since all the world says "Ici" to a dog. Quite complete you see. And there's any amount of receptions, balls and functions, in the diplomatic line, to attend to; and unlimited calling and visiting between. Not the life you or I would get out of bed for, but it pleases 'em and they are working hard. We went on for a day or two into Holland (Amster- and Rotter-dam) which is the most unreal country under the wet heavens! Never conceived how absolutely artificial it is in every way till I saw the farmers making it by dredging it out of the canals. They are manufacturing arms for the Hun's next war, and enjoying enormous and expensive prosperity. It's nice to see the aeroplanes being tried out for the Boches, overhead, and to see the tremendous traffic all round. Virtue, old man, does *not* pay in Continental politics.

(Which reminds me. What of your War and Post War diaries? A good deal of what you foresaw (as you told me) six or eight years ago ought to have ripened by now. Are you going to make any use of it; or are you going to have it locked up in the B.M. with instructions to open it next Armageddon?)[1]

We came home from Ostend, riding on the tail of one of the liveliest gales I have seen in the Channel for a long time, and when the steamer turned end for end to back in, I felt that my stomach and I were going to part brass rags[2] at last!

Now we're back in our valley but we haven't been able to get on the land for months literally. The whole place is a quagmire: the winter wheat dead by the look of it: no manure-shifting possible and the cattle stoaching up every pasture. I've got two bulls—one Sussex and one Guernsey. They live within earshot of each other and behave—like rival politicians. I don't hear (talking of politicians) even the hardiest and hardest-mouthed among 'em prophesying any sort of future for Ll. George.[3] He has just gone out—him and his sunsets and his moun-

[1] See p. 116 above.

[2] To part brass rags: to quarrel. It was a naval expression in the 1890's based on the "bluejacket's habit of sharing brass cleaning rags with his particular friend." [E. Partridge, *A Dictionary of Slang and Unconventional English* (1950), p. 607]

[3] After the War, Lloyd George provoked widespread disapproval of his handling of the Irish Question and the Greco-Turkish conflict, and when, in 1922, the Conservatives withdrew their support from his coalition govern-

tains and his banners of dawn. You said he would. You said the mob threw him up and the mob would throw him down. But I never conceived it would be so completely or so soon. And Squiff[1] is dead—dead in the dug-out that he spent his mischievous leisure in deriding. Oh it's a cheerful world, full of sincerity and altruism. But I *do* believe Baldwin[2] is reasonably sincere and honest, and that some of his followers are too.

---

ment, his ministry fell. As early as 1909, Kipling disagreed vehemently with Lloyd George's social measures and remained his severe critic for decades to follow. [Carrington, pp. 314, 337, 342, 379] In 1906, when Lloyd George was President of the Board of Trade, Haggard wrote him about his experiments with marram grass to stop coast erosion, and Lloyd George appointed him a member of the Commission on Coast Erosion (see p. 66 above). In 1909, as Chancellor of the Exchequer, Lloyd George set up the Development Board (see p. 143 below), on which Haggard was eager to serve because of his interest in agriculture and afforestation, and Lloyd George did in fact propose him. But because of political in-fighting, Haggard's name was struck from the list of Commissioners. [*Days*, II, 209, 221–22, 224]

[1] Between 1908 and 1916 the social reform programme of the Liberal Prime Minister Herbert Henry Asquith (1852–1928) led him into bitter conflict with the House of Lords, whose power he was largely responsible for breaking. His career in the Commons came to an end in October, 1924, when he was defeated for re-election at Paisley. The King immediately offered him a peerage. He accepted and entered the "dug-out" as Earl of Oxford and Asquith in 1925. Asquith was Prime Minister when the Poet Laureateship became vacant on Alfred Austin's death in 1913, and his daughter recalls that her father discussed the problem with her: "The obvious choice was Rudyard Kipling. [But] . . . what weighed with him was . . . that Kipling was inspired and could not write to order. Bridges . . . would be more likely to be able to do so. He wrote, offering it to Bridges." [Carrington, p. 305] As early as 1903 Haggard had "some light acquaintance" with Asquith, and when he read a report of a speech that Asquith made in which he argued for "a vastly increased output of home-grown food," Haggard sent him a copy of *Rural England* and wrote pointing out the virtues of small holdings. [*Days*, II, 149–50]

[2] Stanley Baldwin (1867–1947) had assumed his second ministry (November 1924–June 1929). He and Kipling were first cousins (their mothers were sisters). When they were boys, Kipling was Baldwin's "chief friend" during holiday seasons [G. M. Young, *Stanley Baldwin* (1952), p. 19]; and on Kipling's wedding day, Baldwin came to lunch with the couple at Brown's Hotel. When, on their return from Vermont, the Kiplings settled among the family at Rottingdean, Kipling and Baldwin grew fast friends; and "Stan" and "Cissie" Baldwin were the "first family visitors" to come to Bateman's in 1902. Kipling's biographer tells us that in "the late summer of 1909 Kipling saw much of two friends in Parliament, his cousin Stanley Baldwin and

Are you doing anything with the pen: or are you just answering the letters of the helpless, the crank, the imbecile and the lazy all over the world? That is a whole-time job as you know. And what have you done about our friend Ahasuerus the Wanderer?[1] Also, what are your filmed stories like to look at?[2] I haven't seen a thing for months and months. Recommend me what to attend.

And here I've gone yarning on about nothing. Don't you bother to reply but tell Miss Hector to send a secretarial line at your good leisure.

I'm going off to try to finish a speech—on shipping!—which I'm supposed to say next week.

The wife joins me in her best wishes and I am, as you have always known,

Ever affectionately,
Rudyard.

P.S. Is this (the only religious) limerick on record, new to you? It was to me.

Andrew Bonar Law, and attended one of the violent debates over the Budget." [Carrington, p. 314] In May 1917, Baldwin, then a member of the Cabinet, brought a message from the Prime Minister, Lloyd George, that Kipling could have "any honour he will accept," but Kipling would have none. Baldwin's increasingly liberal views caused an amount of coolness to arise between them. Kipling is supposed to have said that "Stanley is a Socialist at heart," and Carrie "mistrusted him and thought him spoiled by power. Nevertheless [Kipling's biographer adds], the close family friendship was maintained; the Kiplings often stayed at Astley, the Baldwins' home in Worcestershire; were regularly invited to Chequers, the Prime Minister's official country house; often dined in Downing Street." [Carrington, p. 378] Certainly Kipling was able to write his cousin affectionate, consoling letters when Baldwin suffered political reverses [see Young, pp. 154–55]. Although Baldwin was himself lucid and of a literary bent, he frequently asked Kipling to write or polish his non-political addresses, and one of Baldwin's biographers goes as far as to suggest that he modelled his platform personality on Kipling's poem "If." [Bechhofer Roberts, Stanley Baldwin: Man or Miracle? (1936), p. 254] Stanley Baldwin's wife was Lucy Ridsdale Baldwin. [Carrington, pp. 149, 200, 353, 384]

[1] Kipling and Haggard had already discussed the plan for a story that Haggard might write about the Wandering Jew (pp. 125–27 above).

[2] At least eleven of Haggard's novels had been turned into films. Moon of Israel first appeared in 1924 and a second film of She could be seen in 1925. [Scott, 225–27]

"Oh God, forasmuch as without Thee
We are not enabled to doubt Thee,
So grant us Thy Grace
We may teach every race
That Thy children know nothing about Thee!"

Father Knox is supposed to be responsible.

Bateman's, Burwash, Sussex
February 21, 1925

Dear old man,

A simple hell of a day—grey low skies and snow that turns into rain just dribbling out of it like a man chewing a quid.

I've come back from the low game of speech making to an assembly of ship-owners (overwhelmingly Scotch!) in town. Not knowing anything about ship owning—and never, even, having been wrecked —I could speak with perfect assurance and impartiality. Which I did ![1] And this Sabbath morn, the President of the Board of Trade[2] is coming to lunch. Knowing nothing whatever about trade, I shall tell him exactly how to run his own job. And that's about all the news, save that, like a fool, I've bought a couple more stud-book Sussex cows to build up a herd with, and the land is just as wet and untouchable as ever.

And they talk about "small-holdings"—Yah! I wish to goodness you'd look up your old notes on that subject, and let the public know what you think about it now. With the dole in full blast, it seems to me the damnedest folly one could invent.[3]

[1] For Kipling's speech on shipping, see *A Book of Words* (1928), pp. 267–72; for the story of Haggard having been wrecked, see p. 109 above.

[2] Philip Cunliffe-Lister, 1st Earl of Swinton (b. 1884), who has kindly replied to a query about his visit to Bateman's:

I remember spending the day with Kipling at Bateman's, but I do not remember the talk he refers to in his letter. It sounds as if it was about agriculture. That was not my Ministry; but no doubt Kipling knew that I was a countryman and a landowner and had always been interested in agricultural policy.

I remember some young Naval officers coming over from Portsmouth for tea and being struck by the easy way Kipling drew them out about all the details of a new ship they had just joined. [Letter dated May 26, 1964]

[5] Haggard was a strong champion of small holdings; in fact, he saw the small-holding approach to farming as England's solution to her agricultural

Town was swept by a razor-faced East wind and stank of earnest and voluble M.P.'s. As a village London is grossly over-rated.

I want to know if you [are] browzing among your papers and notes with any definite plan made. I ask this because I was talking with Kenyon[1] the other night and he told me, what doubtless you know but I didn't, that the British Museum was the place to store things in that one wanted opened a certain number of years later! One has only got to put the chosen date and instructions on the tin box deposited, and that meritorious national institution will attend to it. I have a whole mass of incredible stuff for war-stories that has come my way in the past few years and I'm thinking of decanting it all in that direction.[2] Elsie in her last letter bids me send you her best love. She is fighting Belgoose domestics and Welsh maids in alternate battles— like Napoleon, but unlike him hasn't any Marshals to help her! I'm doing some damnably bad verses and trying to look over a lot of old stories for a book.[3] Thanks for what you say about the Moon of Israel which I will try to see next time I am in town. Now I'll put this away for a bit and go on with my insane-asylum of a mail. Most people, my dear boy, are incurably mad *and* idle. Here's a female just weighed in with a request for me to hunt up a quotation for her which she can't find. She's been through the book it is in—as plain as print—and 'tis me that has to indicate the precise page. I know they think with their latter ends but they might, at odd times, use their eyes.

---

ills, and for decades he sought unsuccessfully for Government support of his schemes. As with all things he strongly believed in, he wrote, spoke, and campaigned for reform, and the climax of his utterances is to be found in his book *Rural Denmark and Its Lessons* (1911), which resulted from his inspection of Danish farms and farming methods. [*Rider Haggard*, pp. 247–50]

[1] Sir Frederic George Kenyon (1863–1952), Director and Principal Librarian of the British Museum.

[2] Although a number of autograph drafts and manuscripts of Kipling articles, stories, and poems are in the British Museum, the Assistant Keeper of the Department of Manuscripts reports that Kipling's "intention ... [to leave his 'mess of incredible stuff for war-stories' to the Museum] does not appear to have been put into practice." [Letter from Miss J. M. Backhouse dated April 9, 1964]

[3] *Debits and Credits*, a volume of fourteen stories, predominantly about the war, and twenty-one poems, only two of which had appeared in periodicals. The volume would appear in September, 1926.

Out at this speech-making show, I met the Norweegee minister[1] who had just discovered Egypt. He went down there, this year, led, he says, by your Works: and he was immensely full of it and of them. A nice chap with the curious drawled Scandinavian accent, that I can't help liking.

And a chap from Berlin has sent me the corpus of a book of letters from prisoners of the Bolshies, in those northern camps under the Arctic circle—with photos and facsimiles of letters. It's one of the most appalling glimpses into Hell that ever you did see. I don't know when it will be published nor do I expect that our press will take much notice of it.[2] It is the horrible perversion and ingenuity of the torments, moral and physical, that makes one sick. As a breed man ain't much, Rider, unless he is looked after with a club - - -.

Got the more insane letters docketted for the sec. She isn't like Miss H. You've got to tell her in so many words what to say instead of merely breathing a damn across the letter as you chuck it over. She's young but most interested and energetic—specially about the farms and the work on 'em. But when one comes to review one's mis-spent life, don't it seem to you, that most of our time was spent in suffering fools as gladly, or otherwise, as our temperament permitted?

Now I *know* (I've just been doing my Sunday reading) that of all the lies that Paul told, his statement (or implication) that he suffered 'em gladly was the biggest. He didn't—by a dam sight. It soured the little man badly. Likewise (you'll see it in today's Lessons and yester-

[1] The Norwegian Envoy Extraordinary and Minister Plenipotentiary to the Court of St. James from 1910 to 1934 was Paul Benjamin Vogt (1863–1947).

[2] The Northern Camps of Special Designation (SLON), at the core of which were the camps of the Solovetski Islands, formed the base of the Russian labour camp network. In 1925 seven thousand prisoners were being held there. For further details, see David J. Dallin and Boris I. Nicolaevsky, *Forced Labor in Soviet Russia* (1947), ch. viii, which includes a first-hand account of "The Solovetski Camp and Its Inhabitants" by a former prisoner, Mr. Boris Sapir. The British public did not in fact have to wait long for an account of the Russian camps, for in 1926, S. A. Malsagoff, who escaped in 1925, after more than a year in the Solovki, published *An Island Hell* in London. For references to other books about the camps, the bibliography in the Dallin and Nicolaevsky volume is useful, but it provides no clue about the fate of the particular manuscript of which Kipling writes. *Out of the Deep* (1933), with an introduction by Hugh Walpole and a preface by Sir Bernard Pares, contains letters from German colonists from the Lower Volga and Crimea who were inmates of Soviet timber camps.

day's) what perfect *swine* were the Israelites when they started in Bolshevizing the relatively honest Hivites and Jebusites and Hittites;[1] and how wholly unaltered is their racial type: Which reminds me, what do you make of the intended significance of Jahveh saying that He'd "put His Hand" over Moses when He hid him in a cleft of the rock, against the blaze of His Glory? I can't see what was in the translator's mind.[2]

And here, my handwriting is getting too bad even as a mustard-plaster for a sick man. So I'll shut up. Don't you bother to answer unless you care to dictate a few words just to let me know how you feel yourself to be. Half a page'll do for this child.

I've been putting in a spare time of self-examination, rather envying your record. I wish, by the way, you'd get out and have put together, your views, expressed and personal, on emigration.[3] Cook of Australia[4] (a *most* direct man) says that the accursed Dole is knocking emigration on the head.

Ever affectionately,
Rudyard.

[1] Kipling either misdated the letter or finished it the next day. February 22 was Quinquagesima Sunday; the Lesson was I Cor. xiii.1 ff. St. Paul on Christianity ("suffer fools gladly"), II Cor. xi.19, was the Lesson for the previous Sunday. The First Lesson on February 22 covered the first eleven verses of Ex. xxxiii. Verse 2 has the reference to the Hivites, Jebusites and Hittites. But Kipling must have read on to the end of the chapter (part of the Lesson for February 23) because Verse 22 is the one he asks Haggard about in the next sentence.

[2] The Lord is speaking to Moses: "And it shall come to pass, while my glory passeth by, that I will put thee in a cleft of the rock, and will cover thee with my hand while I pass by." Ex. xxxiii.22 (see n. 1 above). I cannot understand why Kipling had difficulty with the passage. The Lord put His hand over Moses certainly to shield him from the blaze of His glory.

[3] Haggard never assembled his writings on emigration. But his views are available in official and unofficial records. The two official sources for his opinions are his report to the Royal Colonial Institute, *The After-War Settlement and Employment of Ex-Service Men in the Overseas Dominions* (London: The Royal Colonial Institute, 1916) and the reports of the Dominions Royal Commission published from 1912 to 1917 (First Interim Report, Cd. 6515, 1912; to Chief Harbours of the British Empire, Cd. 8461, 1917). [For a detailed list of these reports, see Scott, p. 134.] Haggard's opinions were also recorded informally in interviews for the Press and in letters to editors. [For some of these, see the following item numbers in Scott: 241–42, 264, 535, 537–39, 541–42, 548.]

[4] Sir Joseph Cook (1860–1947), High Commissioner for Australia (1921–27).

Bateman's, Burwash, Sussex
February 28 [1925]

Dear old man,

Yours about small-holdings. "Keep your hair on" as the boys used to say. I haven't your Isaiah-like gift of promiscuous fulmination but, believe me, I gave the Board of Trade man pretty much the same sort of stuff as you've written me. But I forgot about work in the woods in winter as a necessary adjunct. I added "all out of me own head" that the small-holder would at once sell out to the speculative builder. Which he dam-well would![1]

Now hear me moan! The land is porridge. We send out whiskey, with the drenches, to the wretched little calves that are now being born; we litter down twice a day and the wet bog swallows it all: *all* my winter wheat is dead. No one has been able to set foot on the land since November and *all* my sheep have foot-rot, so we are mending roads, out of a newly opened quarry (did I tell you) and the men are so bored with past idleness that they are working with interest! Call me a liar, but it's true! I've been up to town to attend one of the P.M. (Mrs. P.M's) receptions[2] and there met approximately two million politicians. *Why* does the type never vary? Was it so in the days of Rameses. But some of the young 'uns aren't so bad—at least they haven't yet caught the damnable disease of window-dressing.

Your tale of old Egypt[3] hasn't turned up yet. Please jog Miss Hector's memory; I want to see it. By the way I don't believe anything ever was "primitive" in the world after the time of the Taung's skull.[4] I bet your early Gippos were as stale and world-used as any one on the planet now. And I bet, too, they knew it. You've gone back pretty far into history of the ages, and behind 'em, but I notice your people are much like our folk. It stands to reason old man that the world's *very* limited modicum of thinking was done millions of years

[1] See p. 134 above.

[2] "Mrs. Stanley Baldwin held an 'at home' at 10 Downing Street yesterday for the members of the Government and her personal friends. The Prime Minister, the Hon. Mrs. Arthur Howard, ... and Miss Betty Baldwin assisted to entertain guests." The guests included the Polish Minister and Mr. Paderewski, Mrs. Churchill, and the Lithuanian Minister. ["Reception—Mrs. Baldwin," *The Times*, February 20, 1925, p. 17]

[3] *Queen of the Dawn: A Love Tale of Old Egypt* was published on April 21, 1925.

[4] The Taungs Skull, discovered in 1924 at Taungs, Bechuanaland, has been identified as belonging to the Pleistocene Age. It is about one million years old.

ago; and that what we mistake for thought nowadays is the reaction of our own damned machinery on our own alleged minds. Get an odd volume of Tyler's *Primitive Culture*[1] and see how far this squares with fact. Not being a philosopher, I haven't the time to develop the thesis.

Now what's my small beer for retail? Oh, there's a young N.O. (almost born at Bateman's) turning up for lunch to show us the girl he's engaged to.[2] Gwynne of the M.P.[3] comes for the night and to-morrow two young married couples (one of 'em Stan Baldwin's daughter[4] and, practically, my child also since her babydom) for lunch. They're both deep in house-building, nesting like young birds with a nestling apiece so far. So, you see, the machine goes on and on. P'raps it has a *vis* of its own to recover this spent world.

Elsie has been really enjoying life. She has a Welsh maid—moody and temperamental—who suddenly developed a lump on her side (small rupture, as a matter of fact, curable by a bandage). *That* didn't matter a jot beside the continuous and exhaustive hysterics which she at once developed in the belief that she [was] falling or splitting in twain! And E. had to look after her! Now the maid is quite well thank you, and as nearly ashamed of herself as any compatriot of Ll. George can be and Elsie is—rather tired. She wrote in her last sending you her special love. D'you know that kid's *very* fond of you? Always was (and so was John) and Francis[5] (the kid who gave you or from

[1] Edward Burnett Tylor, *Primitive Culture, Researches into the Development of Mythology, Philosophy, Religion, Art, and Custom* (2 vols., 1871).

[2] Unidentified.

[3] H. A. Gwynne of the *Morning Post* (see p. 56 above).

[4] The Hon. Arthur Jared Palmer (b. 1896) and Mrs. Lorna Stanley Howard, later the Hon. Sir Arthur and Lady Lorna Howard. The other young couple were Donald Sterling Palmer (b. 1891), elder brother of the Hon. Arthur Howard (1891–1959), later 3d Baron Strathcona and Mount Royal, and his wife, Diana Evelyn. [I am indebted for this information to the Rt. Hon. Oliver Ridsdale Baldwin, 2d Earl Baldwin of Bewdley.]

[5] The Kiplings met Julia Catlin of New York and her two daughters on a journey to Bermuda in 1894, and they remained friends for the rest of their lives. Frances (Kipling consistently misspells her name), one of the daughters, married Dr. Ernest Gerald Stanley, an English surgeon practising in France, and the Kiplings and the Stanleys paid frequent visits to each other. Mrs. Stanley died in 1937, and Dr. Stanley does not recall what incident gave rise to the joke about the cold. [Carrington, pp. 165, 387; letter from Dr. E. G. Stanley dated September 24, 1964]

whom you caught the cold that you wrangled about) has never forgotten. It must be nice to inspire affection at short notice. I haven't the
gift. Like olives and caviare and asafoetida, I'm an acquired taste,
stealing slowly on the senses. . . . Oh, here's a chaste selection from my
mail (since you are off-duty you may as well enjoy a busman's holiday).
(1) Request to put 20 stories into "literary style" for a retired mercan-
tile marine captain on his uppers. Would you like the job? (2) Join
Committee for International Memorial to Byron and help us get 10,
or 15, thousand quid out of the public. Nice, alluring job! (3) Give
away prizes at a modern and progressive girls' school! (*Just* your
style.)[1] (4) Write text-book for Schools on "overseas settlement."
D'you know it's vulgar to talk of emigration, these days? (5) *Ditto, ditto*
to appeal (Allah knows why!) to the natural idealism of the young. (6)
Write "poem" rebuking lazy bricklayers. (7) Take up two or three
perfectly impossible scandals about the price of bread and the importa-
tion of motor parts . . . *Isn't* it just the same old world, and the same
old mail-bag! My dear Rider you be glad you're in bed—even if
those damnable nights are long and even Ecclesiasticus who is my
refuge, doesn't help always. I've had a touch of it and done a deuce of
a lot of thinking—the sum and substance of which is that I wish I had
as straight and high a record as you have of work done. But I never
took on Commissions and now I rather regret it.

Dictate me another letter some time when you're in a better (or a
worse!) temper. Let me hear you cuss the present state of things. I'm
run out of comminations for the moment: but I am

Ever affectionately thine,
Rudyard.

---

[1] Haggard's quick mind enabled him to make the occasional speech from
jottings on an envelope set down in the train on his way to the place where he
would speak. Twenty-nine pages of Scott's *Bibliography* . . . are devoted to an
incomplete list of Press reports of Haggard's speeches. Very often Haggard
used these public appearances as ways of campaigning for his favourite causes.
A school governor has written of such an occasion: "During the latter part of
Rider Haggard's life the Cambridge and County Boys' School . . . got him to
present the prizes at one of its Speech Days, hoping that he would talk about
his adventure stories. Instead, he gave a lecture on agricultural economics. The
Governor who proposed the vote of thanks referred to him as Mr. Rudyard
Kipling throughout the speech. Rider Haggard replied in the character of
Rudyard Kipling." [Letter from Mr. R. F. Rattray, Cambridge, dated August
5, 1960]

Two days later, Haggard did dictate a letter to Kipling, fourteen pages long, in which he takes a backward glance and tries to assess his life's work. Kipling must have valued it enough to break his rule about burning incoming letters, for it survives as part of Mrs. Bambridge's collection of Kipling Papers.

Ditchingham House, Norfolk.
March 2, 1925

My dear Rudyard,

Yours of Feb: 28th gratefully received. I say—whiskey at 12/6 a bottle is worth almost as much, if plentifully administered, as the calf it is meant to cheer. It is a melancholy tale upon the very heavy lands, I know, and how anything is to be made out of them this year, I can't see.

Even here Longrigg[1] is finding great difficulty with the land.—But it was ever thus; if one thing ain't wrong with agriculture, another is. You pays your penny and takes your choice. And yet it goes on for ever. As I have said in the "Farmer's Year," a 1000 years hence it will be exactly the same tale—that is, while there are women to breed and children to feed, and, as I have also said somewhere, you lose money more slowly at farming than at anything else, and unless it be your last copper, there is some amusement in watching it go.

My dear boy, you almost bring tears to my eyes (they are very near them when one is weak) by some of the things you say. For instance, when you compare my humble record with your own, by which it is not fit to stand—but comparisons are odious.

Still is it true that under many disabilities and in the teeth of much official opposition (Lord! how officials hate the outsider with ideas) I have done my best to serve my country to the full extent of my small opportunities which, generally, I have had to *make*. Some fifteen years solid of it I have put in as one of the great unpaid on these accursed Commissions,[2] etc., which really are trying because of the small minds that often you have to fight upon them. You argue and wear yourself out and they vote you down, and then in after years come and say they

---

[1] Haggard's bailiff. [*Cloak*, p. 18]

[2] In addition to the Commissions already mentioned, Haggard served on the Commission on Imperial Communication, the National Birth Rate Commission, and the East African Inquiry Commission.

are so sorry, as now they see that you were absolutely right and they were absolutely wrong.

However, so far as the R. Commissions are concerned, the effort *seems* to have been utterly wasted, that is, if anything earnest is ever wasted in the end. When they had served the Government purpose they were chucked aside on the national rubbish heap at Whitehall.

The only things that appear to have succeeded at all are what I have done off my own bat—such as the "Rural England" work and my mission on behalf of the R. Colonial Institute during the war.

To take the latter first. It was bitterly opposed by the Colonial Office at the time, I never quite found out why. Partly I think, however, from a kind of jealousy of such important matters being put into the hands of one whose findings carried some weight with the Public because they were known, at any rate, to be earnest and honest; and partly from fear lest I should make trouble with the Government of the Dominions at a critical time, or stir up the passions of Labour thereby advocating the settling in them of migrants.

Do you know I found out that they even went the length of writing round to the various Governors to caution them heavily against me? Well, the results of it all were far different from what was anticipated. Instead of angering the Dominions, I conciliated them, and I may say honestly that I converted a hostile Australia to my views, and brought home offers that were worth millions—which were thrown away by our Government.

These developments were received with official amazement, because you see duly appointed missions do not often produce much effect, and the end of it was that they were driven to appoint a Committee upon which I served. Out of the findings of that Committee sprang the present Migration Act,[1] which is imperfect and insufficient enough, but still a beginning—an egg out of which great things will, I hope, grow in time—and, honestly, I believe I had something to do with that egg.

It's all forgotten now (and indeed would be denied probably with indignation) except perhaps by my kindly old friend who thinks I ought to be sworn of the Privy Council, and, apparently, at intervals so informs those who dispense such carrots. Quite without avail of course, for who wishes (especially if of the Conservative faith I have

---

[1] An Act to make better provision for furthering British settlement in His Majesty's Oversea Dominions (Empire Settlement Act), 1922, 12 & 13 Geo. 5, c. 13.

observed) to decorate the manes and tails of worn-out old horses with ribbons? But that don't matter one way or the other. Still honestly I believe the truth to be as I have stated.

The same thing with Rural England. After that Lloyd George consulted me on sundry occasions about the setting up of his Development Board,[1] its possible Chairman, etc. Indeed he went further, announcing that I was to be a member of that Board, sending Ashby St. Ledgers, now Lord Wimborne[2] to me to say so, with the result that, Lord Richard Cavendish[3] in the chair, I attended the preliminary meeting. Ultimately, however, he threw me over to suit a political convenience. So the Board was established without me, to whom no explanations were offered. Only I think I had something to do with its origin.

But what is the use of dragging up all this past history, of which there is plenty more. I only wanted to show you that I have done the best I can single-handed, fighting against principalities and darksome, unknown powers in Government offices, and on the whole, since in such matters one should put oneself out of the question, I am not dissatisfied with the results.

What you say about Elsie touches me. Please tell the dear girl so when you write. Also about John. Lying in bed here day after day, one dissects oneself with thoroughness and alas—a somewhat miserable anatomy appears.

Lack of sufficient principle, or so it seems to me, rashness, want of steady aim (except where the country was concerned of which at heart

[1] The Development Commission administered the Development Grant, created in 1909 under the Development and Road Improvement Fund Act and the Development Act Amendment Bill. The Grant was used to promote "schemes which have for their purpose the development of the resources of the country." [Lloyd George, as quoted in *The Times*, April 30, 1910, p. 9]

[2] Sir Ivor Churchill Guest (1873–1939), 3d Baronet and first Viscount Wimborne, cousin of Winston Churchill. From 1906 to 1909 he was Chairman of the Royal Commission on Coast Erosion and Afforestation of which Haggard was a member. In his autobiography, Haggard recalls their service together on the Commission: "Lord Ashby St. Ledgers was at that time quite a young man whom I liked very much, and with whom I got on extremely well; indeed he was always most kind and considerate to me." [*Days*, II, 209–10]

[3] The Rt. Hon. Lord Richard Frederick Cavendish (1871–1946), younger brother of the 9th Duke of Devonshire, served as chairman of the Development Commission.

I have always been the servant) and of character, liability to be swept away by primary impulses, which you will observe never trouble heroes in really first-class novels, for these turn them on and off with a tap of which the spout is directed only towards the heroine—all these bones and others equally unseemly, such as little secret jealousies, are very large and prominent. But the Powers that made me thus, perhaps to excite strength of repentance and opposition, did give me one great gift which probably I don't deserve—that of attracting the affection of which you speak—though this has sometimes been of a kind that leads to disaster.

For example since I have been so ill I have been much moved (leaving out my own family of whose devotion I need not speak) to observe in what real regard, love I might almost say, I am held, amongst others, by my nephews and nieces, none of whom have anything to expect from me. It is really very affecting.

Always it has been so. I remember when I was a young fellow overhearing my Chief—Sompseu (Sir T. Shepstone)[1] say "I love that boy," as I passed him, and so I think it was with all of them. But they were all much older men than I, and are long dead. Indeed, except yourself and Charles Longman,[2] all my old friends are now gone and: I have only made one new one of late years, Ronald Ross.[3] To tell the truth the sole exceptions in this record of affection were among my own brethren some of whom seemed to resent such small success as came my way, or to find other fault with me.[4] But that is often the case in families—and now they have passed away, and their children take a very different view.

So this is much to be thankful for, especially as I am one of those

[1] See p. 99 above. Sompseu, the name the Kaffirs gave Shepstone, means "Mighty Hunter" [Days, I, 58].

[2] Charles James Longman (1852–1934), eminent London publisher, was a close personal friend of Haggard's and for many years his own publisher. He too served on the East African Commission (see p. 147 below).

[3] Sir Ronald Ross (1857–1932) made major discoveries that led to the understanding and control of malaria and African fever. His contribution to the fight against malaria earned him, in 1902, the Nobel Prize in Physiology and Medicine. Haggard and Ross became friends late in life, and they often went on fishing trips together. [For an account of two of these trips and other material bearing upon the Haggard–Ross friendship, see Cloak, pp. 268–71.]

[4] For an account of some of Haggard's family difficulties, see Rider Haggard, pp. 253–54.

who believe that Love as distinct from passion, does not die. If anything lives, that must—from the Love of God down.

I will tell you a little story. About 30 years ago there came to this village as purchaser of the Hall and all the lands about, a hard-faced Yorkshireman with a slit where his mouth ought to be, who had spent his long life in amassing and inheriting great wealth and now wished to found a family. He detested me out of a kind of jealousy and because to him my name was—Naboth. On every occasion he tried to get around me and to mop up for his son all that was going, such as the Chairmanship of Quarter Sessions, etc., and other public offices, to say nothing of land around me, and at first his son abetted him.

Well, he died and somewhat to his astonishment the son found that he was fighting a bolster which never hit back. The end of it was that he, a very able man in his way but hard like his father, came to like me more and more, till at length not long before his death he was heard to say that he had many acquaintances but only one friend—myself. As was to [be] expected from his ability backed by his wealth, he rose and would probably have been elected Chairman of the County Council next month, also he was to be High Sheriff next year, and so on, perhaps looking forward to a baronetcy for his family at the end. Then Destiny took up the reins and he developed heart weakness. I, too, was ill but one day I thought I was strong enough to go to see him and arranged by telephone to do so. "Delightful," he said to his wife,—"Rider is coming to see me. How Delightful"—a few minutes later he was dead!

It was the same with old Dr. Bright, for many years Master of University College, Oxford, his father-in-law, whom he brought to live in one of his houses here. That odd and rather difficult old boy got very fond of me and when he was dying, it seems that the last words they caught from his lips were—"Give my love to Rider Haggard."[1]—I think, too, I have the warm regard of all the village people in this neighbourhood, all of which makes our mortal atmosphere more pleasant to breathe.

[1] The father was William Carr (1828–1905); the son was also William Carr (1862–1925). The son died on January 25, some five weeks before Haggard is writing. William Carr the younger had married Margaret, daughter of Reverend James Frank Bright (1832–1920), Master of University College, Oxford (1881–1906), author of History of England (5 vols., 1875–1904). [Burke's Genealogical and Heraldic History of Landed Gentry (1952), pp. 256, 387]

I am glad to say that I am somewhat better. I got up yesterday and sat in the old study next door for a little while, but of course my limbs are like sticks and the sight of *meat* is abhorrent to me. You would laugh to see me being fed by the nurse with milk pudding from a spoon just like a baby. Also my rings fall off my hands and there was the deuce of a hunt for one of them the other night—finally retrieved from the seat of my pyjamas.

By the way, I think I saw you had a birthday not long ago.[1] Would you like a present of a ring to use as a seal, for it is too massive to wear, copper I think with a little gold in it. Egyptian 18th Dynasty, and very curious in its way, probably a memorial ring of Akhenaton whose name has been perverted on it, perhaps because it was not lawful to use it after his death as it stood; just as the Zulus in my youth would not mention the names of their dead kings.

Miss Hector will send you an impression of the ring either today or tomorrow, also a copy of a note from Dr. Hall of the B. Museum[2] about it, and you can let me know. If so I should be very glad to give it you, for it is rather fine in its way and came, I think, from the Amherst Collection.[3]

Behold how long a letter I have written to you—with some one else's hand![4] Horribly egotistical, too, I fear, but your remarks brought this on your head. If it hasn't entirely floored you, write to me again when you have time.

Ever your affectionate friend
H. Rider Haggard.

P.S. The miscellaneous correspondent afflicts me also, if not quite so fiercely. But I think the people who annoy me most are those who

---

[1] Kipling had turned fifty-nine on December 30, 1924.

[2] Dr. Henry Reginald Holland Hall (1873–1930) was Keeper of Egyptian and Assyrian Antiquities in the British Museum from 1924 to 1930. Haggard had a collection of Egyptian antiquities, some of which he gave to the British Museum.

[3] After collecting rare books, manuscripts, tapestries, and Egyptian curiosities for over fifty years, William Amhurst Tyssen-Amherst, 1st Baron Amherst of Hackney (1835–1909), realized in 1906 that, owing to the dishonesty of the solicitor who administered his estate, he would have to sell much of his collection. Messrs. Sotheby auctioned off the valuable collection in December, 1908, and March, 1909.

[4] The letter is in Ida Hector's hand, but it bears Haggard's signature.

send one's picture, etc., to be autographed with no stamped addressed envelope for return. It is a regular game; there were two of them this morning. What a lot of people there are in the world who hope to get something for nothing out of me. And often such silly somethings, as you say.

The truth is I fought against this illness too long; I ought to have gone to bed much earlier. But I kept at it sitting on that E. African Committee[1] after dark to suit Lord Southborough's[2] convenience and so forth, and the thing grew and grew until it bowled me over.—

"Queen of the Dawn" has not been sent to you because it does not come out until the 6th.

Bateman's, Burwash, Sussex
(Received 6. March, 1925[3])

Dear old man,

Just a line on my return from town (ghastly N.E. wind, too!) to thank you a hundred times for Akhenaton's Seal (I'm sure he kept it in his Library) which you needn't tell me has no duplicate. It won't be lost—ins'h Allah! And it's going into safe and honourable keeping. I don't care so much about Akhenaton's dealings with it (he probably countersigned a lot of tosh of the Social Progress nature before he was busted) but that it has been yours and that you've given it to me does mean a lot to this teacher of the alphabet.

Have you ever thought, by the way, of having your bed of Ill-ease put into a sitting-room. When I was cut up[4] and fed up with the sight of bedroom crockery and washstands, they put me into a sitting-room —with good effects on mind and spirits. I recommend it. It only gives the nurse a very little more to do.

This don't count as a letter. I've got your long one to answer put by me. We're off on the 12th for a motor-trip down to Biarritz bay for a

---

[1] The East African Inquiry Committee, created in July, 1924, by the Secretary of State for the Colonies, was to examine and report on transportation, cotton growing, control of disease, health and economic improvement, native and non-native economic relations, and taxation of natives. ["East African Inquiry Committee," *The Times,* July 17, 1924, p. 14]

[2] Francis John Stephens Hopwood (1860–1947), 1st Baron Southborough, was Chairman of the East African Committee.

[3] In Haggard's hand.

[4] See pp. 121-22 above.

few weeks. If you can stick it, I'll try and send you a bit of a record of it now and then.

Now to my *dam* desk.

Affectionately,
R. K.

Bateman's, Burwash, Sussex
March 8, 1925

Dear old man,

Yes I value old Akhenaton's thumb-piece but more than that I value your exceedingly cock-eyed p.c. (No I won't sell it for an autograph!) which shows "evidences of design"—and improvement. *Did* you fabricate it lying on your belly, or did you do it from underneath—the thing held above you, as I've done under like circumstances?

You're wrong about "sordid details." I'm *the* expert in 'em. You *can't* be sordider than I've been: but I had the whole messy apparatus in the sitting-room. (You've no notion of the air that a fine upstanding commode gives to a private suite) and it gave the nurse a lot of healthy and innocent employment as long as I couldn't walk. After that I used to totter to the shrine appointed in the next room and so, by triumphant degrees and gradations, to the proper bathroom. (It strikes me you'd better burn *all* this correspondence. It trenches on the — abrupt).

We're off Thursday afternoon and are tidying up odds and ends. Tuesday, I put me in velvet and satin and, tied to a sword, attend a Levee at St. James's.[1] Wish you were there. After that—freedom to come and go in France from hotel to hotel. (You'll be tantalized with accounts of the grub if it's good.)

There's no news except that spring is here (with a hell of a N.W. wind) full of good intentions and on Her way to Norfolk to make you whole again and *exceedingly* fractious, against my return. Don't let your attendants persuade you that you're getting better. Mine tried that trick on me, whereupon I would burst into tears which (I didn't know it at the time) are signs of convalescence. I see our mutual friend George Nathaniel[2] has had a haemorrhage which "may necessitate an

[1] At the levee, Kipling was presented by the Prime Minister, Mr. Baldwin, to H.R.H. the Prince of Wales, serving as Deputy for the King. Presentations to the Prince of Wales were by the King's Command considered as equivalent as presentations to His Majesty. ["The King's Levee," *The Times*, March 11, 1925, p. 19]

[2] George Nathaniel Curzon (1859–1925), 1st Marquess Curzon of Kedles-

operation." We know something about that but I'd like you to meditate on George's notions of personal dignity and bearing when he is being examined (by electric light, same as the Simplon Tunnel) *previous* to the op. If I wasn't a poet, I'd send you a limerick on that exhibition.

Affectionately,

R.

P.S. If you haven't read Doughty's Arabia[1] for a good long time, I'd recommend it now. It's styptic, for one thing, in style and as Culpeper would say, "helps mightily against the emerods." I've tried it.

R.

---

ton. He served as Foreign Secretary in Baldwin's cabinet until January, 1923, and remained active as Lord Privy Seal for two more years. "In March 1925, while staying the night at Cambridge, Curzon recognized symptoms of grave internal disorder. He was taken next day to London and on 9 March an operation was performed." [*D. N. B.*] In spite of Kipling's optimistic note in the following letter, Curzon died on March 20. Kipling first met Curzon in May, 1897, at a "man's party of generals and military," and when, in 1899, as Viceroy of India, Curzon invited Kipling to return to Simla as his guest, Kipling refused because "viceroys, he said, were not much in his line." In 1907, when Curzon was made Chancellor of Oxford, he offered Kipling (and two old friends of Kipling's, "General" Booth and Mark Twain) an honorary degree. This Kipling accepted. [Carrington, pp. 198, 279] Haggard's relations with Curzon were of a somewhat different order. In 1885, when Haggard was enjoying his early fame, he wrote an indiscreet essay about the state of English fiction for the *Contemporary Review*. As it happened, the essay appeared while Haggard himself was away on one of his jaunts to Egypt. So inflammatory was the piece that it immediately evoked rebuttals, attacks, and denunciations on both sides of the Atlantic, with W. T. Stead and George Moore in the lead. Haggard's family and friends came to his defence in his absence. And Curzon, not yet acquainted with Haggard personally, wrote a letter to the editor of one of the papers that had denounced Haggard (very likely Stead's *Pall Mall Gazette*), which, in Haggard's words, "absolutely, utterly, and finally destroyed, squashed and obliterated the whole false case that had been set up against me." But Curzon's letter was never published. In 1919, recalling Curzon's early kindness, Haggard dedicated *When the World Shook* to him. [*Rider Haggard*, pp. 124–26] Kipling and Haggard approved many of Curzon's political policies, certainly his strong stand against Russia, but on Curzon's death Haggard wrote in his diary that "magnificent as it was, and in many ways successful, publicly speaking his career was still a failure. He could never catch the ear of the crowd, his cold and lofty manner was against him. In short, he had not the art of popularity." [March 26, 1925]

[1] Charles Montagu Doughty, *Travels in Arabia Deserta* (2 vols., 1888).

R.M.S.S. "NORMANNIA"
S'hampton
March 12, 1925
10 p.m.[1]

This looks like a regular ocean passage!

A clear cold night, almost dead still, with a full-faced moon that shines *bluish* on the docks and the mouths of the customs sheds. Hardly a soul about except a caretaker or two while we wandered from the hotel, over the railway lines, past "dead" unlighted boats to this packet, which plays at being an ocean-going liner. (We were a long time ahead of the boat train.) And stumbling up the gang-plank in the half-light an aged care-taker hailed us, who had been a Steward on the old *Kinfauns* Castle when the children were little and remembered, not only them, but the Stewards whom they affected and got things out of.[2] A curious and rather a touching talk on the empty deck, while our car, winking in the glare of the electrics, was slung on high and then dropped into the hold—as she might have been an eggshell. There's a funny deep-sea smell about this ferry-boat and the quaintest mixture of day-trip and deep-sea manners aboard her. The Purser has just told me that she (he in her) made 1063 trips in the war across this route "never knowin' what to expect." And during those trips "I didn't take off me trousers of course." They dozed while they could in the day time. But think of the steady strain of it. He wasn't in the least an imaginative bird so he didn't think. He just got *very* fat.

And when I went to the Customs to have my passports visa'ed, the Customs Officer had been on the China-Station (Jardine and Matheson)

---

[1] The name of the ship is printed on the stationery; all else, including the arrow, is in Kipling's hand.

[2] Both Kipling and Haggard sailed on ships of the Union-Castle Mail Steamship Company. Of one of these trips, Kipling's daughter, Elsie, wrote:

Things went according to a fixed routine. First the experienced appraisal of the ship and passengers by the two children, then the unpacking and stowing away of their travelling possessions in the tiny cabins of those days, and then their hunt to discover if any of their numerous friends among the stewards and crew were in this particular ship. A "good trip" meant one on which several friends, from the captain downwards happened to be on board. One special crony was a certain grizzled cabin steward, who could always be counted upon for escorted visits to otherwise forbidden parts of the ship, as well as plates of dessert after the grown-ups' late dinner. [Carrington, p. 298; *Cloak*, p. 219]

and *in sails* during the Boer "war." Sailing ship Torrens. He didn't look at my passport. We yarned in the empty echoing hall for about 20 minutes. Now we're waiting for the boat-train, and my friend Perceval Landon[1] who is coming with us for some ten days of this trip. Hope to see Elsie, by appointment, at Rambouillet on Sunday; she visiting, by happy coincidence her friend Francis Stanley[2] (*your* friend who had the contagious cold) in Paris.

Thence we turn South, I hope and go sun-hunting but as there's snow all over the place, I'll lay you any money we run into it as far south as you please! I wish you were along too. You'd cuss the cold— in spite of the lavish *and* odorous steam-heat—but you'd like the smell of the docks again.

The *Kinfauns* is down the river waiting to be sold—and the ex-Steward specially requested me to take note of her as we go down. *I* can't identify steamers in the dark.

Well, that's all. This is just a kick off to send you good greetings.

I see Curzon seems to be pulling round after his operation; which they tell me was a pretty bad one.

Ever affectionately,
Rudyard.

Hotel du Grand Monarque, Chartres
Saturday, March 14, 1925[3]

Dear Rider,

All the landscape round Havre looked like a new (and rather cheap) bride cake with its light powdering of snow under bright sun on

---

[1] Perceval Landon (1869–1927), barrister, newspaper correspondent, author, was a good friend of Kipling's for many years. They met in South Africa during the Boer War, where Landon was serving as foreign correspondent for *The Times*. Landon was one of the four founders of the Bloemfontein *Friend*, for which Kipling wrote a number of pieces (see p. 44 above). After the turn of the century, Kipling built a cottage on the Bateman's estate expressly for Landon, whose company he enjoyed and whom he wished to see as much as possible when Landon was not off writing dispatches from China, Japan, Siberia, or some other distant point. In 1915 Kipling and Landon went on a visit to the French troops in the field, and in 1917 they travelled together in Italy (Kipling wrote a series of articles about the Italian front for the *Daily Telegraph* and the *New York Tribune* called *The War in the Mountains*). [Carrington, pp. 238, 336–39, 345–46]

[2] See p. 139 above.

[3] Written on hotel stationery; the date is in Kipling's hand.

Friday morn. Just enough *not* to hold up the car and the Seine looking like pewter between the glittering banks.

Too cold for comfort in the early morning as we ran into Rouen (*Nota Bene:* There is an interval of a few hours during which the best of English chauffeurs automatically turns to the *left* in traffic. It is the owner's duty, then, to sit beside him and croak "Right!" at two minute intervals, like a foghorn.) And so Rouen, in an hour and a half. My Lord! What a Doré view of the town and the spires and the looping river from the hill above! All done with a silverpoint in that thin clean air. *All* the hotels of France are under strong reparation and expansion (this comes of not paying your lawful debts) so that stinks of paint and petrol mix with the smell of the upright citizen on all the floors and chased us into our bedroom where, by the way the lock stuck till the maid rescued us! 'Tis a prosperous land and so cheers me when I think how ungodly prosperous the Hun is. Hotel 9/10th void but the streets busy. Went off at once to Rouen Cemetery (11,000 graves) and collogued with the Head Gardener and the contractors. One never gets over the shock of this Dead Sea of arrested lives—from V.C's and Hospital Nurses to coolies of the Chinese Labour Corps.[1] By one grave of a coolie some pious old Frenchwoman (bet she was an old maid) had deposited a yellow porcelain crucifix!! Somehow that almost drew tears.[2] The place is being relevelled for summer plantings and looks, consequently, as bare as Aceldama. But 'twill be all right by the Spring. Then the Cathedral, which I can't love as much as I ought to do, except Joan of Arc's Chapel. That Young Lady by the way seems to be rapidly displacing the Deity throughout France.

Do you know that St. Joseph—*most* accommodating of all Spouses —is always the first of the Saints to be "demobilized" in favour of the latest cult. But, all the same, I did my penance, bare-headed, at the

---

[1] The Chinese Labour Corps was organized by the British Government to work on railways and roads or in factories, mines, dockyards, fields, forests, or in any other non-military spheres. The first contingent arrived in France in May, 1917. [B. Manico Gull, "The Story of the Chinese Labour Corps," *Far Eastern Review*, XV (April 1918), 125–35]

[2] This incident could have inspired Kipling's story "The Gardener" (1926). See p. 156 below. At any rate, on the evening he penned this letter, "he began to write what he described as 'the story of Helen Turrell and her nephew and the gardener in the great 20,000 cemetery.' He worked at it every evening and finished it at Lourdes on 22nd March." [Carrington, p. 385] Another story about a visit to a war cemetery is "The Debt" (1930).

Market above the place where Joan was burned. Also, lit my candles to her in the Cathedral—same as I did at Rheims when the Huns were bombarding. And this morn (time always seems long when you travel) the day broke down in foul rain and wet and we went for St. Andelys [Grand Anely] (switchbacking in mist and feature-shrouding rain) across the big hogsbacks and into the wooded valleys 'twixt river and river. A large-boned country rather like a giant's hunting-field, and fun to take at top speed. Lunched in the hotellized remnant of a XVIth century chateau (and jolly good grub). Then the Cathedral which has some decent XIV century glass. *Colour*, old man, is what *au fond* clinches a creed. Colour and the light of God behind it. That's as near as Man will ever get. Then by side roads (you ought to have seen me reading the map) and by my faultless guidance we crashed into Evreux whose Cathedral is a wonder—but not *the* wonder; and thence to Dreux—more Gothic and sparser; and at last in the tail of a dripping day to Chartres—the great blue-grey bulk of the Cathedral dominating, it seemed, half France. Our old hotel had been modernized, to our immense wrath, and, like Rouen, was full of ouvriers, paint, petrol and noises. Got into the Cathedral on the very last fading of the twilight and it was as though one moved within the heart of a Jewel of the Faith. You know the inexpressible colour-glories of Chartres—all the windows superb and some without flaw or blemish in *any* aspect. Last time I'd seen it the glass was all out, because of bombings by the Hun. Now all the glories were returned—rose window and all and in that last few minutes of darkness overcoming day, the windows burned and glowed like the souls of martyrs. Don't know when I've been more touched in the deeps. I *do* wish you could have seen it.[1] And

---

[1] Kipling wrote a sonnet in praise of the colour-glories he describes here:

Chartres Windows
1925

Colour fulfils where Music has no power:
    By each man's light the unjudging glass betrays
All men's surrender, each man's holiest hour
    And all the lit confusion of our days—
Purfled with iron, traced in dusk and fire,
    Challenging ordered Time who, at the last,
    Shall bring it, grozed and leaded and wedged fast,
    To the cold stone that curbs or crowns desire.
Yet on the pavement that all feet have trod—
    Even as the Spirit, in her deeps and heights,

so back to a damnable dinner in this "modern caravanserai," which was cheered by Elsie's voice on the telephone from Paris where she is visiting; and she promises to meet us tomorrow at Rambouillet. After that, please Allah, we head toward the South; whence, if it be warm, I'll write anon. You can't tell me to stop because I haven't an address: but if you send a line to Bateman's it will be forwarded as soon as we come to a stopping place.

Affectionately ever,
R. K.

Hotel de France, Périgueux
March 19th [1925][1]

Dear old man,

When one has slept in five beds in six days, one gets a little mixed about one's precise position geographically. Anyway, we are beginning to get South at last and find that there *is* a blue sky, tho' the winds beneath it cut like razors under the sun. Not a sign of Spring yet except in the winter wheat and a certain staring hardness—as it might be the coat of a horse before moulting—in the texture of the wayside grass. One nice and absurd adventure overtook us. The man we're travelling with[2] is a friend of the Princess of Monaco who lives at Claridge's, and has a château a bit south of Chartres[3] to which she urgently asked Landon to take us if he went near it by road. She goes herself for a few weeks each year but it is kept as tho' she were there— with variations. Well, we put in for lunch there and found the place was under renovation. But d'you suppose it made any differ? Not a hair! We were received by the Head Bailiff and a pontifical butler in white thread gloves: for they had been warned to expect us. The château itself was "up" for cleaning and painting, etc., etc. Every stick of furniture out in the middles of the vast salons, all carefully covered; with stacked pictures, glasses, bibelots and the whole secular

---

Turns only, and that voiceless, to her God—
There falls no tincture from those anguished lights.
And Heaven's one light, behind them, striking through
Blazons what each man dreamed no other knew.

[1] The address and the date appear in Kipling's hand.

[2] Perceval Landon (see p. 151 above).

[3] Princess Charlotte, Duchess of Valeninois (b. 1898), mother of Prince Rainier III, still owns and occupies the Château du Marche.

guts of an ancient family place, piled, stacked, heap[ed], lumped and protected all among it. The Library was interiorly lined, all over the bookshelves, with sheets of old thick wallpapers (*our* workmen don't think of those little precautions) and one saw vast mirrors down passages reflecting equally stupendous disarrays elsewhere. *But*, like Crusoe's ship, in the middle of the wreckage was an immaculate lunchtable set with many-coloured wines in slim, silver filigree Italian carafes. The Butler formed up and we sat us down to—yes, now I know what a "collation" means! After the hors d'oeuvres (it isn't kind of me to decant this on an invalid but it will do you good) came buttered eggs—not the sort you and I eat at inns and are thankful for, but the kind they serve in dreams. Then veal that the prodigal son didn't get;[1] then a chicken past description; then green peas with onions as big as marbles in 'em; then a cream meringue pudding of sorts with dry wafers; and an exactly ripe camembert. We ate till we rang like inflated hot-water bottles; and every time we looked up we saw the precise butler piloting another course down to us between the reefs and shoals of the stacked furniture; and the eyes of the family portraits looked at us—*on our own level*!—over the backs of sofas and through the backs of chairs. We took ourselves out at last to see the poultry (the Agent insisted) and the garden *and* the orchid house. The poultry lived in brick villas which would have been useful in England for the professional class and they had a water supply that many a parson's wife has never enjoyed. Eight gardeners adorned in the garden and the Head Gardener gave the wife a bouquet of orchids—cypre whats its name and Cattleyes.[2]

Then we climbed statelily (for we were still heavy) into our car and all the magic rolled away behind us.

A nice interlude and quite—quite mad.

I've been trying to know something about old stained glass; and I've failed but I *do* know that, at the Museum at Angers, quite recently discovered, are some tapestries running from the 13th to the 16th centuries which beat anything I've ever seen. Notably one room, hung on two sides with Angels bearing the Emblems of the Passion, against backgrounds of flowers: the whole in a key of blue that rips

[1] Luke xv. 11–32.

[2] Kipling is toying with Cypripendiums and Cattleyas, two of Haggard's favourite orchids. [For more about Haggard and orchids, see his *A Gardener's Year* (1905), especially p. 28, where he mentions growing these varieties.]

the soul open. And everything that Burne-Jones ever tried for is all there—done and finished and nailed down so to speak. Rummily enough, the XIIIth century tapestries deal with the Apocalypse—in reds that are only just tamed by years and in their deadly conviction manage somehow to pull it off and to impress. You know we really *don't* know much when it comes to art. We're too dam clever.

Then, after this revel at Angers, where the last of the stained glass is, we cut across to La Rochelle where—but I won't throw you back by describing the horrors of the yellow and red muckings in the windows of *that* Cathedral. The Port, with its fishing boats and mariners was the thing to see—and the arcaded, almost Spanish-like streets. Nice to notice how the *real* progress of civilization translates itself into improved sanitary plumbing. Four years ago I could have told you a lot about the W.C's of the La Rochelle inn—and elsewhere. Now they are falling into line with the rest of their kind. And to think that twenty years ago I (and a few others) in automobile braved all the horrors of the Unclean South just to make men a little purer and loftier in their habits! But as a race the Latin ought *not* to be trusted with plugs to pull etc., without an examination. Here's really valuable work for the League of Nations.

Angoulême, where we had lunch today, has a semi-byzantine Cathedral, desecrated by some ferocious modern glass but at Périgueux, here, you strike the real, overbearing brute Byzantine of the 10th century; and one realizes what a toss-up it was that our creed hadn't taken a dominantly oriental twist (might have been better if it had, p'raps!). I liked the naked convention of strength and rigidity which doesn't lend itself to internal haberdashery.

We stay here for tomorrow and then drift on to Biarritz—Hotel du Palais. By the time you get this write (or dictate) me a line or two if you feel like it to that gilded caravanserai of all the Unrealities and after that, address to Bateman's where my secretary will send it on, as she gets addresses. *I* don't know where we'll fetch up in the next few weeks. But I've hatched a story which gives me something to do at the day's end (I'm not specially keen on bucketting about all the time) and—please Allah—it may amount to something.[1] I haven't seen a

---

[1] Probably "The Gardener," inspired by Kipling's visit to the Rouen military cemetery on March 14 (p. 152 above). It was first published in *McCall's Magazine* in April 1926 and tells of an English woman's visit to a French military cemetery, where encountering Jesus, she mistakes Him for the gardener. [See Chandler, pp. 101–102.]

paper, so I don't know what the news is—and I don't much care, except that I want to hear from you. Elsie told me that she'd written you. She was looking very well—did I tell you this—when I met her at Rambouillet and so was your other friend Francis.[1]

Now I'll get back to my yarn. This has been a mass of unrelated stodge which you can swallow (or get predigested for you) at your pleasure.

Ever with affection,
Rudyard.

It's a tumbled and at the same time a large-boned landscape.[2]

Hotel du Palais, Biarritz
March 25, 1925. 10.30 a.m.[3]

Dear old man,

I sit facing the Bay of Biscay, surrounded by all the luxuries (from a d——d heating installation which I cannot control to a pink and white stucco salon) and have just got your two letters. Your signature, Sir, is vastly improved and the fact that you can (whether vertical or horizontal) tell good tales is *most* gratifying. I went once outside Chartres to look at the backside of the stained glass and found the organ—tinder-dry for ages—all in little bits being repaired by the light of naked blow-lamps! A fine casual breed our French allies. Otherwise I haven't climbed about much over cathedrals. It's un-alluring to use a vile film word. Apropos, I like your yarn about your film and the Huns.[4] *They* are a nice race, too. They never change and they never will. . . . Now I'm off for a trip to St. Sebastian for lunch: whereof more when I return (D.V.). It's a little warmer here than the rest of snowy blowy France—but not much.

[1] See p. 139 above.

[2] Kipling writes this line under his sketch of the landscape.

[3] This and the two following letters are written on hotel stationery; the dates are in Kipling's hand.

[4] In producing *She*, the director, Leander de Cordova, could not find an appropriate studio in the United States. "All California was searched, but nowhere in America could one be found large enough to take the tremendous sets which the story demands. So the Company journeyed to Germany and there in the old Zeppelin shed near Berlin the picture was filmed." Betty Blythe, the American actress who played the leading part scantily clad, suffered considerably in the unheated shed in mid-winter. ["H. H.," "Intro-duction," *Five Adventure Novels of H. Rider Haggard* (1951), p. 1]

5.20. Back again—and might just as well have been in England as for rain-squalls and general wet. One good thing that cheered me was to see all the fine new red brick factories built round St. Sebastian five years ago, when Spain was rich—all now cold and there's not much shipping in the harbour. I like the Spaniards for not worrying about the rest of the world but I can't love 'em.

So we saw nothing and got an indifferent lunch into the bargain and had indifferent roads. Motor cars and ox waggons make a bad combination—specially when the oxen wear woolly wigs of sheep-skin that fall over their already foolish-enough eyes. . . . And now has come in, by this afternoon's post, your good letter of the 23rd. But motoring *ain't* wearisome. It's all the fun of the road compressed into a few hours; with leisure at one end at least. Of course, if you sit down to 250 miles in 8 hours you'll feel it: but there's no need for these extremities. And consider now a day that gives you a couple of hours in the morning among the caves of the Dordogne—incised and painted Cromagnon piccys of bison, horse, wolf and Rhino traced on the irregularly dimpled roofings and sides of those limestone grottoes, as smooth as candle-drippings. All you hear is, now and then, the one wee drop of water from the tip of a single stalactite. The rest is all warm, stone walled stillness and these inexplicable figures. One grotto we went to, was discovered by the father of the present owner while excavating a potato cellar. It's in much better shape than the more public ones which are lit by electricity and explained by a guide or guidess who— taps the coloured figures with a stick! (The public, of course, is forbidden to touch.) Well, one steps outside and beyond one's own notions of time in such places. Your Egypt is merely a parvenue beside 'em.

Then, a couple of hours later you are at Lourdes. Same sort of looking smooth bluish-white rock grotto in a hill side but instead of incised totems, a lavender and white presentment of Our Lady just in the spot where Bernadette, the peasant girl, aged fourteen, had the visions of her in '58. And all the smooth nodular scarped rock below smeared and covered and runnelled with the gutterings of countless candles—some few hundred of which are always blazing before her, in all spots and at all angles—lighting up and going out like the children of men. And beyond the candles, earnest stricken worshippers, singly or by family, running their rosaries through their hands and praying— well, pretty much as earnestly as Job prayed when his boils were new.

The whole assembly cut off from the outer world by a sort of grille, outside which again, on a concrete flooring in the open air, were lines of benches for other supplicants to the picture with the lavender sash. And sitting high above the rock itself, its altar evidently plumb above the place of the Visions, the modern bulk of the enormous pale-grey blue church and basilica, decorated with gold, mosaic, glass, carvings and everything else that the taste of 1883 could invent, adorn and bedevil. Huge gardens and public spaces round the Church, studded with statues and flanked by huger (but always pale) hospices where the many sick of the summer can wait and lie up when they come to be healed. Miracles do not occur in winter. And outside that again, a long line of booths and stalls selling every variety of holy object—water bottles, crosses, medals, palms, fans; and the weary stale-eyed women in charge alluring the passers to buy. Behind them crags and cliffs of mountainous hotels all getting ready for summer when the miracles begin and the special trains will pour in! . . .

And at the evening's end, soft, quiet, relaxing, *most* English Pau, full of elderly birds with doubtful lungs in plus fours!! That's a fairly large octave to stretch. Never thought I could embrace incised tribal totems and visions of the Virgin (both evidences at least of conviction) in the time one would take to play half a game of cricket.

And here at Biarritz is pure Philistia and wealth and comforts accumulated on fatted comforts: and a wary, close-eyed proprietor with cream coloured hair watching it all—to his profit.

Thank you *ever* so much for the tale of "Her" adventures with the Huns.[1] It's exactly what they would do—energetically and shamelessly —as I've said: but it's also exactly like *you* that the hairy-chinned man should have stuck you for railway fares. Some folk are born to be benefactors: and you, old man, were long ago sealed of that tribe. But he'll pay you back; and I prophesy that "She" will begin to pay you royalty on a big scale. *Only* of course, I can't imagine how the tale could be adequately presented—even by all the means known to film-fakers. Can you tell me when there's a chance of being able to have a look at it? I've got to make pilgrimage there.

This dam Bay of Biscay is roaring, and rolling in, practically *under* my feet, so that I can feel the room gently heaving and tilting and expect every minute to hear the spray swish in at the window. There isn't a ship in sight. A steam trawler came out this morn, had one look at the weather; hooted at it and turned tail for Bayonne. Sensible craft! . . . .

---

[1] A representative of a German company had probably called on Haggard to discuss the possibility of filming *She*.

There are worse things in the world than to lie abed and read your books. I've done it. So I know. But it must give you peculiar satisfaction to run through 'em again: and to find out how big pieces of 'em you've utterly forgotten. Odd, though, that you don't mention "Jess":[1] Whereof I mineself have something of an opinion. . . And here's a streak of low watery sun sloshing in at the window and painting the white wall a ghostly ship's smoking-room blue: which more than over-suggests sea-sickness. But it's better than the Riviera. There's a wind over a few thousand square miles of pine forest which works better than wine. And that reminds me. If you habitually eat British Yorkshire pudding and gravy, it will end by depressing your morale and giving you what I have heard called "tweezies in the trash bag." England's all right to be ill in—owing to the sedative qualities of the air and the inhabitants—but it's no catch for a convalescent. When do you think they'll let you move out a little bit. You tell now of getting up in the afternoons. When will you arise in the morn, and stagger to a steamer—say even as far as Hull—and go "foreign" for awhile? It can't *always* keep up this unspeakable type of weather all over the world. Down here, there is absolutely no sign whatever of spring—not a bloom and hardly a bud. Only the mimosa trees (and they are foreigners by birth) have clad themselves in Jewish gold from head to foot where they can find protection. And I saw one Catalpa, this morning, all ablaze: but of flowers in the grass and by the way, nothing but a few demented primroses.

I think this is enough of a dose for a convalescent at one time so I'll send it off at once: and later turn to your three letters together. We're here for at least a week: so you can easily get in another letter if you feel like it.

Ever with affection,

R. K.

Hotel du Palais, Biarritz
March 31, 1925

Dear old man,
    You may be suffering from insurable diseases (I'm delighted at the

---

[1] Published in 1887, *Jess* was Haggard's first African novel, as distinct from adventure story. It is an anti-Boer tale about love and death during the First Boer War.

victory over the Pirate Company[1]) but you've still got a fine glow of
moral wrath over the sufferings of S. Africa. And you're dead-right,
I believe. The evil that W.E.G [ladstone]. planted hasn't all seeded yet
but (and here's the silver lining) the very mineralization of the sub-
continent is acting, I think as a buffer against the too rampant Dutch.

[1] Kipling's and Haggard's works were mercilessly pirated in the United
States, and both men fought life-long battles for international copyright laws
and for just personal rewards. As early as 1887, Haggard joined Gladstone,
Hallam Tennyson, Walter Besant, T. H. Huxley, and other dignitaries, in
speaking out for an international copyright convention ["An Olive Branch
from America," *Nineteenth Century*, CXXIX (November 1887), 601–24].
Three years later, when London writers were up in arms over American
piracies, Kipling's break with Harper & Brothers (see p. 16 above) received
a good deal of public notice and added more fuel to the general discontent.
In an earlier letter to Kipling, Haggard must have alluded to the settlement he
made out of court with an American film company that had plagiarized his
Cleopatra. Two entries in his diary are apposite: On October 21, 1920, he
writes, "After about a year and a half of effort, I have at last recovered £2000
of the amount due to me, or rather the amount on which we compromised,
from the American pirate . . . Company, for their purloining and
exhibition of Cleopatra. Whether I shall get the rest I do not know but this
sum will enable me to pay my debts for all the various repairs of property into
which I have been forced at a great price on various buildings after the long
neglect and maltreatment resulting from the war." On November 6, 1920:
"I have at last recovered my damages for the shameless plagiarism, to use a
mild word, of my film rights of *Cleopatra* by the . . . Film Co. Of course I
cannot touch them in America, but of what they have taken here I have, after a
struggle lasting for the best part of 2 years, recovered not all indeed, but still a
substantial part. I hope this may be a warning to these people and others. If the
adaptation had been in any way accidental, I might have felt some sympathy
for them but this was not the case. They took my plot, including incidents in it
that were mine alone, but altered the names, and in other ways tried to cover
their tracks. In the end, however, they did not care to face an action, although
they did everything in their power to delay the issue and to wear us down. I
owe the discovery of the proceedings of these people entirely to my friend
Major Cyril [James H.] Davenport [(1848–1941), Superintendent of Book-
binding at the British Museum; author of books and articles on art, decoration,
heraldry], an earnest student of my books and especially of *Cleopatra*, who
chanced to see the film here in St. Leonards and to talk to me of it as my own.
Although I never had an opportunity of seeing it myself, I followed the matter
up with energy and by the help of the Society of Authors and an expert ran
the purloiners to earth." [For more about Kipling and Haggard on piracy, see
Carrington, pp. 124–28, 142, 152, 223, 333; and the following letters to *The
Times* by H. Rider Haggard: "American Copyright," October 11, 1887, p. 7;
"American Copyright," June 5, 1890, p. 8; "Horrors on the Films," Novem-
ber 17, 1891, p. 8.]

A man here t'other day was telling me of the discovery of (and consequent gambling in) platinum. It appears that the stuff—a heavy black
powder—lies out all along a reef of 40 miles and has been traced and
pegged for eighty miles! 'Question, of course, is whether it goes
down but, anyhow, it's a huge proposition and it will draw people.[1]
By the way Hertzog was and is showing himself not equal to his job—
like all Socialists—'cause he doesn't work and doesn't know how to
work. And his Pact with Labour don't work either.[2] All that is to the
good. My own special "moan" is over the state of European affairs
after the war—specially with respect to Hun disarmament. But, I
suppose, every man looks back with a half-broken heart on the failure
of all the things he has tried to bring about in his life. Were it otherwise, O Theophilus—we should be as the Gods,[3] which, all present
information at my disposal advises me that we *are not.*

6.15 p.m. It was a fine—a really fine forenoon of still sea and *hot* sun
and blue sky, behind stone buildings. Didn't quite know what to make
of it; not having seen sun for about a year—so sat bewilderedly on the
beach and grilled. Amazing sensation! Quite like being alive! Then,
after lunch, to see a Pelota game wherein Chiquito[4] (champion of the
world) performed. It was all quite new to me. The great fantastic wall
against which they play their colossal Fives, the cement floor on which
the server stands, the immense size of the court—looks like 70 yards—
and the amazing Implement—the curved basket that they strap on to
their wrists. It's wicker and much more hooked than I've drawn it—
and its width may be three $\frac{1}{2}$ inches at the indent. Anyhow they do

---

[1] In 1923–24 extensive reefs of platinum were discovered in Lydenburg,
Waterburg and Potgietersrus district, and a platinum boom swept South
Africa. [Eric Rosenthal, ed., *Encyclopedia of Southern Africa* (1961), p. 395]
Kipling is disturbed here and later in this letter about the growing power of
the Boers in South Africa and hopes that the lure of the new mineral wealth
will bring fresh English immigrants to the colony and thus dilute Dutch
influence. For a concise statement of Gladstone's South African policies, see
Paul Knaplund, *The British Empire, 1815–1939* (1941), pp. 433–34.

[2] James Barry Munnik Hertzog (1866–1942), Prime Minister of the Union
of South Africa (1924–39), as a result of an alliance between his Nationalist
Party and the Labour Party.

[3] Luke i. 3; Acts i. 1.

[4] Indalecio Sarasqueta (b. 1860). He became champion at the age of sixteen.
He was called Chiquito "à cause de sa petite taille, de sa physionomie très
élégante et de sa délicate complexion." [E. Blazy, *La Pelote Basque* (1929),
p. 71; Luis Bombin Fernández, *Historia, Ciencia y Código del Juego de Pelota*
(1946), p. 43]

miracles with it in the way of catching the ball, and David's sling isn't in it when it comes to returns. One can hardly follow the ball as it is smashed in from the far end of the course. It's three men a side; the rules are beyond me: but it's Fives and racquets in a nightmare. We sat for nigh two hours, on a *most* hard seat watching a game of 50 up. When the men were too winded—it's a punishing game—the marker with no trace of self-consciousness, slipped off his *beret* cap, took position in the centre of the court and sang stanzas of Basque songs— to the huge edification of the crowd. He always broke off, snapping like a dog. You never heard anything so striking as a finale. I shall introduce it in *all* my future verses.

Then into Bayonne shopping (you and I don't feel that way when we come to a new town:) in a moist-feeling evening of soft clouds that made one realize that the whole nature of the year had turned. The Hottentot figs (what the deuce is their Latin name?) in the Hotel garden over against the sea, have realized it in forty-eight hours and are blossoming like exploding shells on turf. The daisies too and the mimosas and a new breath in the wind from out of all these square leagues of pine around us! I don't quite accept your ideas of your travelling days being over; and the fact of calling a disease by a name as long as a probe don't make it any more obscene nor violent than it is. When they cut me open endways, I rejoiced in a lovely lot of names of disgusting import—but words, beloved Rider, to men of *our* calling, do not kill. Put that in your Kaffir Calabash pipe and smoke it. (By the way I'm trying to colour a meerschaum and I wish I wasn't. It's rather like a liaison with a lime-kiln so far.)

I am sorry about Curzon[1]—not because there was any shortcoming in his works—for there wasn't—and the man was a monument and a machine of necessary industry, but because, when he didn't get the Premiership, he went and told everyone of his woe. Here's Lovat Frazer loose in one of the penny piccy Sunday papers faithfully betraying Curzon's moans on that head to the public.[2] And how the

[1] See p. 148 above.

[2] James Alexander Lovat-Fraser (1868–1938), barrister, M.P., writer. In his article, "Is History All Wrong?" he recalls what Curzon told him as a "friend" towards the end of his life. He paints the statesman as a tragic figure and quotes him as having said, "I am a mere cipher in the government. I haven't enough power and influence left to send a messenger across Whitehall." When Curzon failed to become Prime Minister, Lovat-Fraser remembers, "he said that his career was over . . . and that he 'had nothing left to live for in public life.'" [*Sunday Pictorial*, March 29, 1925, p. 10]

Hades a man of decent age can value anything externe to himself and his soul in the way of the world's gauds always beats me. It's right for the young donkey to travail after the carrot: but any elderly ass ought to know that carrots is only carrots and that nothing you get from without in this world is worth anything whatever.

But, then, Curzon had the illusions, and strongly, of rank, Honour, Position, etc. etc. They were all dead real to *him*, and since they seem to have made the spurs and goads that clinched him to his work, they were necessary. But I wish he hadn't uttered so freely of his disappointments—don't you?

This place is more hellish than ever. *I'm* no Christian—Allah knows —but I feel like a Bunyan character in Vanity Fair. And yet, *au fond*, they are no more than idle Englishry bent on having a good time: and, apparently, all-ignorant of the way to get it. Few Hebrews; and, so far as I can make out, no Huns. Last night a "Gala" night—special dinner and elderly people (the young'uns looking on pitying) chucking balloons and coloured paper at each other. The only sensible gentleman I saw was an Aberdeen to whom some people had attached a pink balloon, by the collar. It annoyed him, so he snapped and it burst. Which so amused the inferior animals that they insisted on repeating the performance. Not so, the Aberdeen. He'd been through it and had tested the vanity of balloons. So he took no manner of notice but went on his amiable wriggling career with this thing flying free behind him, till—someone took it off 'cause he didn't amuse 'em. But, no one, 'cept me, saw the depth of the rebuke and the contempt.

Elsie has gone back to Belgium from Paris having bought her raiment. You and I wouldn't be made happy, you know, by the gift of a few pairs of trowsers, would we? How marvellously Allah makes women!—I've sent in a story to be typed and—by Jove Yes—I've done a Sonnet.[1] A real 14-line Sonnet—only it breaks a lot of rules that apparently William Shakespeare laid down for the fabrication of sonnets so, you see, tisn't a real sonnet. But, I swear, it reads all right. And I've written to a lunatic in Florida trying to make him understand that it is *not* my job to transplant him from that remote state to British India where, he says, he was born and for which, he assures me, he is homesick unto death. Now *you* would have sent him a first class ticket

[1] The story must be the one Kipling was composing when he wrote to Haggard on March 19 (p. 156 above). The sonnet is undoubtedly "Chartres Windows" (p. 153 above).

by return post—which was practically what he demanded that I should do.

By some error, I find that I have gone on right up to the end of the 4th page, thinking it was the 3rd; so you'll have to stick it a little longer. What I really meant to tell you was of the disgusting spectacle of two young ladies in the main-street of Biarritz, immobilized by the necessities of two small dogs on the lead, who were of costive natures and hadn't the faintest intention of moving on till they had done their morning duty. I *am* a reasonable dog-lover but I call that atrocious. The wenches didn't care—beyond occasionally tugging each at her respective leash—which, when you come to think of it, must be a bit disconcerting to the person at the other end, if he's engaged.

I've just read this note to the wife who bids me say that she [is] "pityingly sorry" for the male who doesn't understand the joy and solace of shopping. And she *can't* realize that all life here, for me, is a hollow scandal in that I cannot get any decent brand of pipe tobacco. And what one finds is all wet as sea weed from the sea-air.—

I didn't know that one could insure oneself against specific diseases—thought it had to be burglars, or the act of the God: but 12 guineas a week isn't to be sneezed at—at the present price of nurses and—appliances. (I know *all* about that!)

But to come back to where I started—South Africa. Things *are* pretty bad but they're badness on the break—badness that is tired of its own incapacity to make a job of anything. And there *is* a small but a permanent infiltration of decent English on to the land: If we can only have one or two more big mining centres whence the disappointed can drift into farming, that would at least be another help. It's an expensive—i.e. moneyed—class of emigrant that goes to S.A. now, but, owing to the land's peculiarities, I don't see that 'twill ever be otherwise and I've sat up o' nights giving myself headaches over the possibilities of getting more whites out down there. I wish you'd dictate me your views, and I'd cut 'em and pass 'em off to Amery as my own.[1]

[1] The Rt. Hon. Leopold Stennett Amery (1873–1955). Kipling met him, in the early days of the Boer War, in South Africa, where he served as *The Times*'s foreign correspondent at Kruger's headquarters. [Carrington, p. 236] After the Boer War, he went on to work as a barrister in the Inner Temple and, during World War I, served as Assistant Secretary in the War Cabinet. From 1911 to 1945 he sat in the House of Commons. Kipling wrote him about African affairs because from 1924 to 1929, Amery was Secretary of

Aren't you delighted with Balfour's performances in Judaea? The D.M. report that the choir of the Anglican Church at Jerusalem threatened to strike if A.J.B. read lessons there.[1] This, again, confirms my long-cherished theory, that the administration of this planet is entrusted to the charge of an idle-minded but occasionally humorous arch-angel. And the futility—not to mention the danger—of Balfour's messing himself up with things between Jews and Arabs is beyond castigation. There's bound to be unnecessary trouble there—before long.

And now I'll really shut up. I'm hoping you'll have sent another letter amplifying your first. Your letters always cheer me and make me laugh. Rummy! Seeing that *you* are the sick man, but it's all a question of temperament. (*I* come, I am persuaded, of a long line of bankrupt undertakers.)

I think we shall be here for another week. Anyhow, send another letter here, and if we've gone on to Paris it will be duly forwarded. Forgive there being nothing in this note, but four fat meals a day (counting tea as one) don't lead to the cultivation of the intellects.

Ever with affection thine,

R. K.

State for the Colonies, and he was always a keen observer and authority on South Africa (he wrote *The Times History of the South African War* [7 vols., 1909]). [For Amery's memories of Kipling, see L. S. Amery, *My Political Life* (3 vols., 1953), I, 135–36, 220, 441; III, 135.]

[1] By 1925 tensions between Jews and Arabs in Palestine had diminished, fighting was a thing of the past, and observers hoped that time would heal the wounds. On March 25, 1925, Balfour arrived in Jerusalem to open the new Hebrew University. In the face of widespread Arab protest demonstrations, he visited Jewish settlements and holy places, making no effort to conceal his Zionist sympathies. On March 28, a Saturday, the press reported that he would on the morrow read the Lessons in the Anglican Church of St. George in Jerusalem, in order, the *Daily Mail* insisted, "to dispel the prevalent impression that he is a Jew." [p. 9] On Monday the *Daily Mail* reported that because the choir of St. George's threatened to strike in protest, the plan for Balfour to participate in the Service was abandoned. He did, however, come to the Church, and on April 1 he opened the University. [*Daily Mail*, March 30, 1925, p. 9]

Hotel du Palais, Biarritz
April 5, 1925

Dear old man,

Nothing from you for the past few days, and as I've got to pull out of here in a day or two, I'm launching another yarn at you. The Oxford Rugger team is down here and plays a lot of hefty Basques tomorrow, it being the Sabbath. The young'uns can't hold their liquor and, last night, behaved damnably at the Casino (which is Government property and the French don't forget it) jumping the bar, dishing out drinks to all and sundry, making speeches and generally making asses of themselves. Whereupon the head of Police telephoned the Minister of the Interior who said:—"Jug 'em if they do it again." Whereby the Biarritz police are embodied outside the Casino tonight; but the boys have given their word they won't do it again. Fancy *our* feelings if a French footer team did that in England! And 'tisn't as if we were so popular in France that we can let our young misbehave. The English *are* asses.

Today has been miraculous fine—vivid blue sea; clean sky and clean wind and we went out in the car, arriving by vile roads at a height which commanded a trifling foolish view of the snow-headed Pyrenees on one side and the blue-bellied Bay of Biscay on the other— say fifty miles with whole square acres of gorge all around us flaming and blazing, and making thanks to God because it was alive. Also pink almond trees—all blossom and no leaf—like the Socialists. But this isn't much of a life—not in the hotel at any rate. It's full of scented females and toneless-voiced Americans and old hags who gamble at the Casino. One gets so dam' sick of the recurrence of the type; and of the unoriginality of Sin and Vice, and Excess. Also they have ugly legs, which makes me more virtuous than ordinarily.

I've been working—to fill in time—at a study, or sketch of one's wanderings.[1] It won't come to anything but it was like doing scales in a boarding house—it filled in the time. All the fishermen at the absurd little port here have 20-foot motor-boats in which they go squattering out across the waves like badly-ballasted ducks. I watched one man t'other day—an ugly sea and his motor conked out. Up came a bit of

---

[1] Kipling must be working on his *Souvenirs of France*, a series of articles he would publish eight years later. They are not travel sketches, however, but rather an account of his experiences in France, tracing the growth of his affection for France and the French and offering his opinions on French history and politics. [Stewart, pp. 431–32]

a sail and a stick of a mast. He 'verted promptly to the instincts of his ancestors and held her, chopping and smashing into the waves, almost on the edge of a set of sharp-toothed reefs till he had his engine adjusted. Then he got under way again, furled sail, downed mast, and ducked into harbour under his own power. *Very* like life. Also, the wife has bought her a new dress. You and I don't rake the first new town we come to for a pair of new trousers—why? Because, O Rider, we are Superior Animals. Here she cuts in and says we are by *no* means superior, because when the dress is worn, we enjoy looking at it. That *does* rather knock the bottom out of the argument. I'm going to leave this now till I've seen tomorrow's footer match. Then I'll tell you. The children are *all* drinking more liqueurs—regardless. My money therefore is on the heavy-footed Basques!

April 6.

Palm Sunday: And here comes yours of the 3rd (I was hoping it would) with the priceless tales of the drunkard and the leper[1] (shall send it on to Elsie than whom you have no more fervent appreciator). You *do* have bad luck with your equipage. Remember "Karswell" in Australia![2]—I don't marvel that in your damnable weather you get set-backs. All nature is in a conspiracy of course to chill you and gets in under the bedclothes for that purpose. But I note you've contributed two lines in your own fist—not so bad either—which greatly cheers me. No. I don't recall your telling me about your work as an amateur executioner—hope you did it decently.[3] The least one can do on those

---

[1] These are not characters from stories that Haggard published; they must be from anecdotes in the letter.

[2] See p. 88 above.

[3] One of Haggard's favourite tales was how, as a young man in Africa, he had had to execute a Kaffir petty chief because the executioner had shown up "hopelessly drunk." In Haggard's account, the High Sheriff had to withdraw from the spectacle to a corner of the yard, "where he was violently ill. The thing had to be done," Haggard wrote in his autobiography, "and between a drunken executioner and an overcome High Sheriff it devolved upon me. So I stood over the executioner and forced him to perform his office." Justice John Kotzé, Haggard's superior officer in South Africa and a close friend, points out in his memoirs (published after Haggard's) that, though Haggard's distortion could not have been deliberate, the facts were otherwise: "Haggard . . . on the previous day . . . told me he wished to be present at the execution. . . . When the condemned man was brought from the cell and mounted the platform Sir Rider, before the final drop, was overcome and moved away towards the corner of the yard. The Sheriff . . . an old sailor . . . was not the kind

occasions is to be quick and as painless as may be. The breed of Ma-zooku[1] is extinct—white *or* black it has passed away. They'll do what you want now and then—but not often. And they require refreshers in the way of tips.

We pull out of here the day after tomorrow for Paris in a leisurely trek of five days. The roads aren't good. *All* the people here are beastly to look at, and revolting to listen to. By this you will gather that I am in a happy mood. (Have just refilled my Waterman and through some damned legerdemain that I'll look into later, she's—VIOLET!) But they don't please me: and I expect I don't please them. Also, each fine day is paid for by a brute of a wettish gale and cold winds. *Yet*, mark you, there is no air blander or less treacherous than here. Even when you climb seven or eight hundred feet it don't sting or gnaw.

You'll be pleased to learn that the Oxford Rugger team, having all the police with drawn sabres and cocked automatics ready to school them, behaved decently at the Casino last night. So, another Inter-national crisis is averted.

You're dead wrong—for once, Rider—about the French: They aren't safe and they know it. They've been carted once by the U.S.A., and subsequently by England in this very matter of Safety—which means their existence. Naturally they panic. They know what Ger-many is doing and they have known three times what Germany can do. All they get from us is solemn silly lectures about paying up and

---

of man to be overcome in the discharge of his duty. . . . The sentence was carried out by the executioner without any hitch. Later that same morning Sir Rider himself mentioned to me that he felt queer and upset and could not look to see the end. . . . The Sheriff also told me that Haggard's nerves had failed him." [*Days*, I, 112–13; John Kotzé, *Biographical Memoirs and Reminiscences* (n.d.), pp. 487–88]

[1] Mazooku had been Haggard's devoted servant boy in South Africa, and perhaps in the version of the execution tale that Haggard wrote Kipling, Mazooku played some part. Mazooku had rendered his master "Lundanda" (the tall and pleasant-natured one) exceptional service and devotion and once even saved Haggard's life when he had lost the way on the veld (p. 172 below). When, in 1914, Haggard returned to South Africa for the first time in over thirty years, he was delighted to find Mazooku among those who welcomed him back. The newspapers seized upon the reunion and ran stories and pictures of the two men. Before Haggard left South Africa, he saw to it that Mazooku would be provided for in old age. Mazooku appears in Haggard's *The Witch's Head* (1885). For more about Mazooku, see *Cloak*, pp. 51, 64–66, 84–85, 110–11, 223–24, 239–41; *Days*, I, 139–40, 185, 200–202; *Rider Haggard*, pp. 62, 260–62.

not wasting money on military preparations: and, apparently, *we* don't yet see that it's *us* and not France that Germany wants to scupper most. *Do* you imagine for two shakes that the aeroplanes will fly *from* the Rhine across the Channel. And just think for a second what we'd do, if we'd had the guts trampled out of a section of England, thirty by 250 miles. Would *we* pay our debts or put our defences in order first? Go to —— marry come up and quotha, forbye![1]

Will now go down to lunch; then to the Match; and thereafter will tell you how it went. The grub here is sound, nutritious and varied and the waste of the hotel feeds (I've seen and scratched 'em!) ninety of the finest white pigs that ever you did see. But perhaps you're Semitic in your views about pork?

6 p.m. No. It wasn't a gentle game at all. The Basques were in bloody red and behaved as such but, no denying, their passing was cleaner than ours, tho' they did pass forward more than was necessary. The Umpire was surprisingly just and our boys were out of condition —for reasons already named. Consequence we lost—11 to 13: and a huge crowd was very happy. Naturally they cheered the Basques most but they cheered the visitors very much. Queer to hear all the terms of sport translated into the French tongue; and queerer still to see 'em agonize and squirm and have hysterics over the technique of the game. A very warm soft air with a grey sunny haze, so that one sat for two smitten hours and only felt mellow—like a pumpkin.

The tradition of the circuses (we, as you say, are the only land at present that adds the bread) is spreading once more over all Europe.[2] Wonder if it portends the same debacle. . . . *Apropos.* Of course the Dominions don't want emigration: and it's the rankest lying on the part of their politicians to pretend that they do. They've got soft jobs and they mean to keep 'em. Personally, I'm inclined to think it's almost too late for effective emigration—on the present lines. The

[1] Kipling, attuned, through long association, to the French, reflects here the growing uncertainty France felt in the mid-'twenties about the future of Europe. From the French point of view, their security had been seriously undermined by the United States' failure to join the League of Nations, by the treaty of Rapallo between Germany and the Soviet Union, by the British refusal to go along with a French plan to provide the League of Nations with armed forces, by the Dawes Plan for scaling down Germany's reparations, and by covert German rearmament.

[2] Kipling, in paraphrasing Juvenal (*Satire* X:80), may be reflecting on factional disputes in the Soviet Union and on Fascist demonstrations in Italy.

emigré fleeing to save his head or hide is quite a different matter. He may be evoked later.

We shall be in Paris for a few days from Sat. next: so if you are writing address us, *now*, at *Mrs. G. Stanley* (the girl who gave you the cold) *51 Rue des Belles Feuilles, Paris (XVIe)*. Only *do* write if you've time. Never mind what you say; all the letters are duly burned and so you can, if you feel like it, open the door at your pleasure. It's good for a man sometimes to say what is in his heart—even if he *is* running a temperature.

Ever affectionately,
Rudyard.

P.S. Of course the Preachers had to die—Koheleth[1] and all. But it's the afterwards which, I hold, they faced the better, for their present wisdom in life. Anyhow they weren't so likely to be surprised at finding they had to go on living.

51 Rue des Belles-Feuilles
(the house of the child
who gave you the cold!)
April 11, 1925[2]

Dear old man,

Just in from Tours to find yours of the 8th with the *good* news that you've been trekking about in a Bath chair. Hurroo! It isn't quite the same as a Boer pony or even an ox-waggon; but 'twill serve for a start; and you've got the Spring winds in your rear (on reflection this isn't a happy simile: but I'll let it stand).

(While I think of it—*No*. I do *not* believe in a voluntary Capital Levy. I believe in rational economy and trying to make people, occasionally, work. I'm sick of this dam' volunteering of good men for the benefit of the shirker.)[3]

---

[1] Ecclesiastes' original Hebrew name, meaning preacher.

[2] In this and the following letter, the return address is printed; all else is in Kipling's hand.

[3] The vast increase in public debts after the war led some economists to discuss seriously the idea of voluntary capital levies. They argued in the 1920's that such a levy would reduce the public debt, lower interest charges, and thus lighten the general tax burden. Opponents maintained that such a levy would stimulate economic centralization and promote socialism. Haggard's diary (December 15, 1923) shows that he too opposed a capital levy.

Thanks for your attempt at Suicide on the veldt, for that is how it strikes me! I wonder how many men have galloped off in the dawning to their death for a little fresh meat. Lots!—The seeing of the flash of the gun is the real nub of it—to show that miracles occasionally come off.[1]

[1] This is clearly an allusion to another of Haggard's favourite reminiscences about South Africa, the story of how he and his horse Moresco went astray on the veld while hunting:

On a certain morning before breakfast, I wounded a bull wildebeest, breaking one of its hind hocks, and mounting . . . [my] hunting horse . . . started to ride it down. But that wildebeest would not be ridden down. . . . Being thin, notwithstanding its injury it went like the wind, and finally led me into a vast company of its fellows: I think there must have been three or four hundred of them. When once he began to gallop game, Moresco was a horse that could not be held; the only thing to do was to let him have his head. Into that herd he plunged, keeping his eye fixed upon the wounded beast, which in the end he cut out from among them.

On we went again and got into a great patch of ant-bear holes. Some he dodged, some he jumped, but at length he went up to his chest in one of them, throwing me on to his neck. Recovering himself with marvellous activity, he literally jerked me back into the saddle with a toss of his head, and we proceeded on our wild career. The end of it was that at last the bull was ridden to a standstill, but I could not pull up Moresco to get a shot at it. The bull charged us, and Moresco only avoided disaster by sitting down on his tail. As the beast passed underneath his head I held out my rifle with one hand and pulled the trigger; the bullet went through its heart and it dropped like a stone. Then I tied my handkerchief to its horn in order to scare away the aasvogel, and rode off to find the camp in order to get assistance.

All that day I rode, but I never found the camp on those vast, rolling plains. . . . A tremendous thunderstorm came on and wetted me to the skin. In the gloom the horse put his foot upon a rolling stone and gave me a terrible fall that bruised and knocked the senses out of me.

After lying a while I recovered. Mounting again, I remembered that when I left the waggons the rising sun had struck me in the face. So I rode on towards the west until utter darkness overtook me. Then I dismounted, slipped the horse's reins over my arm, and, lying down on the fire-swept veld, placed the saddle-cloth over me to try to protect myself against the cold, which at that season of the year was very bitter on this high land. Wet through, exhausted, shaken, and starved as I was—for I had eaten nothing else since the previous night—my position was what might be called precarious. Game trekked past me; I could see their outlines by the light of such stars as there were. Then hyenas came and howled about me. I had three cartridges left, and fired two of them in the direction of the howls. By an afterthought I discharged the third straight up into the air. Then I lay down and sank into a kind of torpor, from which I was aroused by the sound of

This is written in our rooms here, with Francis babbling to the wife of Elsie's recent shopping visit. Your remembrances have been "conveyed." The answer is that she regrets that she has to be respectful to you. Otherwise, *she* would have pointed out to *you*, that *she* has never been free from colds (specially in winters) since that "fatal rencontre."[1] So there you have it. It's just a question of evidence and as she's my hostess—and has a chef who is an artist—I am venally supporting her. *And* she sends you her best love. She *is* a nice child as ever was: and grows better looking as time goes on. Most of us, you may have noticed, *don't*.

Our tour up was chequered. The roads of France are beyond description, on the main lines—whereby the Duchess smashed a near front spring "pot-holing"—'twixt Angoulême and Tours. Never imagined a road *could* be let down so damnably and completely. A *gritty* road, mark you—palish yellow with an equal light that made the holes almost indistinguishable, till you had got into 'em! And when she was repaired we struck a fresh Devil's track of 70 kilometres from Orleans to Chartres which nearly finished her once more. So she is in the R.R. Garage meditating on her sins. The garages were full of damaged cars and bad words.

Oh, and at Tours, and later at Chartres, was a party of 15 English schoolgirls over here to learn French (15–18) being led round by their head mistress and assistant, to look at stained glass windows. (It's notorious girls love stained glass.) They all dined *en bloc*. You never saw so many (or such meaty) bare arms in all your life. Just young she-Britons of the middle class, with the air (quite justifiable) of owning the earth. Quite cheered one to look at and to listen to 'em.

The English behave badly out of shyness—same as a horse goes through a shop window because he thinks a wheel-barrow is a tiger, only question is *what* made him think that originally. Perhaps the early oppression of the Normans.

Easter Monday. Such a day of sun and woods and daffodils, and the strong nice smell of Paris. Dined at a small restaurant down the street

---

distant shouts. I answered them, and the shouts grew nearer, till at length out of the darkness emerged my Zulu servant, Mazooku. [*Days*, I, 138–39]

Haggard uses the incident of being lost on the veld in *Queen Sheba's Ring* (1910): when the hero gets lost on the desert, the flash of a gun leads to his rescue.

[1] See p. 139 above.

last night after a lunch where I heard French politics discussed from the inside. The comfort is that however low an opinion *we* have of politicians, it isn't lower than their own views of their own colleagues and most intimate friends. They say now Briand will form a Ministry —and no one wants to be the Finance Minister.[1] With a deficit this year of fr. 3,000,000,000—would you?

I'm out today to make arrangements for getting home which we expect to do on the 20th. Going with a car is like travelling with a woman in "a certain condition." She needs a deuce of a lot of attention and cabin room. All Paris is invaded by the Americans and the English, and Notre Dame yesterday was one jam of sight-seers.

I'm in touch with my d——d mail again and my usually sweet temper has gone to bits. All the same I've done some work while I've been away: which is to the good.

The Stanleys make us most heavenly comfortable and I wish you could be here to enjoy the dead country in the heart of Paris. One doesn't hear scarcely a sound in the garden behind the big shut gates of it: and there is one Jack—the big sheep-dog—who looks after the children, whose acquaintance you'd enjoy making, a reserved gent. with a ringing and purposeful bark—*once*: but once for all. Then you stop and find out what he expects you to do.

Send us another line *here* to let me know how you are going out and getting on. Then I'll be home (Ins'hallah).

> Ever affectionately,
> Rud.

The doctors attending Haggard decided, at this point, to take him to London, for more extensive examination and a probable operation. Haggard's daughter has recorded her memories of this period in her father's life:

Looking back on those days, it is obvious that Rider knew the end had come. So in her heart did [Rider's wife,] Louie. On the grey spring morning that the ambulance was coming to fetch him, she was in his room helping with the last-minute preparations. The nurse dressed him and left him in a chair, but he looked down at his overcoat as if

---

[1] Aristide Briand (1862–1932), Socialist, premier of France eleven times. From 1925 to 1932 he was France's foreign minister. But it was Paul Painlevé (1863–1933) who formed a ministry in April, 1925. Briand did not take over the Government until March, 1926.

something were missing, then got up, walked to the table where there was a bowl of daffodils, and taking one out pulled it through his buttonhole—then turned with rather a sad little smile to his wife. How many hundred times she had seen him do that. The last little action of the morning ritual in his dressing-room; for every day the gardener brought in a buttonhole, a rose or carnation in summer, an orchid in winter. Rider was never without a flower. The little incident broke her control—

"Rider," she said, "do you really want to go dear? You have only got to say if you don't and we will send the ambulance back—are you quite, quite sure. . . . ?"[1]

51 Rue des Belles-Feuilles
April 20 [1925] 9.50. a.m.

Dear old man,

Your last dictated letter catches me on the very edge of going off to Boulogne for this evening's boat. You don't tell me *when*, exactly, you go up for your exam; but I'm going to write to Ditchingham when I get back.

One advantage of a committee of experts sitting on one, is that (like Councils of War) they rarely recommend operations. It's the individual surgeon who does that.

More likely 'twill be some kind of treatment—of infinite length and boredom. But you've got the year with you and the love of your friends round you. Bless you a thousand times.

Ever with affection,
Rud.

This city is rotten with politics. Caillaux[2] and his wife—same which shot and killed the Editor—are back in power; he says he is the only person who can "save France!" I'll give him four and a half months to come a heller of a bump!

R.K.

---

[1] *Cloak*, pp. 278–79.

[2] Joseph Caillaux (1863–1944). In 1914, when he was minister of finance, his wife was accused of killing Gaston Calmette (1858–1914), editor of *Le Figaro*, for attacking her husband's private life in his paper. Mme. Caillaux was acquitted. In 1920 Caillaux himself was sentenced to three years in prison for conspiring with the enemy in World War I, but, by the time Kipling writes, he had won back some of his earlier popularity and was again serving as minister of finance.

Bateman's, Burwash, Sussex
May 5, 1925

Dear old man,

Me voici returned (and a d——d dull banquet at the R.A. it was: except that F.E. was richly coopered—a small thing in itself but *not* small when one reflects that his speech was broadcasted. Whereby when I got back to where I was staying, the very maids were aware that "one gen'elman was quite intoxicated." Fancy being effectively and recognizably squiffy in 4,000,000 places at once! Hurray for the March of Science!).[1]

And I've got your note of yesterday; and this, you need not be told, comes to you with my all-love (Bosch locution: but you know what it means) and a sympathy not the less keen 'cause it has been shoved through the same mill.

Don't know what happens to the Philistine in nursing homes and hospitals, but the man who lives by his imagination pays for his gift a thousandfold in such places. The mere smell of 'em makes that terrible machine turn on its alleged owner and rend him to pieces. One pays in advance but—one never gets back the price of one's baseless apprehensions. And the grub matches the wall-paper; and the slow, sickening pully-haully of internal observations sinks one's soul into one's boots. So we are persuaded that our vitality is lowered, which, luckily, it 'ain't, only we feel that way: so it is deadly real. Can you, by any means, relax and let go altogether—either in tears or lamentations. It's better, they say, if one can—all alone. I've tried but stick half-way which was worse than [not] beginning it at all. And atop of that, with the unerring eye of Fate, your son-in-law's trouble.[2] I

---

[1] Although Kipling was a regular guest at the Royal Academy banquet, he was not a member. "F.E." (Lord Birkenhead) had been involved in the Marconi shares scandal of 1912–13, where government officials "were shown to have held shares" in the company that had been awarded the contract for an Imperial wireless chain. [Ensor, pp. 456–57] Kipling's poem "Gehazi" is a bold indictment of Sir Rufus Isaacs, attorney-general at the time of the scandal. "F.E." was among those who had presented the case for the Marconi directors and their friends. [The Second Earl of Birkenhead, *F.E., The Life of F. E. Smith, First Earl of Birkenhead* (n.d.), p. 187]

[2] Thomas Haggard, Rider's nephew (son of Bazett, his elder brother), married Angela, the Haggards' eldest daughter, in September 1907. While serving in France during the war, Tom had come down with rheumatic fever, which disabled him for the rest of his life. At the time that Kipling writes, Tom "was very ill, on the eve of a severe and it was feared fatal operation." [*Cloak*, pp. 198, 268, 279]

suppose it's all a question of degree but, looking into his life as told, 'seems to me that Job got let off rather easy, only a few camels, oxen, slaves and such and bad eczema or septic poisoning. It's modern science that can really terrorize with her rituals and her preparations. But a council of surgeons, as a rule, is a heap safer than one individual with a knife and a theory. They all ride jealous on such occasions, I believe, and operate as limitedly as may be. But there is this—and just this to be said—when the big Machine of Fate is felt and realized to have us in its hold, one gets a blessed incuriousness and content on the matter—on all matters: and the odd feeling that somewhere at sometime the self-same thing has happened before and that, try as one may, one can't put a foot wrong. I *know* that that will come over you as you go up to the table—if you've got to, and it beats any known anaesthetic.

And I've put in a long and wholly absorbed evening over your Young Lady of the Dawn[1]—and—how the *dickens* do you do it? *How* do you keep and outpour the vitality and the conviction *and* how do you contrive to nail down and clinch the *interest* that keeps a man lying along on one elbow till the whole arm is stone-cramped? That's what I want to know. I don't pretend (that'ud be cheek) to judge the book in the least. I only know, in my own person, that it held me as a drug might—but it was a *good* drug. And here am I fiddling and piffling with a tuppeny-ha'penny short-story[2] that I can neither patch, punch, nor pat (try saying that aloud!) into any satisfactory shape. You have the mastery of the incommunicable gift of catching and holding—for the good reason that you breathed your own good spirit into it. (And I ain't good.) Voilà the little difference. *Qua* Stuff—I think the movements, flights and fights before and during the Babylonian Army's battle are as good as anything I've ever touched of yourn. That's no small thing either, old man. And while I read, I was overcome by the ancient marvel, as I lay, that a man's carcass should be such a disgusting, ill-perfumed, vilely-packed bag of tricks while his soul, at that same moment, or almost, should sit cheerily trumpeting above it all!—And therefore all my thanks and—for what they may be worth—my abundant blessings.

Been dining in town and met a lot of people, all identically alike

---

[1] *Queen of the Dawn* (see p. 138 above).

[2] Kipling may have been revising "On the Gate: A Tale of '16," which would appear in *Debits and Credits* (1926). See p. 101 above.

except for their inadequate clothes, and some variations in the crop of hair: and not a thing worth talking of or about in the whole lot of 'em. Came down this morn after rain—as usual: and Chequers, where I spent the week-end was mist and rain all the Sabbath. Francis Stanley's two small adorable babes[1] are with us for a few weeks while their parents go visiting Venice and such places in cars. They make the house talk and echo. We're going (D.V.) to see Elsie in Belgium in a few days—and to a big dinner with Belgoo King and Queen flourishing at the heads of the tables. All very fine and curiously shadowy, and that's practically all the news I have *except* (here's sickness again) Milner[2] is reported as making, already, a good recovery after a "brush" of sleeping-sickness. Never knew before that that long and fell trouble ever contented itself with merely "brushing" one. What *I've* seen of it more resembled the ministrations of a steam roller.[3] I'll be writing again in a day or two. Bless you, and believe in all the affections of your many many hundred thousand friends the world about. And for me I am always lovingly

Rud.

[1] Dr. E. Gerald Stanley writes: "The children who were at Bateman's, May 1925, are my two eldest daughters, Jane and Ursula, aged respectively at that time 4 and 2 years. Ursula was Kipling's god-daughter." [Letter dated September 24, 1964]

[2] Alfred (later 1st Viscount) Milner (1854-1925), journalist, statesman, author, and colonial administrator. He died eight days after Kipling takes note of his illness. In 1897 Kipling, Milner, Cecil Rhodes, and Moberly Bell dined together to celebrate Kipling's admission to the Athenaeum Club. In the following year, Milner welcomed the Kiplings into his circle at Cape Town, where Milner was trying to reconcile Boer and British differences. Kipling came to admire Milner for his personal and professional qualities, and through the years the two frequently exchanged their views, both in person and by letter. During World War I, they worked closely together on the War Graves Commission, of which Milner was Chairman. [Carrington, pp. 195, 211, 309-10, 344; Alfred Milner, *The Milner Papers: 1897-1905*, ed. C. Headlam (1931), I, 240; II, 9, 67, 504; J. E. Wrench, *Alfred Lord Milner* (1958), p. 190] Kipling wrote "The Pro-Consuls" (*Inclusive Edition* of Kipling's verse [1927], pp. 107-108), an encomium to selfless statesmen, as a tribute to Milner. [Chandler, p. 225] Haggard must also have known Milner; certainly, he thought well of him, for in 1909, when Lloyd George (then Chancellor of the Exchequer) asked Haggard to suggest someone who could serve well as Chairman of the Development Board, Haggard suggested Milner. [*Days*, II, 223]

[3] In the Rhodesian type of sleeping sickness, the decline may be unusually rapid, and the patient may die in six or seven days.

Bateman's, Burwash, Sussex
May 7, 1925

Dear old man,

Just a line before I go up to town for a Rhodes Trust Meeting,[1] to acknowledge your note of the 6th. The Lord *is* treating you rough. It's the hanging about indefinitely which makes the life unendurable indeed! I went to ask after Milner who had had a go of sleepy-sickness *but* (and this is a good omen, isn't it: he being 71–72) is now making a most amazing recovery of it. So I went away much cheered—about *you*. I believe in these signs and significations.

It's those d——d specialists who gather round a man and depress him. The first chap M. went to, as the symptoms were coming on, told him quite cheerily that the matter with him was—just senile decay! The effect on an imaginative man you can imagine.

Been to one dinner where I met some Frenchmen and a female Checko-Slovak. My dear old man, we made some new nations after the Peace that might well not have been created. A Checko-Slovak is what came up and fermented after Austria putrified. Otherwise, no news except Spring is late, cold and uncertain. I've lost a calf or two with cold (in spite of whiskey at birth). We *can't* get on the land (it's too squaggy with wet) and I can't do a story that I'm hatching, so that it suits my notions.[2] Hence I'm dull and disgruntled. By the way, has it occurred to you lately that your prophetic "Doctor Thorne"[3] is in a fair way of coming true? Have you noticed how steadily small-pox is digging itself in to certain crowded centres, and (reinforced by the more virulent type now loose in the U.S.A.) is really getting ready to explode. I've been watching it for the last two years—but you foresaw

[1] In 1917 Kipling had accepted an invitation to become a Rhodes Trustee and to help administer Rhodes Scholarships, and for years he worked at his job diligently, frequently visiting Rhodes House in Oxford and entertaining Rhodes Scholars. [Carrington, pp. 344–45, 377]

[2] See p. 177 above.

[3] Actually, *Dr. Therne* (1898), which Kipling confuses with Trollope's novel. Kipling has the subject matter right, however; it is a propagandistic novel written by "one who in other lands has seen and learned something of the ravages of smallpox among the unvaccinated" [pp. 1–2], Haggard's contribution to the continuing controversy over the merits of vaccination. The tale is about an unscrupulous anti-vaccination physician, and it predicts the spread of smallpox to uncontrollable proportions if vaccination is not adopted.

it a good ten or twelve before that. And 'twill be d——d serious. Well, my car is at the door but I wouldn't miss the post.

> Ever with love,
> Rud.

Miss Haggard reports that the doctors considered the operation "entirely successful" and that "Rider lay there, pain more or less kept at bay, quiet and speaking little for three days. Then a new abscess gathered. He lapsed into semi-consciousness."[1]

Kipling's next letter is to Haggard's secretary.

> Bateman's, Burwash, Sussex
> May 13, 1925

Dear Miss Hector,

I am tremendously in your debt for your notes about Sir Rider: and your bulletin of this morning made me feel a little easier.

Seeing that the operation was last Saturday morning and he is reported as reading and smoking on Tuesday, there seems to be a chance of the luck turning.

I'm off tonight for *Brussels* where I shall be staying at the *Hotel Astoria* till Sunday: in case there should be anything to tell or wire in a hurry. I expect to be back in London on the 19th or 20th. I shan't trouble him with a letter unless you tell me.

> Very sincerely,
> Rudyard Kipling.

On the following day, Haggard was dead.

---

[1] *Cloak*, p. 279.

APPENDIX

Plot outline for *The Ghost Kings*, composed by Kipling and Haggard at Bateman's in the autumn, 1905 (see pp. 62-63 above):

[R.K.]

THE GHOST KINGS

Two children of early Natal colonists: Good straightforward English girl (*but with hint of unusual psychic powers in her Mamma*). Mother knows when her husband is killed by elephant out hunting: Mother has fore-knowledge of Weenen Slaughter or may know even before natives know. Girl finds father and mother slain beside waggons one early morning, and lover gone: track of his limp feet dragged in dust proves to her by evidence of native tracker that he is scuppered. Gun and clothes left behind *or* comes with lover to wagon and lover is knocked over.

HERE COMES THE SHOCK:

The Zulus surround her as with intent to ravish. She begins to laugh, and so wins respect given to mad.

She won't leave 'em. They daren't leave her. She runs as fast as they do. Then pres.tly goes away with 'em. Once they flee but are stalled at drift in flood. She appears over bank. They flee and dash: Result. 32 oxen and 27 men drowned. She chances on sandbank and swims across, always laughing.

They flee to Dingaan's Krall. Says Dingaan, "Let us see if any woman on earth can look *me* in the eye. accordingly prepared. She enters as the impis are in place.

[H.R.H.]

She scares witch doctors.

The messengers to Dingaan from the Priest.

King (King of Shapes) bringing answer of the oracle to Dingaan, "The Earth shall swallow him and the King's tongue shall bury him." They ask the mad white girl in payment. "The girl who sees the sha-dows." Little old man soothes her so that she sleeps and afterward is quieter.

They take her away North.

The Ghost Kings Life Tree is blown down by a hurricane. She comes in on the hurricane *laughing* and springs upon the tree.

Now anybody may kill the king. He knows he is doomed, but outwardly there is no sign. All the priests go out to dream each under his own tree hoping to be king.

She (Wensi, the Virgin) protects the Priest King, Nyan, seeing that her only safety lies with him. He instructs her in her arts, her object being to communicate with the spirit of her lover. In early days lover shadow on the ground in a mirror so that she knows him when he comes. Nyan takes her into Hades, shows her all her dead except her *lover*. He wishing to keep swears she has seen the lover "No." He sends out her shadow to seek his shadow on "the great plain." "The wandering of the soul." She sees him. He sees her. Each thinks the other dead. At first he has only has a vague feeling of unrest and a tendency to wander. "Presently," says Nyan, "I will make your shadow strong." He is more and more conscious of her influence. At length he sees the face through thunder and lightning in the bush; it vanishes on waking. He is drawn North abandoning his servants (who bolt at his dream), his waggons; and going on alone month after month, always helped out of dangers by these visions, a sense of pain in his head when he turns from north (like compass), Dingaan's men stop him. He tells them he is following a dream, describes it. They recognize the dream woman, say nothing and let him go North, follow him North a while and leave him.

The rival Priest (Eddo) meets him, asks what he wants. "I follow a dream that lives in North." A Dream lives with us. It is the Ghost that protects the King. The trance meeting. Nyan by his arts knows (water gazing) of the approach of the lover. Detum is to kill him. Eddo, who is next priest, who wants throne determines to save him for he also knows of his approach. The whole Dwarf people know watching from under their trees and the points of dew as still pools in early morning, but keep silence.

(The meeting in the dark forest of the two who think they are spirits, he rising of the sun through the forest *the shadows thrown*, the gradual recognition of humanity. This meeting arranged by Nyan with lover

[R.K.]

on condition that he pays for the *assurance* that he shall join his lover's spirit by death. He is to be sacrificed to *the trees*. JUST TIED UP AND LEFT IN THE FOREST: No enemies against Nyan on lover's part: but a fair bargain because he doesn't want to live (*He is already tied when he sees her*) but he sees the shadow and the will to live returns. Nyan *never* kills a man except by tying him to the trees and he believes in his own sorcery to the extent of believing that the ghost tree will kill. These people have a horror of blood. It's called the *White Death*. Girl is precious, human and rebellious. Wide look into English. Nyan tries to master her by his art but his power is naturally gone. She says, What can you do. My strength is in me. Here is my lover's spear. Will you die by the red death and the blood which is your soul will be spilt abroad, past gathering up. Then you will die, which to you is nothing, but your ghost will too. You will have no shadow. You will not go down among your ancestors. You will be like the little dried bodies of the baby monkies that their mothers leave in the tree tops. Give me my man.

It is true," said Nyan. I think you know that I do not fear any white death.

Nor did you till lately?
I do now. I have my man.
"Oh," says Nyan. I have never known woman.
Call Eddo.
to Eddo: My tree has fallen.
Eddo. I know it. What are your orders.
Nyan. I take his place.
Eddo. And these?
Nyan points North

Curtain

[H.R.H., on back of envelope, in pencil]

Eddo passes lover into the haunted land through the subject guards. Only the priestly initiates have trees but the tribe are all dreamers. The initiates are given.

The struggles of the girl's spirit reach her dead lover.

The Ghost people have no objections to death provided it is the *White Death*.

Die by kind of coma, beri-beri.

G. People pale with living in forest. Haters of sunshine. Movers at night. Her whiteness gives girl a hold. Eddo is carried on necks of four big slaves in a palanquin "daring the sun."

* * *

Plot outline for *Allan and the Ice-Gods* composed by Kipling and Haggard at Bateman's, January 30, 1922 (see pp. 117-19 above):

North Lodge, St. Leonards-on-Sea

[H.R.H.]

ALLAN AND THE ICE GODS

Allan inherits from Lady Ragnall who dies the chest of Taduki with a letter in which she hints at many things. At first he determines to destroy it and shows great virtue in the attempt. But when he looks at and smells the stuff he thinks that he will put it away in the plate chest with some silver she also leaves him in order that it may be analyzed at some future time.

Comes Boredom and Temptation —— Allan on Temptation.

At last he gives way and inhales the stuff. Before narrating what happens to him, whilst disclaiming belief in these manifestations which he attributes to his subconscious self, he points out that there is hope in them, or would be if they were true, since they do suggest that man is a continuing entity. Without such hope he compares his lot to that of the aristocrats imprisoned at the time of the French Revolution, amusing themselves, making love, jesting, but always awaiting the opening of the door and the harsh voice calling the roll of names of those appointed to execution——the end of all things.

The Vision begins——the Wraith of Lady Ragnall acting as showman till at last she fades (? into one of the characters and if so which?).

The scene opens on a green plain——behind it great black mountains capped with snow. In the gorge of the mountains a vast green glacier. The Tribe——forty or fifty people——is gathered round fires of driftwood. Allan recognises himself as the Chief named Wi (the hereditary name of the Chief). It should be spring, but winter holds——the seals have not come, the wild fowl do not pair; some of them flight away to the South.

[R.K.]

The Tribe conceived itself to be all of mankind——by special act of creation. They had come, or had been made "Beyond the Throne whence the God descends," i.e. behind the Great Snow mountain to the North. They had no more time sense than animals. If a thing had lasted from the time the seal appeared in spring till they returned again, it had always existed (Alan was the only one who had the rudiments of the time sense). They said that from time immemorial the world had been split into two tribes——the two little septs of 10 or 15 souls each living on opposite sides of the bay under the Glacier. Consequently they warred, "when their bellies were full."

Had once lived beyond the Throne: but on hearing of Devils (i.e. another tribe) had retreated to be under the personal protection of the God of the Glacier.

Wives here an asset. Alan had two and a head-wife. One married one' first wife officially. Maimena was the only one who knew his third name (told back to him on his death). They had the vague legend of an uniced world—or Heaven—behind them. Perhaps, after one had died, one's "other part" went out into uniced country. They had dreamed about such things. There were noises and bellowings and cracklings in the ice. Some of the very old members of the tribe professed to interpret them and would say on what day the enormous pushed-forward ends of the Glacier would break off or "bear children," as they called it. The great ice rushes were the result of these marriages of the powers.

Originally the valley had been long, level and green—about five miles long. The Glacier had worked its way down it at the rate of perhaps a yard or two a year. No one noticed that it was moving quicker except Allan, who had the curiosity to measure it with two sticks.

[sketch]

(Alan's exploration when the flight from the Valley is inevitable)

[H.R.H.]

Allan finds his soul one awful night under the pressure of doom. He learns to think for others. Mameena, sitting at his feet, sees his eyes change. Pushes her away—for the virtue goes out of him when touched.

Realises that he is up against evil.

[R.K.]

The long vigil ends with his conceiving a plan that shall save not only Maimeema and the child, but the whole of the tribe irrespective of his personal likes and dislikes. He will shift the whole people if he can, but find out the way across the broken ice——that swallowed up the forest. He waits on his "voice" until the dawn. With the dawn the Voice (which is his accumulated sub-conscious experiences as a hunter and explorer co-ordinating all his ideas and observations in the past) begins to speak: at first like the beat of the blood over his ear-drums: then louder and louder——clearly, definitely, cogently is the plan unrolled and when he listens he finds the other side of his heart coldly calculating how much food each of the tribe must carry with him. At the end of the Revelation ——for it is the first revelation to the first Saviour of mankind whereof we have any knowledge——he goes out to walk on the beach——his Garden of Gethsemane: tho' all he is conscious of is that it will be a colder and hungrier trip than he has ever taken.

[H.R.H.]

Someone——the fair witch knew the road but kept it to herself from hate of the race which feared and neglected her——refusing to wed her. He knows that she knows. The Voice tells him that:

She bargains with him to save the tribe if he will marry her (meaning to murder Mameema). In the end the witch funks when she sees the thrashers and killer whales and runs on. Mameema comes back and dies with her. Allan's sacrifice——has no intention of keeping bargain and marrying witch. Determines to die for the Tribe. Looks on himself as already dead.

The corpse of the Forefather of the Tribe that comes down the Glacier and the prophesy connected with it.

One quarto page, entirely in Kipling's hand, contains a pencil drawing of the glacier, with four captions: (top center) "the Throne where the God descends"; (middle center) "noises and cracklings inside the glacier, when the sun shines or when it freezes"; (three-quarters from the top, centre) "faces and threatening figures *inside* the ice of the imprisoned Powers of Destruction"; and (bottom center) "small bay, intense blue with floating ice. The seal lie on the floes."

At the left-hand margin, also in Kipling's hand, is a long list of descriptive phrases, terms and names of characters for the story:

WI = a "personage of predeluvian times." He preached to Mira and Wa who disregarded him: Hence the Flood.
WININI = The Shudderer.
AKA = a pretty woman.
MOANANGA = avaricious.
PITOKITE = a churl, one of the unlucky.
WHAKA = a kind of ill-omen, one who howls.
TAREN = the witch who hides up.
RAHI = the local millionaire in fish hooks.
HOU = the unstable feather.
HOTOA = the slow man.

NAMES:

AH = Who was always afraid.

URK = The old man.

TAH-O = The old woman who talked.

LAN = the girl.

FOH =

DOM =

PAG =

The longer the name the greater the honour of the wearer.

The real name: the hunter's name: and the wife's name told only in his
    ear to carry to the dead as he is dying.

NGAE = The Magician.

MATOURA = Mameena.

KOW = The fish or swimmer.

INDEX